NATIONAL UNIVERSITY
LIBRARY   SAN DIEGO

Challenging violence
in schools

D0888642

EDUCATING BOYS, LEARNING GENDER

Series editors: Debbie Epstein and Máirtín Mac an Ghaill

This timely series provides a well articulated response to the current concerns about boys in schools. Drawing upon a wide range of contemporary theorizing, the series authors debate questions of masculinities and highlight the changing nature of gender and sexual interactions in educational institutions. The aim throughout is to offer teachers and other practitioners grounded support and new insights into the changing demands of teaching boys and girls.

Current and forthcoming titles:

Madeleine Arnot: *Boy's Work: Teacher Initiatives on Masculinity and Gender Equality*
Christine Skelton: *Schooling the Boys: Masculinities and Primary Education*
Martin Mills: *Challenging Violence in Schools: An Issue of Masculinities*
Leonie Rowan *et al.*: *Boys, Literacies and Schooling: The Dangerous Territories of Gender-based Literacy Reform*

Challenging violence in schools

An issue of masculinities

Martin Mills

Open University Press
Buckingham • Philadelphia

Open University Press
Celtic Court
22 Ballmoor
Buckingham
MK18 1XW

email: enquiries@openup.co.uk
world wide web: www.openup.co.uk

and
325 Chestnut Street
Philadelphia, PA 19106, USA

First Published 2001

Copyright © Martin Mills, 2001

All rights reserved. Except for the quotation of short passages for the purpose of criticism and review, no part of this publication may be reproduced, stored in a retrieval system, or transmitted, in any form or by any means, electronic, mechanical, photocopying, recording or otherwise, without the prior written permission of the publisher or a licence from the Copyright Licensing Agency Limited. Details of such licences (for reprographic reproduction) may be obtained from the Copyright Licensing Agency Ltd of 90 Tottenham Court Road, London, W1P 0LP.

A catalogue record of this book is available from the British Library

ISBN 0 335 20584 4 (pb)   0 335 20585 2 (hb)

Library of Congress Cataloging-in-Publication Data
Mills, Martin, 1957-
    Challenging violence in schools / Martin Mills.
        p.   cm. – (Educating boys, learning gender)
    Includes bibliographical references and index.
    ISBN 0-335-20585-2 – ISBN 0-335-20584-4 (pbk.)
    1. School violence–Australia–Prevention.   2. Boys–Education–Australia.
I. Title. II. Series.
LB3013.3 .M55 2001
373.17′82′0994–dc21   00-065269

Typeset by Graphicraft Limited, Hong Kong
Printed in Great Britain by Biddles Limited, Guildford and Kings Lynn

For Ali and Tara

Contents

Series editors' introduction

Educating boys is currently seen – both globally and locally – to be in crisis. In fact, there is a long history to the question: what about the boys? However, it was not until the 1990s that the question of boys' education became a matter of public and political concern in a large number of countries around the world, most notably the UK, the USA and Australia.

There are a number of different approaches to troubling questions about boys in schools to be found in the literature. The questions concern the behaviours and identities of boys in schools, covering areas such as school violence and bullying, homophobia, sexism and racism, through to those about boy's perceived underachievement. In *Failing Boys? Issues in Gender and Achievement*, Epstein and her colleagues (1988) identify three specific discourses that are called upon in popular and political discussions of the schooling of boys: 'poor boys'; 'failing schools, failing boys'; and 'boys will be boys'. They suggest that it might be more useful to draw, instead, on feminist and profeminist insights in order to understand what is going on in terms of gender relations between boys and girls and amongst boys. Important questions, they suggest, are: what kind of masculinities are being produced in schools, in what ways, and how do they impact upon the education of boys? In other words, there is an urgent need to place boys' educational experiences within the wider gender relations within the institution and beyond.

Despite the plethora of rather simplistic and often counter-productive 'solutions' (such as making classrooms more 'boy-friendly' in macho ways) that are coming from governments in different part of the English-speaking world and from some of the more populist writers in the area (e.g. Steve Biddulph), there is a real necessity for a more thoughtful approach to the issues raised by what are quite long-standing problems in the schooling of boys. Approaches for advice to researchers in the field of 'boys' under-achievement' by policy makers and by teachers and principals responsible for staff development in their schools are an almost daily event, and many have already tried the more simplistic approaches and found them wanting. There is, therefore, an urgent demand for more along the lines suggested here.

This is not a series of 'how to do it' handbooks for working with boys. Rather, the series draws upon a wide range of contemporary theorizing that is rethinking gender relations. While, as editors, we would argue strongly that the issues under discussion here require theorizing, it is equally important that books in the area address the real needs of practitioners as they struggle with day-to-day life in schools and other places where professional meet and must deal with the varied, often troubling, masculinities of boys. Teachers, youth workers and policy makers (not to mention parents of boys – and girls!) are challenged by questions of masculinity. While many, perhaps most, boys are not particularly happy inhabiting the space of the boy who is rough, tough and dangerous to know, the bullying of boys who present themselves as more thoughtful and gentle can be problematic in the extreme. We see a need, then, for a series of books located within institutions, such as education, the family and training/workplace and grounded in practitioners' everyday experiences. There will be explored from new perspectives that encourage a more reflexive approach to teaching and learning with references to boys and girls.

We aim, in this series, to bring together the best work in the area of masculinity and education from a range of countries. There are obvious differences in education systems and forms of available masculinity, even between English-speaking countries, as well as significant commonalties. We can learn from both of these, not in the sense of saying 'oh, they do that in Australia, so let's do it in the UK' (or vice versa), but rather by comparing and contrasting in order to develop deeper understandings both of the masculinities of boys and of the ways adults, especially professionals, can work with boys and girls in order to reduce those ways of 'doing boy' which seem problematic, and to encourage those that are more sustainable (by the boys themselves now and in later life). Thus books in the series address a number of key questions: How can we make sense of the identities and behaviours of those boys who achieve popularity and dominance by behaving in violent ways in school, and who are likely to find themselves in trouble when they are young men out on the streets? How can we address key practitioner concerns how to teach these boys? What do we need to understand about the experiences of girls as well as boys in order to intervene effectively and in ways which do not put boys down or lead them to reject our approaches to their education? What do we need to understand about gender relations in order to teach both boys and girls more effectively? How can we make sense of masculinities in schools through multi-dimensional explanations, which take into account the overlapping social and cultural differences (of, for example, class, ethnicity, dis/ability and sexuality), as well as those of gender? What are the impacts of larger changes to patterns of employment and globalization on the lives of teachers and students in particular schools and locations? The series, as a whole, aims to provide practitioners with new insights into the changing demands of teaching boys and girls in response to these questions.

As editors, we have been fortunate to be able to attract authors from a number of different countries to contribute to our series. This particular book addresses one of the key issues for educating boys – the reduction of gender-related violence. While we hear, frequently, about the violences of men and boys against women and girls, we are less likely to discuss violences between men and boys. Yet young men between the ages of 16 and 30 are the most likely group in the populations of late capitalist countries to be injured in violent attacks or fights, and the most likely to be killed violently. Within the school context most of the day-to-day violence is between boys. For the most part, this violence is not dramatic – it can be quite mundane violence, for example, pushing and shoving, that makes the lives of a large number of girls and boys (and, it might be added, teachers) miserable in schools. This kind of petty violence and jockeying for position may also interfere with schools' abilities to produce appropriate environments for learning and academic study. We are very pleased to be able to publish Martin Mills' work on this key issue as one of the first books in our series. Working from a profeminist perspective, he has explored the contexts for the violences of boys (to misquote Hearn 1998). His book, written in the Australian context, is extremely relevant to other countries. It is based on extensive and detailed practical work in schools in Queensland and does a great deal more than trace the theoretical explanations for boys' violence in schools. Drawing on his wealth of experience of anti-violence programmes in schools, he makes practical suggestions for ways of working which can take teachers forward in their approaches to dealing with violence regardless of where they work. Mills does provide some actual examples of ways of working, but the importance of this work is that he does so in a way that makes accessible to others the theories on which his own interventions are based. Thus, readers will be able to use his case studies in innovative and practical ways in their own work with boys in schools and elsewhere. The importance of anti-violence work with boys and young men cannot be over-stressed. It is an issue that has a bearing not only on boys' own school-work and achievement, but on the lives and experiences of all members of the schools community. Mills' work makes that clear and offers some ways of thinking through the issues.

Debbie Epstein
Máirtín Mac an Ghaill

References

Epstein, D., Elwood, J., Hey, V. and Maw, J. (1998) Schoolboy frictions: feminism and 'failing' boys, in D. Epstein, J. Elwood, V. Hey and J. Maw (eds) *Failing Boys? Issues in Gender and Achievement*. Buckingham: Open University Press.

Hearn J. (1998) *The Violences of Men: How Men Talk About and How Agencies Respond to Men's Violence to Women*. London: Sage.

Acknowledgements

I would like to thank a number of people who have been involved in maintaining my enthusiasm and commitment to this book and have contributed to my understandings of the issues covered here. In particular, I want to thank Bob Lingard who has been a constant source of support from the day this book was first conceived. His critical commentaries throughout every stage of the writing process have been invaluable. However, it is the friendship which has developed over the time it has taken to write this book that I most treasure.

Several people have read earlier drafts of this book and have provided valuable feedback, which I have taken account of both in relation to the ideas developed here and the organization of the book. These people include Rob Gilbert, Allan Luke, Michael Kimmel, Debbie Epstein, Máirtín Mac an Ghaill, Shona Mullen, Kath Hearn, Joanne Ailwood and Helen Foley.

In addition to the above people I want to thank a number of other people who have played a key role in the development of my ideas for this book. They include Vicki Carrington, Kathy Roulston, Glenda MacGregor, Debra Hayes, Kerryann Walsh, Paul Brown and Ros Mills. Members of the gender discussion group at the Graduate School of Education, the University of Queensland, have also been significant in this regard; in particular I want to thank Carolyn Baker, Carmen Luke and John Knight. I also want to thank Peter Renshaw and Merle Warry for their support during the writing of this book. Thanks also to Lisa Bridle and Terry Fisher.

I would also like to acknowledge the following people: the students and teachers from the case study sites for their time and input into this project; members of the former Queensland Department of Education's Gender Equity Unit for their assistance with resources and their commitment to projects such as those considered here; the various people (from organizations such as Men Against Sexual Assault, Zig Zag and Brisbane's Domestic Violence Resource Centre) who worked with me in delivering and organizing the programmes conducted in the schools that served as research sites for this book – in particular, thanks to Ben, Cameron and Karen; Kerry Denman for her assistance with transcribing the interview tapes; and also Ali and Tara for selecting pseudonyms for the case study participants and for the two schools. I would also note that some of the arguments in Chapter 4 were first raised in *Gender and Education*, 12 (2): 221–38.

Most importantly I want to thank Tara and Ali for their patience, inspiration and sense of fun during the length of time it has taken to complete this book.

Introduction: challenging violence in schools as an issue of masculinity

Seldom do the news reports note that virtually all the violence in the world today is committed by men. Imagine, though, if the phalanxes of violence were composed entirely of women. Would that not be *the* story, the only issue to be explained? Would not a gender analysis occupy the center of every single story? The fact that these are men seems so natural as to raise no questions, generate no analysis.

(Kimmel 2000: 243)

In April 1999 two boys in trench coats walked into their high school in Columbine, USA, shot dead 12 students and a teacher, and wounded 23 others before killing themselves. The boys had planned their shooting spree in great detail. Three weeks later, in New South Wales, Australia, a number of boys were suspended from seven different schools for creating a similar 'massacre list' of students and teachers as that put together by the two American students (Baird 1999: 5). Such events have served to promote the belief that schools throughout the Western world are becoming like the stereotypic violent American school. For instance, in an Australian newspaper report headlined, 'I fear massacre in our schools' (Patty 1999) a headmistress (*sic*) of an exclusive girls' school, who had visited a number of schools in the USA where she had seen metal detectors, guards, identification badges and transparent school bags, was reported as saying,

> Columbine High School was an affluent school in an affluent area of Denver in a very similar environment to schools in Australia. There has been an accelerating pattern of violence in Australian schools in the past 15 years. The availability of guns, unemployment, homelessness, the disintegration of families and the church and violence in the media. High rates of depression are reflected in the high rates of eating disorders, vandalism, drug use and violence in schools. It's a very dangerous and potent situation.
>
> (Patty 1999: 18–19)

Comments such as these are not uncommon. Violence in schools is clearly disturbing to educators, parents, students and the broader community. However, as with the head teacher above, acts of violence are often attributed to such things as family breakdown (or single mother families); violent videos, computer games, the Internet and song lyrics; lack of discipline in schools and the court system; lax gun legislation; and liberal parents. Issues of masculinity are seldom raised. This is despite the fact that in the majority of instances the perpetrators of this type of violence are male.

This is similarly the case with the concerns being raised about bullying in schools. In much of the bullying literature masculinity is rarely mentioned (see for example, Elliot 1991; Sharp and Smith 1994; Walker *et al.* 1995; Rigby 1998; Smith *et al.* 1999). However, a significant amount of research into school violence suggests that by far the majority of bullying incidents in schools are perpetrated by boys (Milligan *et al.* 1992; House of Representatives Standing Committee on Employment, Education and Training 1994; Sadker and Sadker 1994). Hence, in an essay on the Columbine killings and similar events, Gloria Steinem (1999) made the following comment:

> We will never reduce the number of violent Americans, from bullies to killers, without challenging the assumptions on which masculinity is based: that males are superior to females, that they must find a place in a male hierarchy, and that the ability to dominate *someone* is so important that even a mere insult can justify lethal revenge.
>
> (Steinem 1999: 47, original emphasis)

In this book I want to take up the task of challenging the assumptions, identified by Steinem, on which masculinity is based. This entails demonstrating the ways in which violence has become associated with 'normalized' forms of masculinity and it also involves making some suggestions about the ways in which this association can be disrupted. The book has developed out of work I have undertaken with boys in schools on gender and violence issues and draws on interview data collected from boys, teachers and others who were associated with gender and violence programmes conducted in two Australian State High schools.

Violence in schools

There is often an over-exaggeration of the amounts of violence present in schools. As the Australian Federal report, *Sticks and Stones: Report on Violence in Australian Schools*, states in its introductory paragraph:

> Schools provide a safe learning environment for most children. It is erroneous to conclude that schools are unsafe. In some areas, rather

than being places of violence, schools provide havens and places of safety away from the violent community. The media in its reporting of isolated incidents of school violence has contributed to the community perception that the education system is violent and chaotic. It is easy to form the view that violence is a regular feature of school life. It is not.

(House of Representatives Standing Committee on Employment, Education and Training 1994: v)

Similar comments could be made about schools elsewhere. However, a significant body of evidence does exist which suggests that many boys make life very difficult for other boys and for girls in coeducational schools, and that this is often treated as normal (see, for example, Morgan *et al.* 1988; O'Connor 1992; Milligan *et al.* 1992; House of Representatives Standing Committee on Employment, Education and Training 1994; Sadker and Sadker 1994; Collins *et al.* 1996; Hart 1998; Francis 1999). Based on their research in the United States, Sadker and Sadker (1994: 9) have stated that: 'Tolerated under the assumption that "boys will be boys" and hormone levels are high in high school, sexual harassment is a way of life in America's schools.' In Australia, the Federal *Sticks and Stones: Report on Violence in Australian Schools* states that:

> For many boys being 'tough' was their understanding of what it was to be male. Aggressive play by boys towards girls was often described as 'typical' or 'boys will be boys' behaviour. It was even encouraged. It was the acceptance of this behaviour as normal which was most damaging in the school environment. It was this use by boys of aggression to gain power and dominate which was intimidating and threatening to girls and undermined their whole experience of school.
>
> (House of Representatives Standing Committee on Employment, Education and Training 1994: 14)

The state of play in schools at the moment is thus one where girls and women are often placed in threatening and dangerous situations. In a Brisbane study of the attitudes of grade nine boys to forced sex (O'Connor 1992: 4): 'One in three boys believed it was "okay for a boy to hold a girl down and force her to have sexual intercourse" if she's led him on.' A South Australian study, *Sexual Harassment Between Students: A Report of Teachers' Attitudes and Experiences* (Morgan *et al.* 1988: 35) stated that the victims of sexual harassment were predominantly female (93.3 per cent) and the perpetrators male (88.1 per cent). The *Sticks and Stones* report (1994: 7) stated that: 'The Committee was told that one of the biggest unrecognized aspects of violence in schools was gender harassment. As a component of violence, it was widespread in schools and was largely unrecognized as a violent act.' The report contains further comment: 'Surveys indicated that violence based on gender, together with bullying, were the most systematic and constant forms of violence within schools. In the majority of cases men and boys were the perpetrators of violence based on gender and girls, women and boys their victims,' (House of Representatives Standing Committee on Employment, Education and Training 1994: 14).

The *Listening to Girls* report states that:

> As a part of their day to day routine, girls in co-educational classrooms and schoolyards suffer sex-based harassment from boys and sometimes teachers. Girls accommodate this harassment differently. Some react with hostility and anger, but it causes many to be passive and docile, restricts their access to space, equipment and attention to the teachers, and undermines their feelings of safety, self-confidence and worth.
>
> (Milligan *et al.* 1992: 5)

The report goes on to say that: 'Harassing behaviour springs from and reinforces the idea that boys are the powerful and esteemed sex and that girls' interests and concerns should come second' (Milligan *et al.* 1992: 10).

In these reports there is an awareness that the situation can be worse for female Aboriginal students or students with disabilities and that violence is often directed at gay, lesbian and bisexual students.

The wide-ranging report of Australian schools conducted by Collins *et al.* (1996), *Gender and School Education*, reinforced the conclusions reached above. For instance, a major finding of this study is that: 'Boys are the usual perpetrators of sex-based harassment of their own and of the other sex . . .' (1996: x). However, there is slightly more emphasis in this document on the role that boys play in oppressing each other. For example, they argue that:

> This Study adds to the former evidence of harassment of women and girls, very strong evidence that harassment of boys happens just as frequently, and in some categories more frequently. The harassers of boys are largely other boys. Further, except in the case of a few girls (particularly at Year 6 level when girls are physically larger than boys), our qualitative data suggests that harassing behaviour by girls is often a way of taking part in a game against 'outsiders' controlled by dominant boys. Boys are usually the serious harassers of members of both sexes.
>
> (Collins *et al.* 1996: 164)

It is important to recognize, as Collins *et al.* (1996) have done, that violence by males against males, which is often interpreted as boys being boys or as bullying, is indeed gender-based. Such violence is often a form of boundary policing, usually with a homophobic edge, which serves to both normalize particular constructions of masculinity while also determining where a boy is positioned within a hierarchical arrangement of masculinities.

The role of teachers is also an important consideration in understanding the processes within schools that either hinder or facilitate sex-based harassment. The Morgan *et al.* (1988: 35) study indicates that it is not just students who are responsible for the levels of gendered violence in their schools. Teachers too must share some of this responsibility. Evidence gathered for the report demonstrates that teachers sometimes saw girls as being responsible for their own experiences of sexual harassment. They state that,

> A disturbing number of teachers made comments to the effect that if the girl was a 'slut' then the boy's actions were not sexual harassment. Further comments indicated that some teachers wanted to know what sort of girl she was, before they could make a judgement about the incident being sexual harassment or sexual assault, or who should be seen responsible.
>
> (Morgan *et al.* 1988: 48)

This is a finding supported by the work of Milligan *et al.* who note that:

> Some staff and some students do not believe that the behaviours under discussion actually occur. Others recognize that the behaviours occur but see them as the natural order of things: 'Boys will be boys'. These people tend to see the issue as a kind of hoax being perpetrated by radical feminists.
>
> (Milligan *et al.* 1992: 11)

Furthermore, as the *Sticks and Stones* report comments, teachers are sometimes the perpetrators of sexual harassment. There is other evidence which supports this assertion that girls and women are often also the recipients of unwanted, harassing and/or violent treatment at the hands of some male staff both in the United States (Sadker and Sadker 1994) and in the UK (Mahony 1989). At the same time it is important to recognize that women teachers are also often the recipients of sexually harassing behaviour from male students (see, for example, Askew and Ross 1988; Walkerdine 1989). It is no wonder that Jones (1985: 35) once stated: 'Some of us are now convinced that mixed-sex schools are dangerous places for girls and women and that they exist to further benefit boys as they establish their sexual domination over girls.' There are several issues that need to be picked up from this evidence about male behaviour in schools. The issues of male teachers, of boys' complicity in violence against girls and women, and violence against boys are all important ones and are taken up throughout this book.

In exploring the relationships between masculinity and violence this book draws heavily on interview data collected from two Queensland high schools where I was involved in implementing gender and violence programmes with boys. I remember quite vividly driving home to Brisbane from country Queensland one Sunday evening in the early part of 1996 when I was first starting to work with the boys in these two schools. During that drive home reports began to come over the radio about a mass shooting in Tasmania. A 29-year-old man had gone on a shooting rampage in the Tasmanian historical site of Port Arthur. It was later revealed that he had killed 35 people. The events which occurred at Port Arthur on that day dominated the following week's newspapers and television news programmes. For the first few days the media concentrated on the actual events, on the impact on victims' families and on building a profile of the alleged 'gunman'. The events of the day were recreated by eyewitnesses giving graphic descriptions of what they had seen and amateur home videos being given constant airplay. In order to understand what had prompted his 'breakdown' there were interviews with his neighbours and ex-girlfriends who attempted to provide insights into his 'crazed' behaviour; there were even discussions about his favourite videos. Eventually, as questions began to be asked about the availability of high-powered weapons in Australia, the media focus, along with that of the politicians, swung towards the area of gun law reform.

At this time I was working with a grade 11 (16–17-year-olds) and a grade 9 (13–14-year-olds) class in a Brisbane school, Tamville State High, and with a grade 12 (17–18-year-olds) class in a Sunshine Coast hinterland school, Mountainview State High. During the week that followed Port Arthur, the media and politicians seemed to take little note of the fact that the gunman was in fact that: *a gun man*. An article in Brisbane's *Courier Mail* on the Tuesday caught my eye. It was based on a league table style list of the worst massacres committed by a lone gunman (Bloody toll world's worst 1996). Pictures of these gunmen accompanied the article. That all these mass murderers were men was a fact that had been ignored by most of the newspapers I had read. I decided to use this list as a teaching resource for a lesson in one of the boys' programmes.

I began the teaching session by handing out a photocopy of the article from the newspaper and by playing a song called *Montreal December '89*, by Judy Small (1990), an Australian feminist folk singer. The song recounts conversations and speeches made at a memorial service for 14 women shot at the University of Montreal by a man who blamed feminists for his non-acceptance into engineering at the University (see Faludi 1992). In the song two questions are asked: 'Why is it always men who resort to the gun, the sword and the fist?' and 'What is it about men that makes them do the things they do?' The song also makes the statement that: 'I know there are men of conscience too, who would never lift a hand in anger, who reject the macho way, who hate male violence too.' The students wrote these phrases in their journals and we spent the next 70 minutes discussing some of the ways in which masculinity has come to be associated with violence, and also how it was possible to encourage boys to become 'men of conscience'. This book is an extended exploration of the issues raised for educators as a result of discussions such as this one.

Tamville and Mountainview snapshots

A snapshot of the schools and the programmes in each of these schools is provided here as an introduction to the empirical data used in this book. This brief look at the schools does not explore the complexities and inter-personal dynamics that formed a major part of the schools' cultures and were a contributing factor to how the schools developed their programmes. This is beyond the scope of the book (some excellent ethnographic studies examining the constructions of masculinities within schools include Willis 1977; Kessler *et al.* 1985; Walker 1988; Connell 1989; Mac an Ghaill 1994c; Sewell 1997). Rather, these snapshots serve as a touchstone, as backdrops or reminders of the sites where some of the masculinities considered here were constantly being reproduced, reinforced and contested.

The two schools are located in two very different areas of Queensland, Australia. Tamville State High School is situated in a middle-class area of Brisbane, the State's capital city. This large school of approximately 1500 students prides itself on its 'traditional' ethos. It is strict about uniforms and student behaviour. These qualities are significant in the school's 'marketing strategy'. A large percentage of the students at Tamville come from middle-class backgrounds. However, many of these are not Anglo-Celtic. In particular, the school has a large proportion of students from Vietnamese backgrounds. In addition, many families from nearby 'poorer' suburbs send their children to this school in the hope that they will receive a 'better' education than the one they would receive in their local State High School (one such school has recently closed due to a lack of enrolments).

Mountainview is a rural town situated on the State's Sunshine Coast hinterland. It is approximately two hours by road from Brisbane. Mountainview State High School is the only available high school for students residing in this locality. The small school population of approximately 400 students is largely Anglo-Celtic and the socioeconomic status of the students is varied. One interesting dynamic between students is founded on lifestyle politics. Mountainview is situated in a farming community, a community known for its conservative values. However, Mountainview also has a reputation for its alternative lifestyle communities. Students from these diverse backgrounds seem on the surface to put their differences aside. But, from the occasional comments, it is clear that for many students lifestyle is an issue. This was most evident on the issues of guns and homophobia, and in each instance the boys who held conservative viewpoints were the loudest in expressing their views.

In 1996 these two schools both sought to implement separate gender and violence programmes for boys and girls in their schools. These programmes had quite different origins. The Brisbane community group Men Against Sexual Assault (MASA) initiated Tamville's programme. The Brisbane City Council provided a grant to the group to implement gender and violence programmes in two schools. The coordinator of MASA sent letters around to numerous schools inviting them to apply to have the programme conducted in their school. The two schools which were selected, one of which was Tamville, were chosen on the basis of timetables and other practical constraints, along with the intention to obtain some sort of diversity between the two chosen schools. In each school two grade levels were to be taught, and there were to be separate boys' and girls' programmes.

The female staff for these programmes were largely drawn from or coordinated through community-based feminist organizations, such as the Domestic Violence Resource Centre and the Brisbane-based young women's organization, Zig Zag. In relation to the male staff, these consisted of two MASA workers, a young man recommended by a community organization (one of the intentions of the project was to not only work with school students, but to also provide some young people concerned about gender and violence issues with the necessary training required for them to engage in this form of community work) and myself.

Tamville was chosen due to the commitment that was shown both by a male deputy principal and the school's female Human Relationships Coordinator, Victoria. Victoria was concerned that the school subject Human Relationships Education (HRE) was losing ground in the curriculum and saw the invitation from MASA as a 'good opportunity' to raise consciousness around gender and violence issues. The school was also attractive in that it had 70-minute lessons, which the reference group felt were more conducive to the programme's implementation than the more common 40-minute lesson. However, the school's administration did not appear to be fully committed to the programme. There were some concerns raised by the principal that if the local community knew that the school was doing a programme looking at issues of gender and violence they would perceive that the school had a problem with this issue (this had some research consequences, see below, page 10). In addition, the size of Tamville meant that the students who received the programme were only a minority: approximately 40 students (in both boys' and girls' programmes) out of a student population of 1500.

The Mountainview programme grew out of a Queensland Department of Education gender equity initiative: the 'Inter-Agency Project'. The Department of Education's Gender Equity Unit was engaged in a project to examine how schools related to community agencies.[1] The Gender Equity Unit had done work with Mountainview previously and was keen to see how Mountainview was addressing issues of gender, and in particular masculinity, in their existing separate boys' and girls' camps. Thus, when Mountainview volunteered to be part of this project the Gender Equity Unit welcomed them.

The school's guidance officer, Sarah, was instrumental in the decision to be part of this project. Teachers, parents and some students were particularly concerned about the 1996 group of year 12 boys. The whole year level was considered to be dysfunctional. There had been no school camp for this group of students because teachers were not prepared to go away with many of the students. Sarah was keen to address this behavioural issue in gender terms. For, as she comments:

> I've always had . . . an interest in the construction of gender and how that impacts on behaviour, because I think that a lot of the behaviour management programmes that have been happening in schools just are very superficial without actually looking at the underlying reason why people act the way they do.

As a result of discussions with personnel from the Gender Equity Unit the school decided to pilot a gender and violence programme with students from grade 12 and grade eight. The original idea of focusing on grade 12 students was expanded to include those from grade eight as many teachers in the school considered the grade 12 boys to be 'a lost cause'. In this instance, because of the school's small size, and hence unlike Tamville, all of the year eight and all of the year 12 students were involved. The programmes were also to be implemented through the HRE curriculum. The grade eight programme was be taught in the students' usual mixed HRE classes by their usual teacher. The grade 12 level was to be separated on the basis of sex, and the boys were to be further divided up according to their perceived potential negativity towards the programme. My involvement with the programmes was solely with the year 12 boys' programme, and with the group of boys who were considered to be more receptive to the issues. Apart from the smaller grade 12 boys' class, all of the classes were to be taught by teachers from the school. (I began my involvement as a researcher. However, this expanded as the programme began to take shape.) The smaller class of more recalcitrant boys was to be conducted by a community worker who was involved in private counselling as well as working in schools on gender and violence issues.

My involvement in the two programmes came about in an ad hoc manner. In relation to Tamville, I had been attending a conference/workshop day held by the Gender and Violence in Schools Network in Brisbane. As a result of discussions and participation in some of the activities I was invited by the coordinator of MASA to implement the Brisbane City Council funded school-based gender and violence project in one school. This led to my involvement in the project as both a member of the reference group and as the coordinator and designer of the boys' section of the programme at Tamville. Thus, prior to the implementation of the class-based activities I attended numerous meetings with other members of the project as we sought to identify the main objectives of the programme and to consider some sort of common approach to the issues. I also attended a parents' evening, and, with the female coordinator of Tamville's girls' programme, conducted a teacher in-service on the issues we intended covering throughout the programme.

Some problems did occur in obtaining permission to use the Tamville programme as part of the research for this book. Permission was withheld for a number of weeks. The school's principal was concerned that my research would indicate that there was a problem at the school with gender and violence. However, after some discussion and after I had changed the name of the research element of the programme from 'Challenging Violence in Schools' to 'Promoting Supportive School Environments' permission was granted. This initial refusal does indicate the sensitivity that underpins much social justice work within schools. For instance I know of a Queensland school that was reluctant to tackle the issue of homophobia in case it was considered to be a gay and lesbian school (Mills 1996; also see Epstein 1994: 117; Boulden 1996).

Permission to use Mountainview as a research site was obtained without any difficulty. In this instance, members of the Queensland Education Department had informed me about a boys' project that was being planned in this school. My first contact with the school was met favourably by the school's guidance officer and my subsequent request to the principal to observe the implementation of the boys' programme was treated in much the same manner. I attended several meetings with a deputy principal, a guidance officer, a community worker, a senior policy officer from the Gender Equity Unit and a social work student attached to the Unit in the school term preceding the implementation of the programme. One of the meetings also involved parents. These meetings culminated in an in-service programme for all teachers who were to be involved in teaching the gender and violence programme in either their grade 12 or grade eight HRE classes. In the early stages of this programme I was working closely with the male teacher in the larger group. However, during the course of this programme, this group was also split into two, and I took on the responsibility for working with one of them.

In many ways the programmes in the two schools had similar aims: that is, to disrupt normalized masculinity's association with violence and to critically engage boys in schools with issues of gender and violence. However, the ways in which the programmes developed and were implemented were quite different.

The Tamville programmes were designed externally to the school and were implemented by 'outsiders' with very little input from the school, apart from teacher support in the classroom. In relation to the boys' section of the programme the four men involved in the teaching process had several meetings with each other and with the women who were implementing the girls' programmes to discuss the ways in which we would approach the eight-week programme. In these meetings there was a lot of sharing of ideas and resources. However, it was clear from the beginning that the programmes in the two research schools would have quite different shapes. This was not perceived as a problem.

My original intention had been to observe these types of programme in action. However, my involvement in the project funded by Brisbane City Council enabled me to consider the ways in which I would implement such a programme for boys. In constructing the programme I drew on many of the excellent feminist and profeminist resources available (for example, Curriculum and Gender Equity Policy Unit 1995; Denborough 1995;[2] Friedman 1995; Salisbury and Jackson 1996) and avoided the more men's rights and 'therapeutic' type resources (Browne 1995; Fletcher 1995a, 1995b; for discussions of these men's politics see Kimmel 1996; Connell 1995a; Lingard and Douglas 1999). A unit outline was constructed on these ideas and was intended as a working document that would shape the various lessons presented throughout the programme. The boys in this school generally received the programme quite favourably, although the grade 11 group was probably the more receptive of the two classes.

The Mountainview programme was developed over time as a collective effort involving teachers, a guidance officer, a deputy principal, an Education Department gender equity policy officer and community workers (I'm casting myself as a community worker here, although my status as an ex-teacher now involved in teacher education and in research gave me a credibility I might not otherwise have had). The actual planning of the boys' lessons began at the day-long teacher in-service prepared by members of the Queensland Department of Education's Gender Equity Unit. In the final session of the day the male HRE teacher, Craig, the community worker, Richard, and I planned how we would approach the first few lessons. It was decided that we would adopt some of Richard's suggestions relating to issues of personal power for both groups of boys in these initial lessons. However, once we began implementing these lessons it became clear that the two different groups were responding quite differently to the one approach. In order to cater to this difference, Craig and I began to use the Tamville outline as our model. This too as an approach became redundant in the face of the boys' opposition to the programme. Our response to this crisis led to some positive outcomes. We attempted to encourage the boys to indicate to us how it would be more appropriate to deal with these issues in the school. A suggestion from the students was that grade 12 boys should be trained to work with grade eight boys on these issues. We ran with this idea and this group of boys was then split up into two groups, one of which would be trained to deliver such programmes, and the other which would continue with the existing programme.

The school administration was very supportive of the boys' suggestions. The boys were invited to attend the grade eight camp in the next term and asked to provide grade eight boys with some workshops on issues of gender and violence. The school principal approved a day's release from classes for this group of boys and for Craig, and funded an in-service style programme for the boys. In consultation with Craig and the guidance officer, Sarah, I constructed a workshop that included various activities which the boys could implement with the grade eights and also provided them with a theoretical basis for the programme. This section was delivered by Julie, a principal policy officer with the Queensland Department of Education. Unfortunately, the grade eight camp was cancelled due to a lack of interest on the part of grade eight students. The grade 12 boys were presented with an opportunity to run the programme at school, but this obviously did not enthuse them to the degree that an outside venue might have done. The dents to the boys' enthusiasm did lead to a few problems with delivery and time management. However, it was hoped that the lessons of this programme would provide a basis for future years.

The events at Mountainview represent an opportunity that existed for some boys to engage in a politics which sought to challenge dominant constructions of masculinity. What is of interest here is how many boys who had demonstrated an antagonism towards the aims of the programme in one setting were able to support and, with a group of peers, organize and conduct a similarly orientated programme with younger boys in a different context. This occurrence demonstrates how identification with a particular masculinity politics is not necessarily fixed, but can be shifted and reconfigured in response to particular contexts and events. Tamville and Mountainview, through their boys' programmes, sought to provide boys with contexts and interventions that would encourage a rejection of versions of masculine identity which perpetrate and tolerate violence as an acceptable means of masculinized behaviour. However, it is important to realize that non-dominant masculinities may only be performed momentarily, and that such performances can often be emotionally difficult for boys to maintain (see Connell 1997: 73). Schools thus need to provide a range of support structures that enable students, both boys and girls, to experiment with non-traditional gender performances in a safe environment.

The focus of this book is on identifying the issues that need to be considered in any attempt to challenge the presence of boys' violences in schools. It stresses the need for those in schools concerned about such matters to make the concept of 'masculinity' problematic, especially those masculinized performances that are grounded in misogynist and homophobic rhetoric. There is also a broader intent within the book to promote more equitable gender relations. Normalized forms of masculinity, that is those forms of masculinity which are often assumed to be 'natural', have been implicated in oppressing girls/women and marginalized boys/men through a variety of means, for example, access to legitimated knowledges, distributions of income, public recognition, and exclusion from institutions of power. However, underpinning these forms of oppression has been an implied threat of violence. As Connell (1995a: 83) has commented in relation to the advantages accruing to men from the existing structure of gender relations: 'A structure of inequality on this scale, involving a massive dispossession of social resources, is hard to imagine without violence. It is, overwhelmingly, the dominant gender who hold and use the means of violence.' Hence, while this book is about violence in schools, I hope that it will be part of a struggle for a more gender just society.

Organization of the book

The purpose of this book is to provide a lens through which to approach the development of strategies and programmes that seek to challenge the existence of gender-based violence in schools. Those who intend to engage in such projects have a long and difficult road ahead of them. There are no quick fix ready-made solutions that can be implemented in the same ways in different schools. Every school has its own context or 'thisness' which works to shape gender relations within its grounds. Hence, every school will need to work out for itself how best to tackle the issue of violence; this book seeks to assist teachers, students and others in schools to develop their own responses to challenging violence.

The first part of the book is concerned with the theoretical underpinnings of such work with boys (and men) in schools. The second part focuses more directly on schooling and in particular on curriculum and pedagogy issues in relation to problematizing dominant constructions of masculinity. The book does not provide a list of instructions on how schools should implement work that challenges the legitimacy of boys' violent behaviours. Instead each chapter concludes with a series of activities and questions – referred to as 'strategies for schools' – which a research group, or other interested people, within a school can use in order to stimulate discussion among staff and students or to develop their own strategies appropriate to their own schools. The conclusion provides some principles that need to be taken into account when undertaking anti-violence work in schools.

Chapter 1 of the book explores some of the ways in which violence has become associated with a 'normalized' masculinity. There is a particular focus here on the relationships of dominant forms of masculinity with sport and work, and with the ways in which boy's and men's identities are entwined with their abilities to demonstrate their power over girls and women and also over other boys and men. In order to unshackle violent behaviours from 'normal' ways of being a boy, educators will need to consider ways in which many of the practices considered in this chapter can be demasculinized.

Chapter 2 takes up this theme by exploring the notion of violence as masculine and masculinity as violent. It argues that masculinity has had violence done to it by processes which suggest that there is only one true way of being male. It thus explores the ways in which different masculinities are organized in relation to each other. The chapter suggests that decreasing violent behaviours in schools will require the expansion of the range of ways in which it is acceptable to be a boy. This will mean breaking down the notion that all boys are the same, and focusing on and valuing different non-violent ways of being a boy.

Chapter 3 explores curriculum issues with a focus on one of the more common means by which gender and violence issues are tackled in schools, that is through special programmes for boys. It argues that this is perhaps not the most effective means by which boys' behaviours can be challenged. However, such an approach is often the most strategic way of getting such issues onto the agenda within schools. This chapter provides an account of how one school's programme for boys implemented through a marginalized area of the curriculum served as a means by which this concern could be taken into other areas of the school.

Chapter 4 looks at some key pedagogical concerns in working with boys on masculinity issues. There is a focus here on the popular topic of male teachers and also on the advantages and disadvantages of having people external to the school working with boys on such issues. There is also some consideration given to the notion of 'empowerment'. Many boys in schools face a paradoxical situation. On the one hand they do not feel very powerful while on the other hand their relationships often involve them attempting to exert power over other students and sometimes teachers. This means that simplistic notions of 'empowering' boys need to be problematized. The suggestion here is that teachers must give some thought to ways of developing respectful pedagogies for working with boys which take this paradox into account.

The book concludes (Chapter 5) by presenting some key principles that educators need to take into consideration in their development of work on gender and violence issues with boys in schools. This is not a blueprint for change. There is sometimes a tendency within education to look for simple solutions to complex problems. Such solutions do not exist. Teachers, and others in schools, will need to give consideration to their local context and to negotiate and plan with their local communities appropriate responses to the issues of gender and violence in their schools. The principles offered in this concluding chapter represent a framework within which such negotiations and plannings can take place.

Throughout the book interview data collected from Tamville and Mountainview State High Schools are used to inform the arguments contained in each chapter. At Tamville, interviews were conducted with grade 11 and grade nine boys who had been part of the programme; the HRE coordinator responsible for initiating the programme's implementation and who had sat in on some grade 11 lessons; a male teacher, the science head of department, who had sat in on the grade nine programme; and the grade nine's usual female HRE and science teacher who had been with the girls' programme. At Mountainview, interviews were conducted with grade 12 boys, these boys tended to be those who were most supportive of the programme's aims; the school's female guidance officer; a female deputy principal who had been very supportive of the programme and who had taken a grade 12 girls' group; and the male community worker implementing the programme with the smaller group of boys. These interviews were supplemented by an interview with a Department of Education Gender Equity policy officer who had worked closely with Mountainview High School in order to get their programme off the ground.

A note on men and feminism

This book, in taking as its specific focus men's and boys' violence, draws heavily on feminist theory for it has been feminists who have been central to problematizing dominant constructions of masculinity and their relationship to violence. For example, feminists have been able to identify rape, domestic violence, war, ecological disasters and poverty as consequences of masculinized gender performances (see, for example, Greer 1971; Brownmiller 1976; Daly 1978; Ward 1984; Reardon 1985; Woodhull 1988; Scutt 1990; Bart and Moran 1993; Polk 1994). This is thus a profeminist book. A profeminist masculinity politics is representative of what Connell (1995a: 220–4) has referred to as an 'exit politics'. Such a politics encourages men to 'exit' from those politics that endorse men's privileged positioning within existing gendered relations. It is a politics that seeks to address matters of gender justice from a masculine perspective, which treats feminism as an ally rather than as an adversary. Men who identify with this politics recognize that they approach matters of gender justice from a privileged position; and thus seek points of 'exit' for themselves and other men from privileged positions within existing gendered relations of power. Men's adoption of feminist politics is of course not unproblematic.

There has long been an understandable suspicion by feminists of men's use of feminism (Braidotti 1987; Jardine 1987; Morris 1987; Shoalwater 1987; Cannan and Griffin 1990; Hanmer 1990; see also Kimmel 1998). Inevitable questions include: 'What's in it for them?'; 'Why would a man voluntarily give up his privileged positioning within the existing gender order?'; 'Does this represent a colonization of feminist theory?'; 'Why now?'; 'How will the complexities within feminisms be represented?' The use of feminism in a text such as this one requires that these issues be addressed.

Clearly there are some personal rewards associated with the construction of a profeminist text, some of which do reinforce an individual 'patriarchal dividend' (Connell 1994, 1995a, b), for example, financial gain and academic recognition. However, other issues also motivate some men's support of feminism in their work and personal lives. I find many of those suggested by Bob Connell (1987: xiii) to be illuminative about some men's support for feminism. These include: that even those who benefit from an unjust system, such as men, can recognize the oppressiveness of that system; that gender injustices affect women who men are close to and thus some men have a 'relational interest' (Connell 1994, 1995b: 149) in tackling gender injustices; that some heterosexual men are also injured by the present system; that the inevitability of changes in gender relations means that some men will seek new ways of relating to women; and that men like all human beings have the capacity to develop the abilities to care for others. I would like to briefly comment on two of those reasons, which Connell elaborates on elsewhere (1994, 1995b): that some heterosexual men are oppressed by hegemonic masculinities and that most men have 'relational interests' with particular women, such as daughters, mothers, lovers and sisters. These are important points. However, they can also be problematic.

The first point, that dominant masculinizing processes hurt men and boys too, may be used to legitimate the politics of masculinity therapy, which often construct men as victims. This lets men off the hook. It is important to recognize, as Connell does, that what he calls the patriarchal dividend is distributed, admittedly in different proportions, to most men. The reality that the current gender arrangements are ones that serve the interests of the social group men needs to be kept in focus in any discussion of men's suffering or pain resulting from the pressures exerted by dominant masculinizing processes. Furthermore, it ought to be recognized that the sufferings some men experience in relation to masculinizing processes are brought about as a consequence of the maintenance of an unjust gender order that privileges the interests of the social group men and boys over that of women and girls. Thus, while the issue of men's and boys' pain is one that needs to be addressed when working with boys in schools, feminist concerns about men making this a focus of their work also need to be taken into account (see, for example, Hagan 1992). Being open to feminist criticisms and responding to these criticisms in ways that do not construct men and boys as the victims of feminism is a crucial aspect of a profeminist politics. However, in encouraging boys to engage in a positive manner with feminism it is important to acknowledge, as Kimmel (1998: 59) does, that 'men should want to support feminist reforms: not only because of an ethical imperative – of course it is right and just – but also because men will live happier and healthier lives, with better relations with the women, men, and children in their lives if they do.'

Connell's second point about 'relational interests' has the potential to lapse into familiar patterns of paternalism where men seek to provide protection to 'their' women from other men, that is a form of 'white knightist' masculinity politics. (This was clearly the case for some of the boys who were interviewed for this book.) There is also the tendency, which is often well meaning, for some men to see some women, and in particular their daughters, as being different from other women and as deserving of special treatment as a sort of 'honorary man' (see Bordo 1998). This individualizing of women will serve to negate the social and political dimensions of injustices against women. On the point of men's 'relational interests', perhaps, more significantly for the cultivation of a profeminist politics among some men has been their involvement with feminist women. Many profeminist men have utilized the knowledge gained from these contacts to provide a greater understanding of their own lives and to shape their struggles against injustices in a number of areas, not only in relation to gender. There are perhaps too many complexities involved in the acquisition of a politics to understand fully how any one person arrives at their particular position. The important point is that, as Connell (1994: 5, original emphasis) has commented: 'Support for women's emancipation is always a *possible* stance for men.'

Men's utilization of feminist theory, however, needs to be done in a respectful way. This will mean men acknowledging the privileges that become automatically theirs as a 'birth right' and how this 'birth right' has been integral to the oppression of a great many people. Furthermore, it will entail an active rejection of such privilege (although bearing in mind that despite this rejection, privileges will remain until such time as the existing gender order is reconfigured). This is not a Utopian fantasy. Challenging one's own privilege does have a history. Some white people have engaged in struggles against racial injustices; some straights have supported gay and lesbian liberation; some middle-class people have argued against economic and social inequities that advantage their class over those from lower socio-economic backgrounds; and some men have supported feminist struggles. A commitment to social justice can be a powerful motivating factor in cases of people engaging in struggles against their own interests.

There are of course difficult issues in relation to men engaging with feminist debates. A number of the feminist contributors to *Men in Feminism* (Jardine and Smith 1987) took exception to the term *in*. 'What do men think they are doing *in feminism*?' a number of the contributors asked (Braidotti 1987; Jardine 1987; Morris 1987). This is a valid question. There are a number of debates between feminists and within feminism which are not a place for men, for example, the debates over the extent to which women are made victims by their reporting of sexual harassment. It seems to me that a respectful relationship to feminism in such cases would see men working against the existence of sexual harassment and supporting women in their choices, rather than making suggestions about what women should or should not do. However, there are times when men using feminist theory have to make decisions regarding conflicting viewpoints within feminism.

Feminism is not a unitary body of theory. Consequently, there are often divisions and tensions within feminism. Profeminist men often have to make decisions about which feminisms to be 'pro' in relation to particular issues (see Flood 1997a; Lingard and Douglas 1998 for a discussion of some of the most common issues surrounding profeminist politics). This is particularly the case in this book in relation to masculinity and violence. There are a number of clear differences between the writings of feminists such as Dworkin (1981), Brownmiller (1976) and Griffin (1979) and those of feminists such as Segal (1990), Marcus (1992) and Woodhull (1988) on this issue. In this book, I have found the latter group's analyses of this issue to be more useful for disrupting connections between masculinity and violence. However, while seeing the arguments of the former group, often described as radical feminists, as problematic, I acknowledge their work as having been critical to the placing of men's violence on the political and social agenda.

Throughout this book I have used those feminist theories which seem best to shed light on some of the ways in which schools can engage with the problem of boys and violence. These have been the theories which would seem to indicate that there is a potential for boys and men to change in ways that are less oppressive to women. Such a hope is often contained within the writings and practices of feminists (see, for example, Hagan 1998). For as Jane Kenway (1996: 447) states: 'Most feminists want boys and men to change so that they cause less trouble for girls and women and themselves, so the sexes can live alongside each other in a safe, secure, stable, respectful, harmonious way and in relationships of mutual life-enhancing respect.' This book seeks to support and contribute to such a feminist struggle by looking at the ways in which boys in schools can be encouraged to challenge and reject those masculinizing processes that legitimate men's and boys' uses of violence, and perhaps a little more ambitiously, to encourage boys to understand the ways in which violence has been an integral feature of maintaining an unjust gender order.

Notes

1 In 1997 the Queensland Department of Education was renamed with the more corporate title of 'Education Queensland'. In that same year the Gender Equity Unit was 'downsized' and subsumed under the more generic 'Equity Unit'. However, at the time of the school research the former titles were being used and are thus the ones that are employed here in relation to these materials.

2 A later edition of this article is published in McLean, Carey and White (1996), the 1995 version is used throughout this book.

chapter one

Violence and the signifiers of masculinity

violence is a reference point for the production of boys and men.

(Hearn 1998: 7)

Introduction

In this chapter the practices through which masculinity has become associated with violence and power are explored. This is a necessary step towards developing projects within schools that can challenge boys' violent behaviour, for the capacity to commit violence is one of the most essentialized attributes of dominant forms of masculinity. Violence here subsumes the notion of 'coercive power', that is a power *over* others. It is this naturalized attribute of masculinity which lies at the heart of the network of power relations that maintains existing patterns of gendered privileges. This chapter will demonstrate how assumptions about 'man's' natural proclivity towards violence and desire for coercive power are not natural but are the product of social constructs that serve to reinforce masculine privileges. The disruption of these assumptions needs to be part of the work done with boys in schools.

This chapter explores the ways in which the association between a normalized, or hegemonic, masculinity and violence is constructed through various social practices. The chapter foreshadows many of the arguments in the following chapter, which assert that masculinity has been violenced and violence masculinized. The exploration of violence and masculinity in this chapter is one that needs to be a focal part of work done in schools with boys on gender and violence issues. It is important that boys (and others in schools) come to see that violence and a desire for coercive power are cultural signs which have been imposed on masculinity; that the imposition of these signs works in the interests of particular men; and that signifiers of masculinity which relate to violence are not immutable. This requires boys to engage with the ways in which high status forms of masculinity have acquired their status and to question whose interests have been furthered through this process.

Hegemonic masculinity and violence

Masculinity as a broad category can only exist in a contrasting relationship to the category of femininity. Masculinity is what femininity is not. Hence, while both normalized 'masculinities' and normalized 'femininities' are constructed through social practices that suggest what is normal behaviours for boys and men and for girls and women there are important differences. For, as Arnot (1984: 53, original emphasis) has argued: 'Masculinity in all its various forms, is not the same as femininity – it is after all a form of *power* and *privilege*.' Thus, while a normalized masculinity can be regarded as a 'hegemonic masculinity', a normalized femininity is more accurately described as an 'emphasized femininity' (Kessler *et al.* 1985; Connell 1987, 1995a). It is the normalizing of hegemonic masculinities and emphasized femininities that presents men and women with various legitimated subject positions which construct the existing gender order.

Connell, drawing on Jill Matthews (1984), has defined the gender order as 'a historically constructed pattern of power relations between men and women and definitions of femininity and masculinity' (1987: 98). The pattern of the gender order operating in most Western countries is one that favours the interests of males. Thus, the term preferred by Gilbert and Taylor (1991: 9, original emphasis), the '*patriarchal gender order*', aptly describes the power relations existing within the gender order present in most Western societies. There is a recognition here that 'patriarchy' is a contested term among feminists (see Pringle 1995). However, it is a term that is useful as an indicator of how relations of power within Western countries are balanced in the favour of men. This is not to suggest that it is a unitary, monolithic and totalizing system of domination where all men are pitted against all women.

The power relations that shape this patriarchal gender order are clearly not solely a politics of struggle between masculinity and femininity. For, as Connell (1995a: 37) has argued, 'There is a gender politics within masculinity.' (As there is of course within femininity.) This politics plays its role in maintaining the subordination and domination of girls and women within Western cultures. However, this politics also has repressive consequences for some men. Connell identifies four broad categories of masculinity that are engaged in this politics: hegemonic, subordinate, complicit and marginalized (1995a: 76–81). He refers to the way in which these masculinities interrelate as the 'social organization of masculinity.' (This is explored further in Chapter 2.) These categories of masculinity are useful as descriptors of male performances, rather than as denoting the qualities of particular boys and men. Males rarely demonstrate a coherent or consistent form of masculinity, and it is possible to see particular or individual boys or men operating at different times and in different contexts in a number of these categories. This chapter is concerned with the ways in which hegemonic forms of masculinity are represented within Western cultures.

The term hegemonic masculinity can be problematic (Donaldson 1993). Hegemonic masculinities are high status forms of masculinity which have been constructed as those masculinities that demonstrate 'normal' masculine behaviour (see Kessler *et al.* 1985; Connell 1987, 1995a). However, this form of behaviour might not be that practised by most boys and men. Rather, it serves as an idealized form of masculinity by which boys and men can be measured, by themselves and others, to determine the extent of their 'manliness'. Furthermore, hegemonic masculine behaviours do not always reap benefits for the person who displays these behaviours. For instance, one only has to think of school boys whose hypermasculine behaviours might impress sections of their peer group, but inevitably leads to school failure (see, for example, Willis 1977, and see Francis 1999 for responses to Stephen Byers' view of this issue, the former British education minister), or the sportsman/boy who does great damage to his body in the pursuit of status. The status and interpretations of hegemonic masculine behaviours are also nuanced by factors such as class, ethnicity/race, age and sexuality. For instance, hegemonic masculine status in Australia is often linked to excessive displays of heterosexual activity (encapsulated in such notions as the 'stud'). However, when performed by Black boys the excessiveness of this activity is valued quite differently within dominant sections of society from how it is valued when performed by white boys.

Hegemonic masculinities are also contextual constructs in that a particular form of masculinity acquires hegemonic status only in certain situations. Thus, the hegemonic nature of the subject position from which a boy or man operates will depend on where he is (for example, in a pub, in a boardroom, on a football field, at a university, on the street or in his home) and with whom he is (for instance his 'mates', his mother, his father, his boss, his colleagues, his lover, his staff or alone) in those places. However, there are common elements within all forms of hegemonic masculinities. These elements relate to a man's strength (physical, intellectual, of character and/or of willpower), rationality and supremacy over those (constructed as) 'inferior' to him. It is these masculinized attributes that are demonstrative of a masculinity which normalizes the association of masculinity with violence. And it is this normalization that shores up privileged men's position within society.

Signifiers of masculinity

The following section examines some of the ways in which a boy's or man's ability to dominate others act as signifiers of masculinity. In so doing it makes general references to the processes of schooling. These signifiers of masculinity impact on most males within Western societies. However, it should be noted that responses to them will vary in a multitude of ways, and that not least of the factors affecting these responses will be issues of race and class.

Horsfall (1991: 80–87) argues that sport, work, alcohol and power over women are important signifiers of masculinity. Power over other men should also be included in this list. These signifiers of masculinity clearly associate violence with a blueprint masculinity: that is a form of masculinity which shapes all 'true', or 'normal', masculinities. These signifiers are given meaning in various institutional contexts. Schools are one of Western societies' major institutions where the masculinization of what is valorized in each of these signifiers is re/produced. Sport is a major component of the curriculum, and 'boys' sports' invariably are the most prestigious of the sporting curriculum. Furthermore, these sports tend to be those which glorify the strong, tough, aggressive, competitive, and hence violent, boy.

Schools, aside from being workplaces for teachers, also provide students with a very realistic and instructional role-play of a gendered life in the workplace. These include the ways in which gendered roles in schools are distributed among teachers and the way in which masculinized subjects/ occupations are more valued than those which have been feminized. Females who move into these traditionally male spheres of influence have to contend with males seeking to protect the masculine identity (and hence value) of these subjects/occupations. Thus, girls/women who move into masculinized subjects/occupations experience numerous barriers, including sexual harassment and intimidation, to their successful participation in these areas.

Alcohol use and abuse start to appear among teenage students at secondary schools. While alcohol may not actually appear within the school grounds its presence can often be felt in discussions between students about their out of school social activities. These discussions tend to be at their most boastful when males are describing their activities. Alcohol is an important signifier of masculinity and has obvious links with masculinized violence (see for instance Polk 1994; Cannan 1996). However, it will not be considered in any detail in this book as its valorization does not have the same legitimate status within school curricula and structures as do other signifiers of masculinity. (It should be noted, though, that many schools recognize the importance of this issue, and run some very constructive and worthwhile programmes dealing with alcohol abuse.)

Power over women dominates the gender processes within the school. It is not only built into school structures and curricula but also shapes the relationships between male and female students; male and female staff; and male students and female staff. This power can range from male students' often unthinking domination of class space and school space down to conscious acts of intimidation and sexual threats against female students and teachers (see Morgan *et al.* 1988; Walkerdine 1989; Milligan *et al.* 1992; Gilbert *et al.* 1995: 51–8; House of Representatives Standing Committee on Employment, Education and Training 1994; Sadker and Sadker 1994; Stein 1995; Collins *et al.* 1996). There is evidence to suggest that these threats are often carried out, sometimes to the point of rape (personal communications with rape crisis workers).

Power over other men has been ritualized in most Western societies as a signifier of masculinity. This has occurred not only through sport, but also in areas seemingly as diverse as: the valorization of war in traditional victory and commemoration parades; the schoolyard fight; and 'poofter' bashing (see Connell 1995a: 83). Masculinity is often at its most 'glorious' when it represents the domination of other men. Power over women is an assertion of what is perceived to be a 'natural' state of affairs. However, the domination of other men represents a 'true' competition where the 'best man wins'. This competition is alive and well in schools in most Western industrialized societies (Walker 1988; Martino 1999).

These signifiers of masculinity are evident in most Western schools. For example, this can be seen in Walker's (1988) ethnographic study of an all boys' Australian urban working-class secondary school. There is a clear hierarchy of masculinities within this school. At the top of the hierarchy is a group known as 'the footballers'. Walker says of this group:

> The superiority of heterosexuality, of machismo demonstrated through athletic and sexual prowess, physical strength, drinking and appropriate verbal display, along with the monopoly of the English language spoken with a traditional Australian accent, were the shibboleths of footballer culture.
>
> (Walker 1988: 39)

In each of the signifiers of masculinity there is an association of maleness with coercive power. Dominant images of the 'ideal man' portray him as competitive, strong, aggressive when crossed and as a good 'mate' (mate here referring to friendships between males as opposed to sexual partner). This image is true of the action hero, the football star, the business magnate and even the popular politician. The physical, sexual and, sometimes, intellectual prowess of these heroic men is beyond the reach of most men. However, the ideal forms the basis of hegemonic masculinities. Thus, for instance, the jungles of Vietnam can serve as a metaphor for suburban and inner-city streets, the stock exchange, schools and even the family. This metaphor creates a frightening picture when it becomes obvious that the violence at play in these settings is far more representative of the 'real' violence of war, where the victims tend to be women, the young and/or the poor, than of cinematographic violence. The ways in which these signifiers construct an 'idealized' man requires that they be explored in more detail. The following exploration will draw on interview data collected from boys who had participated in gender and violence programmes run through their schools.

Sport as a signifier of masculinity

Sport is an important signifier of masculinity. Indeed as Burstyn (1999: 33) has noted, in an era when many of the great master narratives have been undermined and have lost their explanatory powers, 'one master narrative – the one of hypermasculinity – survives and thrives through the culture of sport and its erotic, heroic, masculine idealisations.' The sporting arena is a site in which the validity and status of a boy's/man's gendered identity can be asserted, challenged and negotiated. In the following section, I critique the role of sport as a 'community of practice' (see Fitzclarence *et al.* 1997). This does not mean that sport per se is as an activity devoid of worth. Sport may be beneficial to health and the development of motor coordination skills; it can provide a supportive communal activity when conducted in an environment that encourages participation, friendly rivalry and fun. It can also be very satisfying to perform particularly challenging or difficult skills successfully. However, there is a more negative side of sport: a side that is implicated in reinforcing dominant gendered relations of power. It is this side that I examine here.

There have been a number of studies analysing how sport is integrated into the processes that preserve existing gender relations (Bryson 1987; Messner and Sabo 1990, 1994; Thornton 1993; Disch and Kane 1996; Jefferson 1996; Parker 1996; Schacht 1996; Fitzclarence *et al.* 1997; M. Mills 1997b; Wedgwood 1997; Burstyn 1999). So significant is sport to the gendering process that Bryson (1987: 357) has argued that: 'Sport needs to be analysed along with rape, pornography, and domestic violence as a means through which men monopolize force.' This monopolizing of force is apparent in such popular discourses as those that describe masculinized sports, for example various codes of football (such as rugby, soccer and gridiron), as an outlet for men's naturally aggressive tendencies. The assumption is often that it is better for boys and/or men to use up their aggressive energies on the football field, where it can be tightly controlled within a set of rules, rather than in social situations where a man's uncontrolled aggression may have fatal consequences for others.

This was evident in some comments made by Peter, one of the grade nine boys from Tamville:

I just like to get, you know, run and it relaxes ya. You know it calms you down and stuff like that. I think it's important for men to do sport but you don't have to be good at it, you can just to do it.

Peter is a young Aboriginal boy who has experienced significant violence in his life and he speaks of what it is like to be in a fight:

I've had fights and that, I fought my cousins and stuff and friends, other friends and that, and it's like, it's hard, like the pressure's on saying, 'Oh no don't be chicken, you'll smash him, you'll smash him,' like that. And like you just get so, like I do, I get so psyched up and I go out and I, and I, you smash the person up. Like you want to keep going. That's like what I find happens to me. You want to keep going. You want to do it more and more.

It is perhaps because of this involvement in fighting that Peter's teachers have encouraged him to take part in sports such as football.

I like I love sport. My teachers have said, in my previous schools, have said, that I am a very talented sportsman. See I like running and football and stuff. I made it for a rep side on football and stuff like that. But well you see . . . it's just different, men are like good at different things. Like I like sport and that so I really find it relaxes me and you know it gives me what I like to do to have a good time. Have a game of football or run or something like that.

This encouragement, as well meaning as it might have been, may be contributing to the construction of Peter as a naturally violent boy who needs an outlet for his aggression. In this pathologizing of Peter, social factors, for example racism, are ignored. It is not surprising that Peter has taken up football as his sport.

Sport is hegemonized. Sports with the greatest hegemonic status are those that can operate as proving grounds for masculinity. These tend to be the sports that have a strong emphasis on violence, for example, various codes of contact football (such as rugby and gridiron) and boxing. These sports valorize the extremes of masculinity: aggressiveness, strength, speed, competitiveness and domination of the opposition. In Australia, soccer is often considered to be less violent, and hence less masculine, than some of the other forms of football; however, it too has an important masculinizing role in those countries where it occupies hegemonic status. Holly (1985: 56) notes the significance of soccer (football) in England:

football occupies a mythological place in our culture. It is the celebration of male skills and stamina and football matches are the arena for male competition and violence. One of the defining features of football is the systematic exclusion of women. It also monopolizes television space, playground space and reinforces substantial male ownership of many aspects of the environment.

(Holly 1985: 56)

The importance of sport as a signifier of masculinity is often most evident in young men. In many instances a boy's identification or lack of identification with sport, especially masculinized sports, serves as a benchmark by which the value of his masculinity can be socially determined (Sadker and Sadker 1994: 209–15; Gilbert and Gilbert 1998: 60–72). This is well captured by Sabo (1994) who, in his description of why he took up American football, states:

> Like a young child who learns to dance or sing for a piece of candy, I played for rewards. Winning at sports meant winning friends and carving a place for myself within the male pecking order. Success at the game would make me less like myself and more like the older boys and my hero, Dick Butkus. Pictures of his hulking snarling form filled my head and hung above my bed, beckoning me forward like a mythic Siren. If I could be like Butkus, I told myself, people would adore me as much as I adored him. I might even adore myself.
>
> (Sabo 1994: 83)

Sabo's comments are supported by numerous comments made by the Mountainview and Tamville boys. For instance, those made by James:

> In year nine . . . I came to this school . . . I was a nobody. Like I was one of the people that no one knew. That sort of didn't really get picked on, but was just one of the people that was out on the side. Like never talked about . . . never nothing. Just a nothing man so to speak. But I started playing basketball and it just so happened that I had a natural gift at that sport and it just worked out really good. I was playing basketball when I was year nine and I was better than most of the year twelves. And that way you just sort of get status in the school. You get a name for yourself. Sort of everyone . . . like you start getting friends and stuff. So I don't know it's just been lucky for me I guess.

It is apparent that sport plays a major role in the construction of masculinities, either in terms of a rejection, ambivalence or acceptance of a sporting ethos, in both working-class schools and middle- and upper-class schools (see Connell *et al.* 1982; Walker 1988; Mac an Ghaill 1994c: 108). Those boys who do not measure up, the effeminate, the overweight and the underweight and who do not compensate for this by engaging in other masculine activities, often related to alcohol, motor bikes or cars, are usually made to suffer the consequences of their lack of 'masculinity'. For instance, as Wade states: 'You know, you see . . . you see big fat guys who don't like sport, and then you see, you know, guys who are really fit and they often tease the people who can't do sport or stuff.'

There is a clear desire on the part of those boys who are not good at sport to be so:

Joseph: Yeah it's good if you're good at sports. Like I'm not (laughter) . . . 'Cos like some people are like built to be athletes. Different builds and stuff too.
Martin: And does that make a difference in how you're treated?
Joseph: Yeah.
Martin: In what ways?
Joseph: 'Cos, you like everybody knows ya if you're good at something. And you're talked about a lot if you're good at something.
Martin: Would you like to be good at sports?
Joseph: Yeah.

According to Harry from Mountainview, sport is also seen as an important means of making friends. Oscar supports this, 'It would be hard to find, like, find friends out of the sport area I guess. I guess, that's like a lot of the way that guys meet other guys.' Bryce, makes a similar point,

I'd like to be good at sports because then . . . you get out you get to know more people as well. Like and then you get real heaps of friends through sport because if you know someone they know heaps of people and then sort of you get to know everyone around the place.

This importance that sport plays in a boy's life may well have long-term consequences for the gender relations within which the boy will later find himself. For instance, the dependence on sport for friends can have detrimental effects for women who are involved now and later in a sportsman's life. Those sportsmen who are involved in team sports are often expected to put the interests of the team above those of the women in their lives. A man's identity can thus become inextricably linked to that of his team. (Similar comments can be made about men who participate in sport solely as spectators – see Burstyn 1999.) This not only works to oppress any nurturing, loving, caring and sharing emotions in a man's intimate relations, but also to reinforce the masculine privileging of the public over the private.

This privileging does not only occur through men's involvement in team sports for it is not only in such sports where men learn to put the interests of women second to their sport (see for instance, Connell 1990). A man's dedication to success in the public world of sport will often see him prioritizing his lifestyle in such a way that women do not interfere in his potential success. However, it is in team sports where the camaraderie between players, a camaraderie which is often likened to that of warriors in battle, is a valorized aspect of the masculinizing processes of sport.

These relationships between men in a sporting team, though, are often fragile and based on a shared activity: the match. A player's sense of oneness with his team is in constant threat of being removed should he demonstrate any weakness. Hence, players play when injured, they take risks on behalf of the team, and they show little compassion for the bodies of their opposition. A team player will often suffer from a form of performance anxiety. He must perform, and he must perform masculinely. One of the greatest disasters for a sportsman is to be dropped from the team (see, for example, Messner 1992: 72–4). To demonstrate weakness is to become the 'other': 'a woman' or a 'pansy'. The colloquialism that: 'You are only as good as your last game' ensures that sportsmen are under constant stress to perform. Engaging in the practice of violent sports is thus not a cost free exercise for many players.

These sports promote an instrumental view of the masculine body. This view plays a major role in those constructions of masculinity that encourage players to position the interests of the team over those of their own bodies. This was clearly evident in Australia during 1995 in the much documented and highly lauded actions of Trevor Gillmeister who dragged himself out of hospital in order to captain Queensland in a rugby league State of Origin game against New South Wales. His actions were regarded as the selfless act of a warrior who was putting his own health on the line for the sake of his State. In 1999, billboards throughout Queensland carried a poster advertising a sports drink that utilized an image of Gillmeister being carried on the shoulders of his team mates with the caption, 'The stuff legends are made of'. This 'loyalty' to the team can have quite negative effects for the player, for as Messner (1992: 71) comments: 'The instrumental rationality that teaches athletes to view their own bodies as machines or weapons with which to annihilate an objectified opponent comes back on the athlete. The body-as-weapon ultimately results in violence against one's own body.'

This is not a problem that faces only top level athletes, but also those young, and sometimes older, sportsmen who play sport for 'fun'. The valorization of a top sportsman's qualities have an effect on those aspiring to success. The seemingly distant violence of, for example, professional football can manifest itself in very 'real' situations. For instance, the traditional Queensland versus New South Wales State of Origin football (rugby league) series is hyped into a (civil) warlike frenzy with such slogans as 'State against State and mate against mate' (see McKay and Middlemiss 1995). The slogan of the 1997 Super League competition was 'When two tribes go to war'. The fights between opposing players usually receive prominent attention in commentaries and media reports to the point of glorification. During a particularly violent series in 1995 an 18-year-old male was killed in a local Brisbane football match in an incident involving another 18-year-old male whose on-field behaviour closely resembled that of the

State of Origin footballing 'heroes'. It was not until mid-1997 that this young football player was finally acquitted of a charge of 'unlawful killing'.

It is worth noting that there is currently an increase in women's engagement with sports like soccer, rugby union and rugby league, and also in some instances, an increased recognition of the spectator value of such women's sports, for example, the final of the women's 1999 soccer World Cup was a huge TV audience and spectator success in the US, perhaps because of the US team's achievement in making this final. However, media coverage is still largely focused on men's games and the participation rates of boys and men in these sports is still much higher than it is for girls and women. The football field is constructed as a form of men's space. It is an arena in which the demonstration of the extremes of masculine behaviour such as aggressiveness, strength, speed, competitiveness and domination of the opposition is required. It is something that only men play because according to popular wisdom it is only men who have these qualities and abilities. Messner (1990) refers to an interview he did with a white professional man who stated that a woman might be able to do the same job as him or his boss, but she would not be able to take a 'hit up' from a famous American football player, Ronnie Lott. And, giving Messner's American example an Australian and a British context, it could quite justifiably be argued that the majority of women could not take a 'hit up' from Gordon Tallis from the Brisbane Broncos or Tim Rodber, the English rugby international. But then how many men could? Very few, I would suggest.

The sleight of hand that allows the social grouping of men to be identified with those who demonstrate the 'manly' virtues of power and controlled aggression serves as a legitimator of women's oppression in relation to men. This can be seen in one comment by a boy (Sean) from Tamville:

> I think some points . . . need to be more equal. Especially like with work. Most guys get the higher paid job and they've got secretaries and stuff like that but it's becoming more equal still nowadays. People are starting to even out a little bit but I still think the males dominate a little bit more . . . but then sometimes in the sporting field, I think oh if people want equal rights then it should be equal rights in the sporting field.

For as long as women are seen not to be able to compete with men on the sporting field then they are still considered to be really unequal/inferior. Equal opportunity legislation, which to a limited extent has reshaped the public world, can simply be treated as a compensatory measure for women's natural inferiority. The arena of violent sports exists as one public venue that has not been touched to any great extent by liberal feminism.

However, the association of such sports with particular forms of masculinity not only reinforce men's general domination over women, they also work to reinforce existing class and ethnic/race relations (Burstyn 1999). At the same time that the ability (perceived or otherwise) to play sports such as football serves as a means of uniting men as the superior sex, it is instrumental in privileging certain men over others. It has been argued that for many men who experience masculinity as 'other' there is a desire to prove one's manhood (see Kimmel 1996). Football provides an arena where this may happen. Thus as Messner (1992: 82) notes: 'young athletes from lower-class backgrounds, especially poor black males, were far more likely than their middle-class counterparts to become committed to careers in violent sports.'

For many of these men sport provides an arena for a demonstration of their manhood and consequently earns them a societal respect that would otherwise not be forthcoming (see Messner 1994; Burstyn 1999; and also Jefferson's (1996) account of the ways in which racial and class factors impacted on the construction of the boxer Mike Tyson's subjectivity). Messner (1990: 105) picks up on this desire for respect elsewhere: ' "Respect" was what I heard over and over when talking with the men from lower status backgrounds, especially black men. I interpret this type of respect to be a crystallisation of the masculine quest for recognition through public achievement.'

However, the limited options which are available to non-white, non-middle-class men and the ways in which these masculinities are constructed in contemporary masculinity politics ensures that working-class and/or ethnically/racially marginalized men continue playing violent sports for longer periods than their white middle-class counterparts. Although this may elevate the masculine status of particular marginalized men for the duration of their involvement with sport, it has significant consequences for ethnic and classed gender relations. For instance, in Australia the over-involvement of particular social groupings of men in football or boxing reinforces dominant images of working-class and/or Aboriginal men as being more aggressive and violent than white middle-class 'civilized' men. These marginalized men are seen as being well suited to such sports, but not to activities which require intellectual ability. The complex nature of masculine politics shaped through dominant masculinizing practices, such as football, is captured well by Messner (1990):

> For middle class men, the tough guys of the culture industry – the Rambos, the Ronnie Lotts who are fearsome 'hitters,' who play 'hurt' – are the heroes who prove that men 'we' are superior to women. At the same time, these heroes play the role of the primitive other, against whom higher status men define themselves as modern and civilised.
>
> (Messner 1990: 103)

Football thus also serves to position those who play particular types of football, for example, Aboriginal and/or working-class men, as inherently more violent than white middle-class men (as was perhaps the case with Peter above). The racism and classism of this essentialist association of violence with working-class men and men from marginalized ethnic/racial backgrounds is played out in many areas of society. For instance, in Australia, it is more likely that a working-class or Aboriginal man will be convicted of crimes of rape and domestic violence than a white middle-class man, despite evidence which indicates that class and ethnicity have little bearing on who commits such crimes (Scutt 1990). Further, violence here becomes associated with something embodied within the individual. The structural nature of violence perpetuated through institutional practices that maintain dominant gender, racial/ethnic and class relations go unquestioned. Thus, the performance by certain men of hegemonic masculine practices does not necessarily lead to long-term privileges for those men. These performances are often more important for the collective benefit of men, and in particular privileged men who often do not take the risks associated with hegemonic masculine performances.

This does not mean that sport is unimportant for white middle-class men. For instance, Connell *et al.* (1982: 93–4) identify football as a 'visible masculinizing process' within private boys' schools: the domain of white middle–upper-class masculinity. However, there is an obvious class dimension to the ways in which male sports are organized. For instance in Queensland, as in England and Wales, rugby league is clearly associated with working-class males and rugby union with middle- and upper-class males. This latter sport's association with privileged males and 'gentlemanly' pursuits was, until quite recently, denoted by its spirit of amateurism. It was a sport that men played because of their love of sport, not because of a concern with anything so 'common' as money. Its association with the upper and middle classes has also been reinforced by its lack of appeal to the 'common' man and its elitist connections to the most privileged private schools in Australia.

However, like rugby league, the contact nature of rugby union works to provide middle- and upper-class men with a hegemonized form of masculinity. The toughness, the competitiveness, the aggressiveness, that is the 'maleness', of these kinds of football all develop skills and attitudes well suited to the business and professional worlds. However, while white middle-class men may have a significant attachment to their sporting history, and a few may continue to play competitive violent sports past their prime, most privileged men seldom continue an involvement in such sports past either school or university level. Their manhood has already been proved, and will continue to be proved in the world of work.

Work as a signifier of masculinity

The changing nature of the workplace and high levels of unemployment in the Western world have been integral in the production of tensions within masculinity politics (see, for example, Willott and Griffin 1996; Fine *et al.* 1997). This tension is captured well in the recent British movies *The Full Monty*, *Brassed Off* and *Among Giants*. The globalized economy and the proliferation of non-industrial, service orientated styles of occupations within the West has led to high levels of unemployment in a number of traditionally masculinized industries. Contrary to some popular assumptions though, these changes are not representative of a reorganization of gender relations, but of a reorganization of global capital, which in turn has effects on gender politics. However, the frequent citing of these workplace changes as an example of how men are currently an oppressed group, gives an indication of the importance of the public world of work to a man's identity, and his relationship to women and other men.

Traditional concepts of work are thus fiercely clung to as signifiers of manhood, and as such are integral to the production of relationships between masculinities and also of various relationships between these masculinities and femininities (Collinson and Hearn 1996). Men's traditional work practices have a foundation in class, and work sites have served as places where issues of men's domination of other men are often played out (this is taken up later in this chapter, see pp. 44–8). Class analyses of the workplace, though, have often ignored the ways in which gender is a feature of the practices being undertaken within those sites. However, as Cockburn (1985: 168, original emphasis) has argued, '*work is a gendering process.*' This is clearly evident in the way in which gendered boundaries are created and policed through work environments. There are close links between the overt violences of rape (both inside and outside the home), 'domestic' violence, sexual harassment and 'poofter bashing', and the subtle violences constructing the institutional arrangements of masculinities within workplaces, including schools. The subtlety of the violence being done through these institutional arrangements lies in their ability to normalize existing gender/sex/sexual relations of power.

Traditionally waged workplaces, along with the streets and all other public spaces, have been designated as male space, while the home, or private (unwaged) space, has been designated the territory of the female (although this has not necessarily protected women from the 'master of the castle'). The effect of this has been to separate women from societal centres of power and to devalue, or not recognize as proper work, women's unpaid work (see Beasley 1994). The traditional male perception of women and the workforce was typified in Cockburn's (1985: 185) study of working women and men; from her interviews with men she noted that, 'In contrast to the way men represent themselves – as striving, achieving, engaging in the public sphere of work – they represent women as static, domestic, private people, as non-workers.'

This can be seen in some of the comments made by students at the two schools. For instance, Julian, a grade 11 boy from Tamville, states: 'Like only my Dad works, my Mum stays at home to look after my sister and I, but she, you know, really doesn't want to go back to work.'

The construction of the public as male has served three functions. First, it has enabled a silencing of women's positive contributions to national political projects. Second, it has served to protect incursions from women into this masculinized space. And, third, it has legitimized, as women have become increasingly involved in the public world, a hierarchical positioning (and gender segmentation) of occupations based partly on their 'masculine' or 'feminine' characteristics.

The denial of women's unpaid work as 'real' work has served to negate their contributions to national economic, social and political processes. Beasley (1994) refers to the presence of 'sexual economyths' in dominant economic theories. Sexual economyths are: 'implicit or explicit economic assumptions or principles which systematically marginalize and/or exclude women' (Beasley 1994: ix). She develops through her work a feminist economics that goes beyond a concept of work as that which only occurs in the market place. An attention to what constitutes work, how traditional perceptions of work have been constructed and why women carry out the bulk of unpaid work in society is an important consideration in developing an understanding of how particular forms of work have become signifiers of masculinity.

There have been a number of feminists who have examined how the economy has been historically structured and supported by institutional arrangements in such a way that women have been excluded from or disadvantaged in the public world of work (see for example, Cockburn 1983, 1985; Waring 1988; Kelly 1991; Apter 1993; Pringle 1994; Hollway 1996). The assumption that it is women's responsibility to look after children has been instrumental in the creation of these arrangements. To some extent this is picked up by one boy, Will, a grade 12 student from Mountainview:

> I agree with equality and . . . but also you we have to we still have to take . . . acknowledge our past and what happened then. Where the lady was just a beautiful figure and who cleaned the house or, and satisfied the husband when he came home from work. So I think, I don't know if we can ever really be equal because women have babies and their work must be affected by that and they got to bring up children or else the world will end.

The pervasive belief that it is the responsibility of women to bring up children serves to disempower women in the public sphere. Of the boys interviewed, it was perhaps Julian, a grade 11 boy, who provides the clearest example of how this belief can shape popular discourse:

> *Julian:* I reckon . . . like when they had . . . used to have you know women didn't get paid as much as males . . . you know a woman

would work for ten or 12 years, live at home and then they'd get married and then you know have kids and stay at home. Now there'd be . . . okay the few that wouldn't stay at home they'd go to work, but I think the families were a lot better off. I don't think there was as many divorces and all that sort of stuff then.

I think that was the worst thing they did . . . women want all these rights. And now there's a few . . . the do gooders I suppose . . . that want that but I don't think it's any better off . . . And you know after they brought in these new laws I think everything went up, everything got dearer and you know made it harder for them . . . now both families . . . both parents have to work.

I think that was . . . that's sort of bad for the kids I suppose. I suppose my Dad earns a lot, a lot more money than when he was younger now he's got a good job and that and he . . . like Mum doesn't need to work but I don't think if it . . . if she had to work she'd really want to. She's been out of work for so long I don't think she'd really want to go back. It's just the way things are, I don't know. It's either your wife wants to work, well let her. But I think if they have kids and that they should stay home with them you know from when they're babies 'till primary . . . late . . . middle primary school so that they you know . . . they're not just shoved into day care centre. I think that's the worst thing for them.

Martin: What about if men wanted to stay home with them? How would you feel then?

Julian: Ah, oh depends if they are gonna support them. It depends what you do.

Martin: And the woman went out and worked?

Julian: Yeah oh . . . there's a few cases of it I hear.

Martin: Do you think it's okay?

Julian: Yeah it's all right in some ways. In some ways it's not. It just depends on what you do. You know if you can support your family and you can do that well fine you know. Like some people . . . the farmers they look after their kids while the wife's doing something you know picking or something like that you know.

Many of the assumptions Julian makes here are not atypical. These assumptions include those which suggest that: women should earn less than men; women who do not stay at home to look after their children are not acting in the best interests of their children; working women are responsible for the breakdown of the family; women would only want to work if the husband cannot provide for the family; and women's work is inferior to that of men's (in Julian's view the man is the farmer, the woman is his wife).

The nuclear family, valorized here by Julian, is a significant institutional arrangement that works against women's interests in the world of work

(Pyke 1996). In such families childcare responsibilities have largely fallen to mothers. This has meant that women's opportunities to work have been limited, despite the existence of childcare centres, which have been blamed for all sorts of societal ills. Childcare facilities only cater for work carried out between certain hours (how difficult is it for a woman executive, single or with a male partner, who has children to attend late night meetings?). Further, lack of part-time work in professional organizations has ensured that women who take on childcare responsibilities are limited in the types of work they are able to secure.

There have in recent times been some improvements for women in the world of work. However, these have been limited (Walby 1997), and they certainly have not been to the extent that many articulating a men's rights politics suggest. For as Mahony (1998) has commented:

> Within a restructuring of capitalism the patriarchal cage seems to have been rattled by a belief that men are losing economic ground to women. There is indeed an issue emerging in some areas of the labour market . . . But for white male elites the 'natural order' is not about to be overturned and any panic in that direction is unfortunately unwarranted with women constituting fewer than 5 per cent of senior management in the United Kingdom and United States (2 per cent in Australia), 5 per cent of UK Institute of Directors and less than 1 per cent of chief executives (Collinson and Hearn 1996).
>
> (Mahony 1998: 42)

Hence, even though many women have entered into the workforce on a full-time basis this has often been into unskilled monotonous work (such as shop assistants, checkout operators and production line workers in factories), or, when more highly trained, into service type industries (such as tourism, nursing, secretarial work and banking). It should also be noted at this point that, for many women, entering the workforce has been an economic necessity, not a choice or career move. This is especially the case for women from low socioeconomic backgrounds who do the vast majority of society's unskilled, non-unionized and low paid work. The legitimacy of the existing arrangement between women and work has rested on the natural attributes associated with hegemonic masculinities and emphasized femininities.

Dominant constructions of femininity and masculinity imply a subordinate–dominant relationship. This relationship exists within the world of work. Women's traditional unskilled, skilled and professional work is positioned as inferior to its masculinized counterparts in these various categories. Several factors have contributed to this. Not least of these has been the construction of femininity as servile, as demonstrating a natural capacity for caring and as lacking a natural affinity for technical know-how (despite evidence to the contrary, see Wajcman 1991: 15–16). Equally important has been the construction of masculinity as dominant, strong and having a natural affinity with technology (these differences have enabled the legitimation of the unequal pay between 'men's' and 'women's' occupations).

Cockburn (1985) provides a demonstration of how mastery of technology has been a signifier of masculinity and how this signifier has served as a means of maintaining unequal relations of power between men and women. She argues that 'The technical competence that men possess and women lack is an extension of the physical domination of women by men' (Cockburn 1985: 7). Furthermore, as Wajcman (1991) demonstrates, the uses to which technology has been put by men has served to make technology an instrument in the oppression of women both directly and through its re/production of existing gender ideologies.

The learning of how males and females are positioned in relation to technology is integral to the gendered relations of the school curriculum. It is not difficult to see how ingrained the associations of technical subjects with a boy's education and the non-technical subjects with a girl's education have become, especially in situations where students have been provided with opportunities to 'choose' their subjects. A look into any elective technical drawing class, in any mixed school (I would suggest anywhere in the Western world) will provide a picture of a higher proportion of boys than girls, likewise for physics and computer-based subjects. An opposite picture is likely to be observed if one looks into a secretarial studies classroom, history classroom or art classroom. Boys (and others) in schools need to be made aware of the gendered curriculum and the limiting of life choices that such a curriculum provides to both boys and girls, as well as giving consideration to which subjects provide privileged post school pathways to students.

I do not want to suggest that girls should be coerced into science/technology type programmes. This is obviously problematic, as it valorizes the masculinized section of the school curriculum at the expense of the now feminized humanities curriculum. This attempt to provide girls with 'equal' opportunity rather than 'different' opportunities works to reinforce masculinist ways of seeing the world (Grosz 1995: 54). This was picked up in a previous study where a female teacher complained that her school's 'girls into science program' was trying to turn 'girls into good little boys' (Mills 1995). This is a point made by Wajcman (1991):

As with science, the very language of technology, its symbolism, is masculine. It is not simply a question of acquiring skills, because these skills are embedded in a culture of masculinity that is largely coterminous with the culture of technology. Both at school and in the workplace this culture is incompatible with femininity. Therefore, to enter this world, to learn its language, women have first to forsake their femininity.

(Wajcman 1991: 19)

This raises issues of the 'masculinization of science' and the desirability of such a science for either male or female students (see Kelly 1989; science has also been racialized, see Harding 1993, 1998).

Campaigns to encourage girls into science/technology areas of the curriculum continues the process of valorizing the science/technical subjects at the expense of feminized arts/humanities subjects. An effect of this is to further devalue women's achievements in these feminized areas. But, of course, also at issue is the power that is being denied girls through their exclusion from acquiring technical know-how. These are important considerations for educators concerned with curricular justice. However, I would like to avoid a specific focus on these issues here.

What is more a concern for this book is boys' avoidance of humanities/ arts type subjects and also their treatment of girls who do enter into non-traditional areas. The problem of boys' lack of involvement in the arts/ humanities areas is that these are the subjects that are most likely to expose boys to possible non-hegemonic masculine subject positions. Boys need to be exposed to a wider range of opportunities to experience difference than is currently being catered for by the existing curriculum.

The treatment of girls entering into traditional male space in schools should also be a major concern of gender equity and social justice programmes in all schools. In line with equal opportunities programmes in the workplace, there have also been successful initiatives within schools to encourage girls into non-traditional areas. These initiatives and programmes have enabled a number of girls/women to enter into subjects/occupations 'normally' the preserve of men. However, these programmes have seldom considered the boys in the classroom and how constructions of hegemonic masculinities have worked to protect science/technology from intrusions by women and women's issues. Such a consideration of boys/men and the masculinization of science/technology is essential for enabling women's access to science/technology and to enable feminist critiques of them in order to transform their current role in maintaining the patriarchal gender order. For as Wajcman (1991) has argued:

> Men have to learn that technology is not 'theirs' and give up the privil-eges and power that go with this construction of masculinity. Ulti-mately this depends on transforming gender power relations which in turn requires changing the nature of work itself so that childcare and housework can be equally shared. Access politics alone cannot succeed because the institutions themselves are founded on gender inequality.
>
> (Wajcman 1991: 164)

However, it appears that men have been far from sympathetic in their treatment of women who have sought to enter into male dominated fields. There is for instance an assumption that women are taking men's jobs (Fine *et al.* 1997; Kimmel 1998). The actions of males like Lepine, who shot 14 women in an engineering class at the University of Montreal 'because they were 'all a bunch of fucking feminists' (Faludi 1992: 89, see also Stato 1993), may represent an extreme male reaction to women's entry into a masculinized domain of work. However, the attitudes expressed by Lepine reflect a widespread view of males in such fields, or men who would like to enter into these areas but feel prevented from doing so by feminist affirmative action policies. Perhaps the greatest indicator of how men have resisted women's participation in 'their' industries has been the high levels of sexual harassment in these industries.

Evidence indicates that sexual harassment is a daily reality for women working in traditional male spheres of employment, although of course not peculiar to these spheres (see Stanko 1988; Schneider 1993). Comments made by some girls in North Queensland schools give a very vivid picture of how this harassment works to protect the masculinity of particular subject areas (Gilbert *et al.* 1995: 55–6). Many of the girls in this study avoided subjects that were dominated by boys, because,

> They expected, with good cause, that they'd get teased and humiliated. If they dressed in the appropriate mechanics' clothes for Metal Module subjects, for instance, the boys would laugh at them and make disparaging remarks about their femininity. If they dressed in swimming togs when they were in a Marines Studies class, the boys would embarrass them by making offensive remarks about their bodies.
>
> (Gilbert *et al.* 1995: 55)

This harassment should not be constructed as a product of male sexual desire or of boys' hormones at work. Such an essentialist construction ignores the effects of this harassment and the contexts within which it occurs. Bhattacharyya (1994) argues that:

> Harassment is usually made possible by a power imbalance between groups – men can harass women, whites can harass blacks, straights can harass gays, because the harassed group suffers wider social disprivilege. The activity of harassment reiterates this skewed relation, puts the harassed party back in his or her place. His or her identity feels less negotiable and fluid and more painfully certain. Harassment is a way of ensuring people who are already having a bad time are painfully aware of their predicament. It serves as a reminder of local power relations, while reproducing the same patterns. We can think of harassment as a threatening restatement of the status quo.
>
> (Bhattacharyya 1994: 82)

Thus, sexual harassment in male dominated areas can be seen as a practice that serves to restate the existing gender order, a restatement made necessary for patriarchal privilege, due to disruptions to this order brought about by female incursions into the realm of the masculine.

However, as Stanko (1988) has indicated, sexual harassment does not only occur in these overtly male dominated areas of life. It occurs throughout institutional arrangements wherever women/girls are primarily defined by their gender/sexuality. Thus, it is no surprise that the practice of sexual harassment is found throughout all forms of classrooms and schools as well as in workplaces (see Jones 1985; Morgan *et al.* 1988; Herbert 1989: 167–71; Stein 1993, 1995; Sadker and Sadker 1994). Milligan *et al.* (1992) in *Listening to Girls* deduce from their research evidence that sexual harassment is a feature of most schools. In relation to one particular 'good' school they state:

> The weight of evidence in this school, and from many others in the consultation, is that sex-based harassment is endemic in co-educational schools, in both classrooms and schoolyards. It is highly likely that most girls in most co-educational schools experience it.
>
> (Milligan *et al.* 1992: 10)

It also needs to be recognized that sexual harassment in schools is not restricted to high schools. The 'Users' Guide' to *Enough's Enough! Sexual Harassment and Violence*, a resource kit for primary schools (Queensland Department of Education 1994: 7) states that: 'Sex-based harassment (or harassment on the basis of being a girl, or a 'feminine' boy) is common in primary schools' (see also Walkerdine 1989; Thorne, 1993; Skelton 1996; Warren 1997; Danby and Baker 1998). The sexual harassment of girls/women by boys/men has to be a prime concern of programmes addressing the role of hegemonic masculinities in perpetuating the patriarchal gender order. Sexual harassment is one of the primary means by which boys/men can assert their power over women.

Power over women as a signifier of masculinity

The ability of boys and men to demonstrate their power over girls and women lies in the extent to which they can defend their own image of masculinity both from attacks from within and without. This entails constructing images of girls and women that best complement their masculine image of themselves; proving their supremacy in male defined public spaces; and violently suppressing any images of femininity or masculinity that serve to delegitimize their power over girls and women.

The use of physical violence by boys against girls is seldom articulated by boys as a legitimate act. Numerous boys I have interviewed argue that it is wrong for men to hit women. For example, Than states that, 'You shouldn't hit girls because they're more ... they're weak.' He goes on to say that people would tease any boy who hit a girl at school. This is supported in an anecdote by another student:

> *Paul:* If you find out someone . . . like you can't really stop guys going against guys, but if it's a guy going against a woman, it's you know pretty unfair . . . Like at the school I've only seen one person hit a girl and he got beat up pretty bad.
> *Martin:* By other boys?
> *Paul:* Yeah.

In both instances these boys recognize that many girls and women get hit at home. This happens at home according to Paul, 'Because there's no one really to stick up for them.' In one instance a grade 12 boy (James) told a story of how a friend of his had intervened in a situation of domestic violence:

> I did work experience with a builder whose name was Brian but anyway one of his mates used to beat his wife and he knew about it and Brian's done a lot of karate like he's a black belt and stuff. And for a long time there, Brian just let it go by, you know he didn't really worry about it. But then one day it sort of just went . . . it got a bit overboard. Like the husband found out that his wife had done something . . . like this is only recently . . . this is about say it would be about 18 months ago. He found out that his wife had done something. He was over at Brian's place and he went to get in the car and he went 'That's it I'm going to really beat her this time.' Brian ended up just going up and taking the keys off him. Went, 'You're not going anywhere mate.' And it's like Brian had sort of tried to stop him a bit before but he'd never really interfered. Like she'd gone to the police and they had just said there's really nothing they could do about it . . . But anyway Brian just took the keys off him that time. And the guy was just sort of . . . he was trying to get the keys back and stuff and Brian just said, 'Look I'll give you the keys back but if you put one finger on her you're a dead man.' . . . So he got the keys back and I think he went back and . . . slapped her anyway but the next day . . . the next time Brian saw him apparently he gave him a fair bit of a beating . . . And since then I think the marriage has broken up.

These attitudes towards violence against women do not mean that physical violence against women and girls is universally condemned by these boys. There are several things happening here. For example, these comments suggest that among many of these boys, it is becoming increasingly illegitimate for men to use violence against women. Some of the reasons why this is seen to be so are problematic, for example, Than's statement that boys should not hit girls because girls 'are weak'. The recognition, though, that such acts are unacceptable can be an important starting point from which discussions on gender and violence can be initiated. However, violence against women, the existence of which most of these boys acknowledge, implies that women need to be protected from 'other' men. Thus, even though violence against women is not legitimated by these boys, violence still works to make women/girls potential victims. Hence displays of physical violence are not always necessary to demonstrate power over women. In many instances, it is enough to 'know' that men are stronger than women, as evidenced by the sports men play and the work they do, and that women are always potential victims.

There are also other means by which men/boys can demonstrate their power over women. For instance, power over women can be demonstrated by coercive displays of power that produce fear and seek to make victims of women/girls through desktop and toilet graffiti. Such graffiti can quite legitimately be referred to as pornography. Feminists have long identified the role that pornography has played in constructing for men a violable image of women (see, for example, Brownmiller 1976; Dworkin 1981; Griffin 1981; MacKinnon 1989; see also for feminist debates over pornography, Segal and McIntosh 1992; Walters 1997).

These images in schools play a role in shaping the way in which males see females: that is as primarily sexualized beings. Furthermore, they mark out the space of the school as masculine. (It is interesting to note in Connell's (1989) paper on the interplay of masculinity and schooling, that in one school, activities that went on among the 'hoods' in a presumably masculinized space, along with smoking, were talking about women and going through pornographic books.) The pervasiveness of these sorts of images within one particular English school is described by Jones (1985). They took the form of both 'art' and 'woman-hating' graffiti. An example of this 'art work' was a large painting depicting a woman's dismembered body, which was hanging in the school foyer. Graffiti that described female teachers and students as 'pros' and 'slags' could be found in various areas of the school. Drawings of erect penises were used to mark out male ownership of the school space (of note was the extent to which a 'Girls are Powerful' poster was destroyed by these symbols of masculinity combined with the comment 'we're here to stay'). Jones identifies this type of graffiti as misogynist propaganda in that it serves to normalize the violence existing in gender/sex/sexual relations. For as Jones (1985: 27) argues, 'The central themes of domination, control, humiliation and mutilation of women by men serve as propaganda by which men learn it is acceptable to abuse women and girls.'

Power over girls and women is also demonstrated through a bodily domination of public space. The dominance of school space by boys reflects the broader dominance of public space by men (Askew and Ross 1988; Thorne 1993). In any visit to any co-educational school during a recess break I would confidently predict that it would be apparent that the biggest most open public space, usually the school oval or playing fields, would be dominated by boys. In Thorne's case study of a Californian elementary school she notes that, 'On school playgrounds boys control as much as ten times more space than girls' (Thorne 1993: 83).

The correlation of a masculine domination of school space with domination in a non-school public space can be seen in the Australian study by Walker (1988). 'The footballers' in his study not only dominated the school oval but also spaces in the nightclubs they attended. Walker's school is an all boys' school. However, some of the experiences of a 'feminized' group of boys known as 'the three friends' are representative of the experiences of many girls within coeducational schools. These boys, who were constructed in opposition to the footballers because of their interest in drama and dislike of competitive sport, were forced, out of a consideration for their own safety, to occupy a small room within the school during lunch times. In mixed schools boys take up far more space both in the school grounds and in the classroom (see Spender 1982; Holly 1985; Thorne 1993: 82–3; Warren 1997). In the Milligan *et al.* (1992: 8) report it was clear that in many schools the only spaces that girls could call their own were the female students' toilets.

Power over women is signified by the silencing of both women and men who seek to disrupt the existing patriarchal gender order. The preserve of male space is policed through this silencing. It is a silencing that is often the product of fear. This can be seen in an example from Walker's (1988: 102) study:

> B: Well, I went to the beach one day, in the night. And uh, she took off her bra, right? I wanted to touch her boobs. She hit me here 'n' I went pow! pow! pow! (C laughs loudly) I hit her; she was on the ground, and she goes, 'what did you hit me for?' 'Shut up mole!' (Slaps hands together)

When one boy, A, attempts to intervene in the discussion by stating that he has different views on the treatment of women he is silenced by C's comments, 'Yer a poof, yer a poof.' (Walker 1988: 102–4). This last comment served as a reminder to A that aversions to violence and siding with women against men is a traitorous act which can result in expulsion from the dominant masculinity. A number of boys I interviewed also commented about how any attempt to raise issues of gender and violence would lead to ridicule. This was demonstrated in a discussion with Greg:

> *Greg:* Oh they're scared to speak out in case they . . . I don't know . . . just in case they say the wrong thing . . . And stuff like that.
> *Martin:* And what would the wrong thing be?
> *Greg:* I don't know. Someone might think they're queer or something like that.

An indication of some of the difficulties boys face in raising issues relating to sexual harassment is provided by another grade 12 Mountainview boy, Will:

Martin: Do you think that you could talk to your friends or your peer group about issues to do with gender and violence? Would you feel comfortable?

Will: Name something specific?

Martin: Say if you were really concerned about a high degree of sexual harassment in the school or if you'd seen it, do you think that you could say, 'I really don't like that type of behaviour'?

Will: I'd love to say 'yes'. But no, definitely nope.

Martin: Why not?

Will: Um well it's a peer, peer thing again and it's just . . . since they'd probably be the ones that were doing this (laughter) it's a bit ridiculous. But some times it's all in good fun. I mean boys will be boys that sort of thing. But it's just something they do. I mean it happens and it's that tradition thing again.

Martin: Yeah and do you think that, that other boys . . . that it would be difficult for boys to criticize other boys' violence?

Will: I'd say that's very difficult to say. I mean I've got a pretty good group of friends but I don't think, I don't think I'd say that to them like (laughter). It's just something . . . it's not something you can talk about.

Fear is a major controlling emotion operating within existing gender relations. For many women and girls this fear is engendered through the ever-present threat of sexual violence. The ubiquity of this violence serves to prevent many women from disrupting emphasized femininities. For instance, it works to enforce the naturalization of heterosexual relationships by encouraging girls/women to seek the protection of a male partner (Mahony 1989). Furthermore, as Kitzinger (1994) states in relation to the silencing of lesbian femininities:

> In an oppressive heterosexist society it is not necessary, most of the time, to beat up lesbians, or to murder or torture us in order to ensure our silence and invisibility. Instead, a climate of terror is created in which lesbians 'voluntarily', and of our own free will, 'choose' to stay silent and invisible.
>
> (Kitzinger 1994: 127)

Other such climates of terror exist that serve to prevent disruptions to the notion of male power over women. Rape and sexual harassment are considered in Chapter 2 in relation to their role in protecting male interests. However, it is worth demonstrating here how the normality of these practices produce these climates for girls/women and others.

A demonstration of a normalized rapist mentality is clearly evident among a number of Walker's 'footballer' group. They refer to attempts to meet women/girls as 'hunting'. One boy (V) made the following comment during a school dance, being held in conjunction with a girls' only school, in relation to what he and his friends were going to do after the dance, 'We're gunna take as many as we can. But even if there's only one we'll fuck her' (Walker 1988: 108).

V's comment here can be seen as being part of a broader rapist culture where sexual violence against women is a legitimate act. These comments by the 'footballers' also demonstrate the observation made by Burstyn (1999: 169) that sport culture encourages men's sexual violence against women. For example, she points to evidence on such violence in the United States, which indicates that: 'One of the most highly visible patterns in recent years is the findings that rapes on college campuses are being performed by team athletes in numbers significantly out of proportion to their presence in the student population' (Burstyn 1999: 169). Attitudes and practices that support a rape culture are not of course restricted to male working-class or sporting cultures. For instance, various comments made by Australian judges have demonstrated an acceptance of rape as part of controlling women (see Scutt 1994: 136–7).

Rape, 'domestic' violence and sexual harassment have become naturalized aspects of the patriarchal gender order. However, their presence may at times be representative of a violence applied against women when the naturalness of this gender order is threatened. Such violences are a reaffirmation of the 'proper' arrangement of gender relations. They serve to demonstrate to women that men will not be 'emasculated' by challenges to their masculine privilege of power over women. As such they give credence to Horsfall's (1991: 68) comment that: 'Male violence against a female can be seen to be a desperate attempt by the perpetrator to prove to himself that he is a male.' Sexual violences, such as rape, 'domestic' violence and sexual harassment, can therefore be seen as producing a climate that serves to signify male power over women.

Power over other men as a signifier of masculinity

Climates of terror primarily affect girls and women. However, particular social groups of boys and men can also be the targets of such terror. Two such social groups have been gays and/or boys/men from marginalized ethnic/racial backgrounds. For instance, the horrific murder of the Wyoming gay student Matthew Shepherd in the United States in 1998 underscores the terror that many gay men and boys experience throughout the Western industrialized world. A similar terror also confronts many men from other marginalized backgrounds in their engagement with the public world. For instance, in Brisbane, Australia, in 1995, a former police officer related how officers from his station regularly went in search of Aboriginal men for the sole purpose of beating them up. Anglo-Australia has a long history of unprovoked brutality against Aboriginal people. There is also a clear link between this violence and the maintenance of cultural and racial hegemony. However, there is a definite gender dimension to many of the differing forms of violence that Aboriginal men (and gay men) experience in contemporary Australia; and the effects of this violence are tied into maintaining the patriarchal gender order. For instance, in relation to the violence against Aboriginal men, the gendered element of this primarily racist violence can be seen in its effect of asserting the victory of a particular masculinity, non-Aboriginal, over a subordinate Aboriginal masculinity. It identifies the perpetrators as exemplars of a victorious, conquering masculinity.

It is this power over other men that works, as Connell (1995a) has demonstrated, to create categories of subordinate and marginalized masculinities. This is explored in Chapter 2, however, it needs to be stressed here that violence has been integral to the creation of these categories. For instance, masculinity does not reserve its brutal repressions for non-Anglo men. Inside traitors to masculinity also often live under a constant threat of violence. Such inside traitors consist of male homosexuals and men who challenge the naturalness of the gender order (for some chilling accounts of the effects of homophobia on high school lesbians and male homosexuals see Ward 1995; also Butler 1996; Martino 1997; Flood 1997b).

The extent to which male homosexuals are positioned outside dominant constructions of masculinity and the role of homophobia in policing masculine behaviour were starkly obvious in Tamville and Mountainview. Throughout the course of the programmes at the two schools homophobic attitudes were constantly displayed. In the follow-up interviews the extent of a number of boys' dislike for homosexuals was expressed. The reactions to the potential 'coming out' of a friend included the following:

Than: I won't play with him any more

Joshua: I would tell him to fuck off.

However, some were more tolerant in their homophobia. For example, Isaac said:

I'd probably . . . like as long as he like . . . he like didn't try anything on me, I'd treat him just the same as I treated him before.

A similar response was made by a boy, Sean, from the same class:

Oh . . . I've never really been put in that situation before so I never . . . I wouldn't know what I would do. And if he was coming on to me I'd just tell him to piss off . . . Um it's not that hard to tell him to do that but if he's just a friend and he knew like what I felt then how he felt and if he was still acting the same way and didn't change I'd still think oh yeah . . . I still think he'd be all right to hang around with and stuff like that.

Another boy was not quite so certain:

> *Martin:* If someone did say they were homosexual how do you reckon they would be treated?
> *Greg:* Depends, it depends who they were. If they were like your friend or . . .
> *Martin:* If they were a friend that would be okay?
> *Greg:* . . .
> *Martin:* How would you treat him?
> *Greg:* Ah shit. (Laughter) . . . I'm not sure hey.

In response to the question, 'What would happen to a boy who said he was gay?', Joshua comments: 'He would get the shit beaten out of him.' James said:

> I don't know. I think some people would just shrug and go, 'Oh well leave him be,' and like there might be a few others that sort of would like to get in and beat him up . . . But if he like sort of came out and like professed his love to another boy or something I think then he'd start to be beaten up pretty bad.

There was an attitude that if it was kept hidden, not flaunted, that homosexuality in a friend could be tolerated. For instance,

> *Than:* Like if he acts like that, I won't go around with him anymore. But if he doesn't, he just acts different when you're not there, that's okay.

And,

> *Martin:* And how do you feel about homosexuals?
> *Paul:* I pretty much hate them all.
> *Martin:* Yeah?
> *Paul:* Like there is some nice ones that just mind their own business but I don't like the ones you know that dress up in all that drag stuff and that you know.
> *Martin:* And why's that different for them?
> *Paul:* Because like we don't go around like saying that we're . . . we're heterosexuals . . . So they shouldn't go around going oh we're . . . we're a bunch of fags.
> *Martin:* How would you feel if one of your close friends told you . . . ?
> *Paul:* I'd probably beat him up (laughter).
> *Martin:* Really?
> *Paul:* Yeah.
> *Martin:* Why?
> *Paul:* I just don't like them . . . I've been brought up that way.

The potential of being a recipient of violence due to this labelling is emphatically demonstrated in a comment made by a student in Walker's (1988:

100) study, 'B: If I find out he's a poof: "Fuck off poof! (slaps hands) There, y' fuckin' poof!" I'll fuckin' 'it 'im.'

This homophobic response to the perceived potential homosexuality of a particular boy who is opposed to violence against women/girls is evidence of the policing effects of homophobic discourses. This policing of the boundaries of hegemonic masculinities leads to the repression of masculinities that threaten their hegemonic positioning. Homophobia is an important aspect of this repression. It is a form of repression that permeates societal relations within schools (see, for example, Butler 1996; Epstein 1997; Flood 1997b; Martino 1997; Gilbert and Gilbert 1998). For as Epstein and Johnson (1994: 204) have argued,

> In strongly homosocial situations, such as boys' schools and school-based cultures of masculinity, homophobia is often a vehicle for policing heterosexual masculinities. Men habitually use terms of homophobic abuse against peers who deviate from hegemonic masculinities.

Such abuse works both through and within institutions. It may not always be as overt as in the above comment by 'B', however its effects can often be just as brutal (see Bartell 1994). The horror with which many boys and men treat male homosexuality can be seen as a product of its potential to undermine traditional constructs of masculinity (Edwards 1990: 114; see also Kaufman 1994; Kimmel 1994; Mac an Ghaill 1994a). Pronger (1990: 2) makes this point well when he states that: 'In our culture, male homosexuality is a violation of masculinity, a denigration of the mythic power of men, an ironic subversion that significant numbers of men pursue with great enthusiasm. Because it gnaws at masculinity, it weakens the gender order.'

However, it should be stressed, as Donaldson (1993) does, that there is nothing inherently counter-hegemonic in gayness. Many gay men in recent times have adopted the hypermasculine qualities associated with hegemonic masculinity (see, for instance, Freeman 1997; Burstyn 1999). Male homosexuality undermines traditional aspects of hegemonic masculinity, which rely on the domination of women for sexual gratification, but this does not necessarily translate into a rejection of constructions of the male as a 'superior' being. It may even, among some gay men, reinforce this notion.

Constructions of class-based masculinities also weave complexities into analyses of masculinity and men's oppression of other men. Perceived intellectual and physical attributes, and a concomitant division of labours, serve as markers of classed masculinities. Hypermasculine attributes are often associated with working-class men, a situation that can sometimes be reinforced by working-class men's denotation of bosses as effeminate and weak (Pyke 1996). Such interpretations of middle-class and upper-class masculinities serve as a means by which working-class men can protect their self-respect in situations where men in management positions clearly have power over them. However, they do so by denigrating women.

The four signifiers of masculinity discussed here, sport, work, power over women and power over other men, are imbued with the spirit of violence. Wherever one looks within institutional patterns of gender relations shaping the current gender order, one finds violence. It is a violence of suppression and oppression and of power over others. It is a violence that has suppressed the voices of women and girls, and other marginalized men and boys. It is a violence that has filled the public domain with a hegemonic masculine presence, leaving little room for those who do not fit the 'norm'. It is a violence that makes those marginalized from the hegemonic norm experience fear as part of their everyday reality. It is a violence that underpins Western national political projects.

Conclusion

Sport, work, power over women and power over other men all act as signifiers of a masculinity that is premised on the domination of others. These signifiers are not lost on boys in schools. Male students have a firm image in their minds of what constitutes an 'ideal man'. The signifiers of masculinity indicated in this chapter are those that serve to provide a boy with 'manly' status. The boy who is good at sport, who is competent in the 'right' kinds of work, and who can demonstrate his power over girls/women and other boys/men is one who is likely to achieve recognition from his peers, if not the authority structures within his school. This recognition is clearly attractive to boys, and especially for boys who have little access to institutional power and/or financial resources.

However, these 'achievements' do not come easily for most boys. They have to work hard and take risks to achieve the social status 'manliness' offers. Furthermore, the status hegemonic masculinity offers is often fragile. Boys are continually expected to prove and reprove their masculinity. This may see them causing great pain to others or engaging in self-destructive activities, for example high alcohol consumption or playing sport when injured. Achievement of this status within a school context is also not a guarantee that the boy will gain greatly from the benefits of the patriarchal gender order. In many ways such boys act in ways that lead to others becoming the beneficiaries of the system. (Chapter 2 examines Connell's (1995a) concept of 'complicit masculinity', which explores this theme.) The boys who are held up as exemplars of masculinity are often those who have prioritized achievement of hegemonic status over academic aspirations, and for many of these boys this involves protest activities that reinforce their class and/or racial status (see Willis 1977; Connell *et al.* 1982; Sadker and Sadker 1994).

The desire for manly successes, and consequently societal respect, is also complemented by a fear of being one of those subordinated boys/men who provide a means by which other boys can assert their manliness. There are significant numbers of boys in schools who experience violent behaviour directed at them because of the type of boy they are. Most boys are aware of this. It is the possibility of attracting such attention that works to keep boys 'in line' and to produce a silence among boys about issues of gender and violence. Thus, in order not to attract such attention, boys have to distance themselves from any actions that may bring their masculine status into question. This often means that many idealized 'manly' values are over-emphasized by those boys who have the potential or desire to achieve hegemonic masculine status and those who wish to avoid being the recipient of violence. Weaknesses have to be covered over, alignments with girls and subordinated boys need to be kept to a minimum and a commitment to hegemonic attributes needs to be demonstrated at available opportunities. Fear therefore plays a major role in maintaining the gender order from inside challenges. This fear helps to perpetuate the normalization of violence as a masculine attribute.

Programmes that seek to work with boys on issues of gender and violence need to confront the existence of this fear and the state of affairs from which it is generated. Boys need to explore the ways in which idealized forms of masculinity have been constructed and the costs associated with attempts to achieve the status awarded to those who meet the standards of current constructions of hegemonic masculinities. That these costs are met both by marginalized others (for example, girls, women, male homosexuals, non-aggressive males, non-Anglo males) and many of the men/boys who perform hegemonic displays of masculinity is perhaps an important consideration in these explorations. This should avoid the 'boys are oppressed too' discourse, for men and boys as a group benefit, in the form of the 'patriarchal dividend', from unjust gendered relations of power. However, some men benefit more than others, and ironically some boys/men who represent the 'ideal' man become casualties of the masculine processes that prop up privileged men's positioning in the gender order (Mills 2001). Investigating these themes is likely to promote defensive reactions from boys. For many boys confronting issues of their own power is very difficult in a world in which they do not feel powerful (Fine *et al.* 1997). Thus, boys often draw on anti-feminist backlash discourses in order to explain their sense of powerlessness (Faludi 1999). However, at the same time boys are not prepared to relinquish notions of their inherent superiority over girls/ women because of a perceived physical supremacy.

One of the biggest obstacles facing educators who want to promote gender justice programmes within schools is thus the seemingly impermeable construction of masculinity's relationship to violence. The fragility of hegemonic masculine status means that boys who perform well in high-status activities are not likely to make an identification with an 'exit politics' their first priority. Nor are those who wish to avoid becoming isolated from their peers, and perhaps even become the recipients of homophobic abuse and physical violence likely to attract attention to themselves by engaging in activities that subvert the existing gender order. Attempts to further gender justice require an analysis of the socially constructed relationship between violence and masculinity. The following chapter explores how masculinity has been violenced and how violence has been masculinized.

Strategies for schools

The boys in this chapter spoke about their feelings in relation to sport and work and in the process demonstrated their attitudes towards girls and women and 'other' boys and men. However, there is always a certain 'thisness' or uniqueness about every school context. The activities suggested here will serve to assist people working on boys' issues to develop a more localized understanding of gender issues in their schools.

- Spend a week talking to students, both boys and girls, and teachers about the 'most popular' boys in the school. What is it about these boys that makes them popular? How do these boys solve conflicts? How do some of these boys treat girls? Is the label 'most popular' attributed to different groups of boys according to whom you talk? If this is the case, what are the different characteristics of these groups of 'most popular' boys?
- What are the attitudes towards sport in the school? Which sports are most valued within the school? How is this evidenced (e.g. in school assemblies, newsletters, prospectuses, etc.)? Who plays these sports? What roles do girls play in these sports? How important is sporting prowess to the boys in your school?
- If in a high school, do an analysis of the subject selections made by students in your school. Consider the degree to which boys and girls choose non-traditional subjects. Which subjects are most valued within the school? Do girls and boys do these subjects in equal numbers? How are boys and girls who choose non-traditional subjects treated by their classmates and others? Do any of these students experience harassment because of the choices they have made? What about post-school pathways? Where do boys and girls from your school go after completing their education?
- What are boys' attitudes towards girls in the school? How do these attitudes differ among boys? What do boys think about gender equity, sexual harassment policies and so on? How do boys regard non-traditional post-school pathways? How do girls in the school feel they are treated by boys? How do responses differ among girls? What aspirations do girls have about their adult lives?

- How is difference recognized and valued within the school? How prevalent within the school are negative attitudes towards gays and lesbians? Does this come from teachers and students? Which boys most often attract homophobic insults? Why? What about racism? Do you ever hear racist insults in the school? Does the school have an effective anti-racism policy? Does it have an effective sexual harassment policy?
- Over a limited amount of time, do a rough tally of the incidents of homophobic comments made by students and teachers within the school.
- Prepare a statement about the state of gender relations within your school. Divide it into two sections. In the first section outline the ways in which dominant constructions of gender are reinforced within the school. In the second, outline the ways in which your school is challenging dominant gender constructions. In both sections consider the role of teachers as well as students.

chapter two

The violencing of masculinity and the masculinization of violence

'Violence', it seems clear, cannot simply be equated with 'masculinity'. Neither are unitary phenomena. There are many different types of violence, some legitimated (from sport and beating children to policing and warfare), and some not (from corporal punishment in state schools to rape and murder). It is easier to understand and attempt to change men's engagement in these practices if we see them as operating relatively autonomous to each other.

(Segal 1990: 269)

Introduction

The previous chapter examined hegemonic masculine performances and some of the signifiers of such performances: sport, work, power over women and power over other men. It is apparent from these signifiers that violence is a major component of normalized masculine performances. This violence is often used to protect boundaries of privilege. However, violence is not only used in a reactive way by men but also proactively. For instance, the violence of football and much domestic violence are part of a process that serves to demonstrate men's power over women. Violence here comes to represent men's 'superior' physicality to women, a feature of many discourses that serve to legitimate the existing gender order. It makes little difference in this sense that currently one of these forms of violence, football, is legitimate and the other, domestic violence, illegitimate. Both types of violence are usually based on the premise that it is only men who can engage in such violent acts (although some men's rights activists have begun to argue that women also commit acts of domestic violence, see Farrell 1993). This has the effect of enabling men to monopolize access to violence, to construct men as a unitary gender category and to construct violence as an inherent feature of masculinity.

These constructions have widespread support. For instance, within both dominant constructions and within some feminist constructions of masculinity two assumptions abound: that there is a unitary masculinity which serves as a blueprint for normal masculinities, and that violence is the preserve of the masculinities shaped through this discourse. In working with boys in schools these assumptions need to be disrupted in order to provide male students with opportunities to develop non-violent conflict resolution skills. This requires exploring some of the ways in which these assumptions have come to be normalized. This chapter provides a discussion of these assumptions and thus examines how violence has been masculinized, and how in the process violence has been done to the concept of masculinity.

The discussion that takes place in this chapter serves as an indication of the pervasiveness of the association between masculinity and violence. In working with boys (and with adults) in schools there is much to be done to demonstrate that this association is a social construction which works against the interests of gender justice. If schools are to be places where the legitimacy of violent practices are to be disrupted, it is important that this work is done (Hinson 1996). Unfortunately, discourses which suggest that masculinist violence is inevitable are quite resilient to disruption. However, challenges to dominant perceptions of masculinity and violence are possible, and schools can act as sites where these possibilities are realized. It should be noted here that many boys have an emotional investment in these constructions, which makes challenging the legitimacy of existing representations of masculinity very difficult. This is taken up in later chapters. This chapter focuses on disrupting the assumptions that there exists a unified 'true' masculinity and that violence is an essential quality of this masculinity.

The violencing of masculinity

The assumption, that there is one true masculinity, does violence to the concept of masculinity. It negates the existence of a multiplicity of masculinities, some of which by their very definition have an aversion to violence (see, for instance, Christian 1994; Connell 1995a: ch. 5; Messner 1997; Pease 1997). This is not to suggest that violence has not been a significant weapon in the armoury of hegemonic masculinities: a weapon that has been used to maintain dominance over 'othered' masculinities and all femininities. It is clear that the primary perpetrators of rape, 'domestic' violence, incest, war, environmental vandalism, and other crimes of violence have been men. Furthermore, it is clear that the greatest beneficiaries of such crimes have been men. However, the silencing of masculinities, other than hegemonic masculinities, delegitimizes many of those masculinities that have the potential to challenge existing gender, class, race, ethnic and sexualized relations of power. It is on the unitary concepts of these relations that dominant constructions of 'othered' masculinities are based.

However, gender is not a fixed unitary attribute (see, for example, Gatens 1983, 1996; Grosz 1990, 1994, 1995; Young 1990, 1995, 1997; Flax 1992; Gunew 1993; Yeatman 1993, 1994, 1995a, b; Huggins 1994; Ang 1995). Neither can it be particularized by categories of race, ethnicity, class and sexuality. This argument is explored in the work of Segal (1990) who identifies numerous forms of masculinity, which cut across boundaries of class, race, and sexuality (see also Connell 1989, 1992, 1995a; Westwood 1990; Evans 1992; Buchbinder 1994; Hearn and Collinson 1994; Mac an Ghaill 1994a, b, c; Sewell 1997, 1998). Black masculinity is a case in point. It is apparent that there has been a dominant unitary representation of Black masculinity in white society. This masculinity has been constructed through masculinist colonialist discourses, which have stressed physical prowess and sexual attributes and desires (interestingly enough attributes that form the basis of white hegemonic masculinities). This construction of Black masculinity has legitimated numerous oppressions against Black men, in numerous white societies, and in some instances has prevented solidarity actions between non-Black women and Black men and women.

Essentialist constructions of Black masculinity serve to mask the multiplicity of Black masculinities thereby enabling the maintenance of racist stereotypes. Black masculinities in non-Black dominated societies are thus formed in a context where racist discourses predominate (Mac an Ghaill 1994b; Marriott 1996; Sewell 1997, 1998: Wright *et al.* 1998). However, numerous other discourses work through Black men to give Black masculinity a variety of forms. These forms may, for instance, be exploitative of women; they may be supportive of feminist women (regardless of race); they may see violence as a means of dealing with problems facing them and their community; or they may chose non-violence to solve such problems. Segal (1990: 203) states in relation to this point, 'In looking at the oppositional meanings inherent in Black masculinity today, the stress is on diversity'.

A similar comment could be made about homosexual masculinity (Connell 1992). The stereotypical camp/feminine image of the male homosexual does not hold true for a range of homosexual masculinities. For instance, displays of tough aggressive masculinity are not restricted to heterosexual males. There has in recent times been an increasing valorization of the 'masculine' within various male homosexual communities (see for instance, Segal 1990: 144–57; Burstyn 1999: 217–19; and also Pronger 1990; Miller 1998). Furthermore, the Western male homosexual cannot be assumed to be white (Mac an Ghaill 1994a, c; Marriott 1996).

This does not mean that it is impossible to talk about men as a category. Masculinizing discourses affect all men. For example, as mentioned in Chapter 1, it is very difficult for boys to avoid being affected, either positively or negatively, by their relationship to sport. However, it is import-ant to recognize that masculinizing discourses are nuanced by factors such as class, race and sexuality, and thus that there is a dominant expectation of how various categories of men will behave. It is also important to recog-nize that these are not the only discourses which are available to boys and men.

Masculinities are acquired through various processes that shape numer-ous subject positions for boys/men. Some of these positions have been shaped through discourses that have emphasized the 'manliness' of violence and domination. However, the sometimes competing, although sometimes com-plementary, discourses stressing the 'manliness' of responsibility and the need to stand up for social justice (occasionally referred to as the 'Truth') have played a part in producing a range of masculinities that have rejected individual and/or institutional violence. Furthermore, some feminist dis-courses have created a number of possibilities available to men, which allow a range of emotions and capacities for love and caring sometimes denied by dominant discourses of masculinity.

A male tendency towards violence is thus not 'natural'. Signifiers of hegemonic masculinity serve to make this link, as do a number of other discourses. However, in each instance where this link is made there is a construction of masculinity as a unitary category. This naturalization of the connection between masculinity and violence was clearly evident in a number of comments made by boys interviewed for this book. Natural reasons for men and women's different propensities for violence included: 'testosterone'; 'human nature'; 'god'; 'it's just how we are' and as 'something that just happens.' Thus Will argues that: 'God has given them (men) more physical power. So they use the advantage as they can, it's human nature I suppose.'

It is perhaps reasonings such as these which led Wade to conclude that men and women are 'a different race.' For Peter masculine nature is trans-lated into a frightening urge to fight:

See with boys and men I reckon, I don't know, something in them snaps. Like in us we've got the fighting urge. Like I don't know, it's just fight and kill, 'Yeah come on you cunts, come on you bastards,' and stuff like that, you know. Take on the world sort of stuff like that.

In some instances 'natural' reasons were combined with a prehistoric tradition (reminiscent of Bly 1991 and Biddulph 1995, 1997), for example Oscar comments:

Well I often have arguments about this. I believe it's in men's nature because we were always hunters and that's just a . . . behaviour that we're brought up with and it's in our genes and that's just the way we've been earlier so it would be very hard to sort of get that out of us I guess.

In other instances boys saw a combination between nature and social conditioning as a cause of men's violence. For example, Julian states: 'to a degree it's born, you know. And then to a degree it's brought up in them you know by their mothers and you know other people.' These boys are not alone in this naturalistic construction of masculinity. Even those discourses that appear to be working on the margins of gendered relations of power construct similar representations of men. For instance, there is a worrying tendency within the men's movement to support the existence of a naturally aggressive male. Bly's (1991) *Iron John* is a prime example of this. Similar sentiments can also be found in Australia in the work of Biddulph (1995). For instance, Biddulph comments: 'It's known that boys' testosterone levels increase when they are placed in ongoing situations of threat and danger, and that this leads to even more aggressive behaviour' (1995: 143). Biological explanations for aggression such as this are of course comforting to men who have felt that their 'deep masculinity' (Biddulph 1995: 28) or the 'Iron John' in them has been squashed through a number of discourses, not least of which has been feminism.

These masculinist discourses represent a long tradition of blaming women for men's violence. Kimmel (1996) examines how men in America have sought to unleash their repressed manhoods by engaging in various masculine rituals. It is sometimes argued by such men that this repression has occurred as a cost of the civilization of men, a civilization which has been brought about by women. Thus, for many of these men, male explosions of rage are explained as the product of the civilizing of men. The anger at women, which such men sometimes express, is captured in the now infamous statement of Robert Bly that if women try to tell a man what to do he should 'bust them in the mouth' (quoted in Kimmel and Kaufman 1995: 40).

This apparent need for men to have a natural outlet for their masculinity has not been missed by some boys. For instance, Oscar states in relation to why men resort to violence to solve problems:

> I think this suppressing of males' . . . I don't know fighting instinct, I guess you might call it is partially at fault because I don't know many males may seem . . . seem to think that they have to take it out on something and as a result it's their wives, so yeah I'm not really too sure how you could solve such a problem . . . I guess you can only suppress it to a certain extent but then you see in some cases it's suppressed too much and people tend to snap . . . For instance these men that bash their wives I believe that a lot of things they suppress, not just like physical hitting and that sort of thing is suppressed, but their emotional feelings and all that and they bring it out on their wives. If you had some sort of outlet to be violent, that didn't harm anyone, I believe that that would be a lot better and you wouldn't bring it out like in society.

Essentialist notions such as these take the responsibility for violence away from the perpetrator. They imply that illegitimate male violence in a 'civilized' society cannot be helped. However, it is not just men who have articulated concepts of an essentialized masculinity.

Some (pro)feminists[1] have also used essentialist arguments to explain the predominance of male violence. This is understandable many of the dominant institutions within industrial societies that serve as a means of reinforcing men's privileges demonstrate a significant propensity for violence of one sort or another. This violence is particularly evident when the privileges they impart are threatened and/or when normalized gender positions are rejected. It has been the way in which men have used violence to preserve/reinstate their privilege within these institutions which has led many feminists to suggest that men are essentially violent and aggressive. One institution, for example, which has given credence to essentialist constructions of a violent masculinity is the heterosexual nuclear family.

The family as an institution of oppression of women and children has long been a major concern of feminism (Thorne 1982; Ward 1984; Scutt, 1990; Horsfall 1991; for comments made by school girls in relation to family violence see Herbert 1989; Gilbert *et al.* 1995). Normalized constructions of the nuclear family produce a seductive image that leads many women to 'voluntarily' enter into such an arrangement (Weedon 1987: 16) despite evidence which indicates that: 'The most violent institution in society after the police and the military is the family' (Schostak 1986: 129). Furthermore, institutions that primarily appear to serve women, such as social security, often have a dual character in that they can also work to protect the patriarchal family arrangements at the expense of women's needs and safety (see for instance, Dale and Foster 1986; Bryson 1988; Horsfall 1991: 31–2).

Violence as a means of policing dominant representations of masculinity and femininity is also starkly obvious elsewhere in the patriarchal gender order. Dominant representations of masculinity have been protected from 'inside' challenges through the normalization of, and often state sanctioned, homophobic violence (see Altman 1971; Comstock 1991). The most repressive, and demonstratively violent, of society's institutions are closely associated with masculinity and often work to protect the legitimacy of men's violence against women. These institutions include the legal system (see for example MacKinnon 1989), the military (see Reardon 1985: 52–8, who has argued that misogyny is 'the mother's milk of militarism') and the police (see Hanmer *et al.* 1989). Rape and pornography have also been significant features of these institutions' practices (see, for example, Brownmiller 1976; Griffin 1979, 1981; MacKinnon 1989; Stock 1991).

In her landmark work, *Against Our Will*, Brownmiller (1976: 15, original emphasis) argued that: 'From prehistoric times to the present, I believe rape has played a critical function. It is nothing more or less than a conscious process of intimidation by which *all men* keep *all women* in a state of fear.' The works of radical feminists like Brownmiller have been significant for their contributions to bringing into popular discourse the existence of male violence against women. However, such positions suggest that a male conspiracy exists to which the possession of a penis automatically makes one a co-conspirator. This is problematic on two fronts. First, male violence against women, and support for or condoning of such violence, can become an irreducible condition, and thus a potentially forgivable condition, of masculinity. Second, it dooms to failure attempts by males to engage in political projects with the purpose of challenging male violence.

I do not want to trivialize or negate feminist comments, such as 'All men are potential rapists', which have been derived from works like that of Brownmiller. It is important for men to accept that this is an obvious reality for many/all women: a reality which has been constructed from damning evidence against men. The point being made here is that this reality serves two purposes. First and importantly, it identifies the prevalence of men's violence against women and children and can thus serve as a means of setting up structures to challenge, and to support survivors of, such violence. However, second and more problematically, it also serves to assist in maintaining the state of fear, identified by Brownmiller herself, which works in men's interests in controlling and dominating women. Thus, the suggestion I want to make here is that the link between violence and masculinity is not 'natural'; rather, it has been a social and political project that has served to protect male interests.

Essentialist explanations of male violence do little to disrupt this project. However, there are also some non-essentialist positions regarding gender that also reinforce existing gender relations. Many of these positions place the responsibility for male violence on various structural features. For instance, one of the boys in this study, Harry, states that 'girls are placid' because, 'They're not really brought up like boys are. In their childhood they're given dolls and boys are given little cars and they crash their cars and . . .' However, he realizes that not all boys are violent because he is not. Thus, Harry argues, some boys are violent because of the 'way they're brought up. Their parents . . . if their parents are violent and drink too much they'll be violent. Or . . . because they were beaten when they were a child or they didn't get enough attention and they want a lot of attention.'

Sean also looks to the structural relations within the family to explain how boys can be deterred from using violence:

> Just got to be brought up differently . . . obviously a fair bit comes from when they're younger. The male used to beat . . . the husband used to beat up the wife and like the kids used to see that and think,

'Oh yeah that's all right that's allowed.' Stuff like that so I guess you've just got to be brought up differently. Parents have to act sensibly to bring children up the right way.

Structural accounts of violence, such as this, are common. However this determinism discounts the agency of people within those situations. Peter provides a most lucid account of how such deterministic views of gender are founded on uncertain principles:

Well I grew up watching my Dad batter the shit out of my Mum. See he used to drink rum and that would make him go mad. When we'd come home, him and Mum would have an argument and he'd ahh he'd ahh like hit her around. And it's sort of hard for me to talk about it like but uhm, I just you know ahh I, I always said when I was older I'm never going to let him touch my mother again, I'm never going to hit a woman or anything like that . . . that was just like a nightmare. Every weekend like on Saturday nights and stuff I'd just have to run behind this wall sort of thing and just watch Mum get the shit beaten out of her and I'd want to do something but I was too little to do anything you see and it was just, shit, I'd just wish it would stop and stuff like that. And that's why see I had to go to the guidance officer for the school cause I, I was getting into a lot of fights and they said, I had to tell them about my past and stuff and she said that's mainly why I get angry and stuff like you gotta like . . . and uhm that's why I'd never hit a girl or a woman or anything like that. Just, it's just not on.

Peter's response here brings into doubt many of those assumptions, expressed by the boys above and others, which suggest that young boys learn how to relate to women from the way men have treated the boys' mothers. There are times when boys' bonds with their mothers will be such that the behaviour being performed by their fathers, or whoever, is anathema to them. This is not to wash away structural features. Peter admits that he has a problem with violence, and this may well stem from the way he has been brought up in a violent home. However, nothing is certain or predetermined by structural relations. It is important not to deny the agency of those working within these structures to bring about change.

Structural relations that are created within nuclear families, workplaces, schools, and various other state organizations certainly play a major role in the legitimation of masculinized attributes associated with violence. These institutions are usually based on patriarchal privilege and engage in differing processes that valorize the masculine over the feminine. Each of these institutions also constrains disruption with the threat of sanctions against those who might seek to alter their structural arrangements, thereby legitimizing force and control as a means of maintaining 'order'. Thus structural features, while not being totally responsible, are certainly implicated in normalizing the relationship between masculinity and violence.

Some theories of men's violence do wash away these structural features by pathologizing the perpetrators of violence. Excess of violence is often portrayed as the actions of a sick man or men. For instance Issac comments: 'I think it's just a genetic thing but that will only . . . there'll only be a minute number of people that are violent.'

There was a lot of discussion in the classes at Tamville and Mountainview about men and violence after the Port Arthur shootings in Tasmania (see pp. 5–6). Many of the boys explained the gunman's actions in relation to his mental health, for instance he was described by one boy, James, as 'just one looney that comes along every now and then.' Attitudes such as this prompted Joshua to comment: 'I think you should get a like a license and a . . . like sort of a mental check on people who have automatic guns.' Wade describes the, at the time, proposed gun laws as a 'crock' because, 'Just one foolish man did it and then like the whole of Australia gets the blame for it.'

In order to understand how masculinity has been constructed alongside violence it is important to consider the ways in which violence, desire and fear are integrated into normalized masculine subject positions. In the introduction to this book a question asked by the Australian folksinger Judy Small in relation to the massacre in Montreal was noted. This question asks: 'Why do men always resort to the gun, the sword and the fist?' In order to avoid essentialist and socially determinist answers to this question it is important to explore how this association has been a political project, which feeds off men's insecurities. Many of these insecurities stem from men's constant need to demonstrate their commitment to dominant constructions of masculinity in order to receive the rewards that go with successful hegemonic masculine performances and to avoid the repercussions which active rejection of such performances often attract. This need has done much to masculinize violence.

The masculinization of violence

In recent times a number of feminists have sought to identify the ways in which violence has been masculinized to the detriment of women. The focus in this literature has often been on men's sexual violence. For instance, Segal (1990) argues that rape cannot be 'naturally' associated with the phallus. She states,

> But what, apart from lack of inclination and possibly access to weapons, is to prevent a woman (or marauding gang of women) from buggering a man with bottle, fist or tongue, or from demanding orgasm through

oral sex? These are, after all among the most common forms of male sexual assault on women, and well within women's capacities should we so choose. (Feminists long ago rejected the misleading definition of 'rape' exclusively as forced penile penetration of the vagina).

(Segal 1990: 235)

An important element in Segal's comment is women's lack of inclination, in relation to men's inclination to rape. If we can accept that violence, including sexual violence, is not naturally male, it has to be asked why it is that a violent culture has become such a central feature of patriarchal societies. Ian suggests that, 'Girls can be violent if they want to . . . But they just don't really. I reckon they could if they wanted to be.'

Why women 'choose' not to be violent raises important questions, which are beyond the scope of this book. However, the arguments of Marcus (1992: 391) are significant here: 'Masculine power and feminine powerlessness neither simply precede nor cause rape; rather rape is one of culture's many modes of feminizing women.' She argues further that, 'Rape does not happen to preconstituted victims; it momentarily makes victims' (Marcus 1992: 391). Thus rape, and all other forms of violence against women, rely on constructions of masculinity and femininity that treat violence as inherently male and women as victims. Brant and Yun Lee Too (1994: 7) have stated, in relation to the construction of women who complain about sexual harassment as 'victims', that: 'The weak, feckless victim is an image of misogynist myth.' Feminist actions throughout this century (not to mention women's activities throughout history) exist as an indictment of this myth.

This leads to the second flawed assumption relating to the denotation of violence as a natural component of a unitary masculinity: that is that violence is the sole property of males. In order for masculinity to retain violence as its possession, women must be constructed as being unable to use violence. Many of the boys at the two schools perceived women in such a way. For instance, Julian in outlining his reasons why 'some' sexual harassment is a problem, positions women and girls as victims:

Oh some of it goes too far. Some of it . . . some people (girls) in certain cases they're delicate and they shouldn't do those sort of things to other people. I don't think there's a real lot of people in society, it's only the cases that you hear that make it so bad . . .

Peter, who often tries to respond to issues of gender in a positive manner, explains the differences between men and women's natures. For Peter, men not women are the perpetrators of violence:

Maybe because it's girls have got like such a gentle nature, you know. I mean like I don't mean to sound sexist or anything but like they've got babies and stuff like that. Mainly, I know a lot of my friends' dads and that they go out to the pub and that after work on weekdays and that and have a bit of a charge and stuff like that and . . . They you know and then like some of them sometimes they come home beaten up like just out of a fight. Had a fight and stuff like that. You know.

Peter has hard evidence in front of him to prove that women have different natures from men. Julian too does not want to appear sexist but:

I think women depend more on the more feminine side. Not being sexist but they're just you know they're not fighters or you know they're not . . . you know wanting to fight. Mainly males do I think just you know some being king or whatever.

During the course of the programmes being implemented at the two schools there was significant discussion about the availability of guns in Australia. The activities of the gun lobby, which was seeking to prevent Federal government legislation making licenses for gun ownership more restrictive, was the source of much debate. It was apparent from numerous pieces of news footage that it was mainly men who were attending the pro-gun rallies. The boys provided several reasons for this. For instance, Harry thought that this was because shooting is 'seen as a more masculine sport' and that when a gun is shot 'you make big bangs.' Joshua's rationale was along the same lines:

Probably because women probably wouldn't have guns as much as men because they don't like the . . . it's too hard to have . . . um carry and stuff. It's hard to hold . . . and it's probably too noisy and stuff for them.

As was Than's: 'They just don't like to be . . . weak. They can't hold up a gun or something. It might be heavy.'

Issac, who knows that women are able to use guns (his aunt and cousin both belong to a shooting club) notes that they do not go hunting:

Yeah, because it's out in the, you know, rugged . . . Some women just don't like it out in the bush. Because they like all the comforts . . . creature comforts like showers and cleanliness. They don't like to be dirty . . . I guess that's one thing you'd have to be when you're out shooting.

Women's dislike of hunting is also picked up by Luke in a frightening indictment of men's relationship to violence:

A lot of women use guns too. On the ranges. Women mainly use pistols. Men use the semis more often. They do the hunting. If you come across a wounded pig. You need to be able to shoot more than once or you're . . . I think men like the power . . . the power to take a life.

Women's perceived inability, or unwillingness, to hunt is presumed due to a number of factors associated with femininity, for example cleanliness.

However, this construction of women as being too 'delicate' or too 'weak' to use violence as a means of fighting back against violent men is being contested by numerous feminists.

Many feminists argue that denying women the property of violence can work to maintain male dominance over women. This is a point made by Marcus (1992) who argues for women to reject subject positions that construct a 'rape script' within which women are passive victims. She presents an argument to women which states that 'we must develop our capacities for violence in order to disrupt the rape script' (Marcus 1992: 397). This political position was very much in evidence in a poster I saw on the wall of a doctor's surgery in the early days of writing this book. The poster was produced by Brisbane's Rape and Incest Centre in conjunction with an arts worker (Sally Hart). It depicted, superimposed upon text dealing with rape, a surrealistic devilish woman encircled with large bold red words reading 'EYES, NOSE, THROAT, GROIN' and a message underneath stating 'Don't be too polite girls . . . hit him where it hurts'.

A similar sentiment is expressed forcefully by Andrea Dworkin:

> We are in a war. We have not been fighting back to win this war. We are in need of political resistance. We need it with our lawmakers, with our government officials. We need it with our professional women. We need it above ground. We need it underground too . . . I am asking you to organise political support for women who kill men who have been hurting them . . . I'm asking you to stop men who beat women. Get them jailed or get them killed . . . I am asking you to look at every single political possibility for fighting back.
>
> (Dworkin 1991, quoted in Chisholm 1993: 30)

The assertiveness of the arguments put forward by Marcus, the Brisbane Rape and Incest Crisis Centre and Dworkin present a dangerous threat to masculinities that are founded on men's domination of women. They undermine a masculinist construction of femininity. Furthermore, the femininities proposed through this feminist discourse seek to appropriate a major tool that in the hands of men and boys has served to police the boundaries of masculinities and femininities.

It is interesting, and perhaps an indication of the fragility of dominant representations of masculinity, that men's rights groups are also beginning to argue that women can be just as violent as men. A number of these groups have been pushing the line that men experience just as much domestic violence as women do. Evidence of course proves otherwise (see, for example, Scutt 1990; Polk 1994; Jackman 1996). However, what is significant here is that men who would normally subscribe to all the manly 'virtues' of hegemonic masculinity are prepared to admit that women can beat up men. In one instance, a Brisbane man even took a Brisbane feminist organization, the Domestic Violence Resource Centre, to the Human Rights

Commission, because they refused to provide him with counselling after he alleged he had been subjected to violent attacks from his wife (Jackman 1996). It is difficult to ascribe motivations to this action and the enormous support he received from the Queensland based Men's Rights Organization. However, a possible reading of this action could be that the fear that feminism has provided women with access to violence, with which they can resist dominant constructions of femininity, has stung such organizations into a reactive mode. This fear does appear to be more widespread than simply existing in the minds of men's rights activists.

The extent to which this threat is feared by men can be observed in the treatment of women who have killed men, especially when the killing has taken place in the public sphere (R. Mills 1997). These women have often been constructed as mad, as freaks of their gender, not female (often identifying them as 'lesbians', see MacDonald 1991: 5) and sometimes as not human (for example as vampires). In whatever way they are constructed, women who kill men disrupt the patriarchal gender order, 'for if women usurp the traditionally male role of aggressor, and if they do it successfully, men fear that their ultimate weapon – their physical superiority over women – is gone' (MacDonald 1991: 239).

There may also be a concern on the part of some men that women may arrive at the point where the mystique of violence no longer holds: in other words, the myth, which states that in order to use violence properly one has to be a man, will be exploded. Furthermore, once women acquire the ability to use violence a fear exists that they may in fact be able to do 'it' better than men. This fear is demonstrated in discourses shaping the attitudes of European anti-terrorist squads. MacDonald (1991) identifies a strong belief among these groups that women freedom fighters/terrorists are far more dangerous than their male counterparts, thus prompting a general attitude of 'Shoot the women first'. This notion of the dangerous woman is captured in some comments made by Bill: 'Ah girls are (violent) as well. You don't see it as much about. Once they get going they're worse . . . They just come out and go psycho.' In addition, Issac notes that, 'it is changing like there are a lot of girls becoming just as violent.'

It is possible that the argument that women may be as good if not better than men at being violent has the potential to lapse into egalitarian feminism and a valorization of the masculine violent subject. However, the argument presented here is not one which proposes that women should adopt violence as a means of disrupting existing patriarchal practices. This is obviously a contentious issue for feminists (see Chisholm 1993; Brant and Yun Lee Too 1994) and it is not one with which I want to engage. Rather, I am simply seeking to demonstrate that violence cannot be constructed as an inherently male attribute (a point recognized by both feminists and men who are defenders of patriarchal states, for example anti-terrorist squads) and that casting women as victims serves to reinforce dominant constructions of femininity. An acceptance of these points is a necessity for working with boys in schools on gender and violence issues, and I suggest for maintaining a hope that the patriarchal gender order may be reconfigured into a gender order which is more representative of the interests of both females and males.

The intention in this book is to explore the means by which dominant masculinities and their dependency on male violence can be disrupted in order to create spaces for male subject positions that challenge normalized ways of being a boy, or a man. The opening up of these spaces will involve making public the effects of and assumptions present within dominant representations of masculinity. There is a primary intention here to expose the presence of male violence within the patriarchal gender order as a social and political project, rather than as a 'natural' product of masculinity. However, it should be noted that the men's rights' arguments that 'women are just as violent as men' (Farrell 1993) serve to trivialize the extent of the violence to which women are subjected by men. This is not the position taken here, nor should it be one used with boys in schools. The point being made here is that there is nothing natural about the dominant perception of men and women's relationships to violence.

Underpinning work with boys in schools should thus be the assumption that masculinity and violence are cultural and historical constructs (see, for example, Segal 1990; Horsfall 1991; Connell 1995a) and a belief in the necessity of deconstructing these constructs. This latter project will entail disrupting discourses that naturalize and normalize the relationship between masculinity and violence, and hence also those discourses which construct a unitary masculinity based on men's propensity for violence. These disruptions will serve to open up spaces for alternative masculinities, which are less oppressive to others, to surface. However, this disruption will not be an easy task for there is an overwhelming amount of evidence that suggests the contrary.

Feminist, and other, discourses can quite clearly, and legitimately, link masculinity with violence. Most forms of violence are perpetrated by men. However, the connection is problematic if the link is seen to be 'natural'. The naturalization of this link can serve to dismiss boys' and men's acts of violence as either 'boys will be boys' behaviour or as the transgressive actions of a particular individual. In both instances the wider social picture, which indicates how violence is employed to maintain the existing gender order, is ignored. A more useful analysis of the linkages between men and violence is one that seeks to explore how the naturalization of this connection has been constructed through dominant discourses that serve to make violence the property of hegemonic masculinity. This can be seen in the attempts to keep women out of front line military action, male homosexuals out of the armed services, restrict corporal punishment in schools to males and largely to exclude girls from playing typically violent male sports, such as rugby.

In Australian society, as in most others, violence has been masculinized. A long-term improvement in gender relations will only occur when it has been emasculated. There are a number of sites within society where disruptions to the dominant construction of violence can take place. One important site is that of the school. Schools in both their formal and informal organization serve as powerful gendering and violencing agents. Thus, as a matter of social justice schools should seek to play a role in both regendering and deviolencing dominant constructions of masculinity. Such a process will entail an exploration of the ways in which different masculinities have been socially organized.

The social organization of masculinity

The work of Bob Connell (1995a) is most useful in exploring this social organizing of masculinities. For while there are a multiplicity of masculine performances not all masculinities have an equal status within a masculinist gender order. The vicarious ways in which men perform their masculinities do not occur in isolation from other masculinities and femininities. There is a social organization of masculinity (Connell 1995a; see also Brod 1994). Recognizing the existence of this organization is crucial to understanding the ways in which power is implicated in the formation of masculinities, and thus how male violence is a political issue not a pathological one.

A valorization of a violent masculinity within the current social organization of masculinity provides men with an indication of how they should perform their gender in order to be considered a 'real' man. Dominant representations of masculinity portray men who perform a version of hegemonic masculinity as 'real' or 'natural' men. However, such 'real' men are seldom 'natural'. Very few men can actually live up to the criteria that signify such a man, and those who do have to work very hard to maintain it. However, the masculine benchmark that these masculinities provide serves as a means to police existing gendered relations of power. This policing effect of masculinities makes the social construction of gender a justice issue.

The current organizational arrangement of masculinity is one that predominantly serves the interests of white, middle-class, middle-aged, heterosexual men. However, men marginal to this category of masculinity do at specific times also receive some of the societal benefits specific to being a man. It is an understanding of how these benefits accrue and of the costs that others face from this association of masculinity with violence which needs to form the basis of working with boys on gender and violence issues in schools. The interpretation of these benefits and costs within a justice framework has the potential to engage boys in schools with what Connell (1995a) has referred to as an 'exit politics.' This politics seeks to engage men in a contestatory relationship with the patriarchal gender order. In order to explore the possibilities of boys engaging in such a politics, there needs to be some consideration given to the ways in which social organizations of masculinities are played out within schools. This section provides a consideration of this, and in so doing draws heavily on the work of Connell (1995a).

Connell identifies four ways in which men engage with existing gender relations. He terms these four performances of masculinity as: hegemonic, subordinate, marginalized and complicit. Hegemonic masculine practices are those that serve to naturalize the dominance of men over women. Subordinate masculinities are performed by those men whose behaviours, demeanour and way of life pose a threat to the legitimacy of hegemonic masculinity: for example the masculinities of gay and 'effeminate' men. Complicit masculinities are those masculinities that do not embody hegemonic processes, but benefit from the ways in which hegemonic masculinities construct the gender order. Marginalized masculinities represent the nuancing of masculinities by factors such as class, ethnicity and race. This social organization of masculinity is at work within the gender regimes operating inside institutions such as schools. In any attempt to intervene in masculinity politics at the school level this organization must be a major concern.

Hegemonic masculinities

The men, both real and fictional, who make up the hegemonic category of masculinity represent an embodiment of exemplary masculinity. They are the men who demonstrably meet the criteria set by the signifiers of masculinity outlined in Chapter 1. However, the identification of hegemonic masculine performances is somewhat complex. There is a clear bodily representation of hegemonic masculinity which does not necessarily resonate with the amounts of institutional power that a man wields (Donaldson 1993).

Many of the white middle-aged men who form the powerful elite in Western societies, politicians, generals, bankers, company directors and media owners, do not have the bodies nor the physical trappings typically associated with hegemonic masculinity. However, as Connell (1989: 298) states: 'A man who can command this power has no need of riding leathers and engine noise to assert masculinity. His masculinity is asserted and amplified on an immensely greater scale by the society itself.'

Such men are performing versions of hegemonic masculinity. For these men the power they exert over women and other men does not necessarily manifest itself physically, although it might (Scutt 1990). However, there is a clear threat of violence underpinning their power, a violence which they can distribute without taking any risks. A clear example of this occurred at a union demonstration in Canberra in 1996. The demonstration was organized to protest against proposed changes to federal industrial relations legislation. A splinter group broke off from the official Australian Council of Trade Unions (ACTU) rally, to occupy the federal parliament. A significant amount of violence occurred during this incident and both police and demonstrators were hurt. (There are a number of interesting gendered observations that could be made about this incident. Most of the demonstrators were male, and much was made of the injuries sustained by a female police officer.) John Howard, the Prime Minister of Australia, commented in that night's news that he would not be bullied.

In this instance Howard cast himself as a strong man who would not give into the bullying, or illegitimate violence, of the trade union demonstrators. He was perhaps seeing himself as the John Wayne, Clint Eastwood, Mel Gibson or Arnold Schwarzenegger of Australian politics. However, unlike the characters these men play in the movies, his body is seldom 'put on the line'. There are others who can take the physical consequences of his stand against the 'bullies'. For the majority of boys at school this form of power is something to which they have no access. Their power rests on coarser attributes: their physicalities.

In the early days of the boys' programme at Tamville, Arnold Schwarzenegger was held up by a number of boys as being their perception of an ideal man; often he was described as the man they would most want to be like. However, it was not so much the personality of Schwarzenegger that they wanted to identify with, but his body. Many boys, in particular the younger boys, the grade nines, were most concerned about the size of their muscles. One grade nine boy (Than) from a Vietnamese background commented about his body building activities: 'I want to be like . . . big built see . . . I want muscle not fat, like the chest I don't think is big. It's improving at the moment but I'm still working on it.'

Perhaps the desire to be an 'Arnie' is not so much driven by an urge to be powerful, although there is a clear element here, but out of a wish for safety. The same boy talks about the importance of arm wrestling as a demonstration of strength among his friends:

Than: Yeah, most boys do arm wrestle.
Martin: Are boys who are stronger treated better?
Than: Yeah. Like they . . . they don't get picked on by other boys because they have a reputation that they're quite strong.

Those boys interviewed were very clear about which boys are at most risk from their peers. They are the 'smaller kids', the 'smart ones with glasses and nerdy type ones' and the 'skinny ones.' Oscar commented that: 'naturally the weaker ones will be picked on more than the stronger ones, because . . . no one wants to pick upon the stronger ones.' Many of the boys could think of specific instances: 'John Street he gets picked on a lot because like he's very dramatic and stuff like that . . . he's "Unco" . . . he's uncoordinated.' There is a clear policing of hegemonic activities as normal and natural here. For instance, it is not only the boys who do not meet the bodily expectations of hegemonic masculinity, but also those who 'willingly' transgress its dictates who can also become the targets of violence. For instance Julian notes that some of the boys who are picked on in schools are:

> The shy ones, the ones that don't socialize all that much you know they do their own thing and they do things that are like real boring. Read books all the time (laughter). That sort of thing you know.

The pictures many of these students paint of boys' lives demonstrate how masculinity is constantly having to be proved. Hegemonic masculinity is fragile. Those boys whose behaviours best fit hegemonic standards have to be constantly prepared to act out and to defend this form of manhood. For instance, Oscar recalls a fight he had 'ages back':

Martin: And how did that occur?
Oscar: Ah just teasings. I just got sick of it and just hit him.
Martin: Did things change after it?
Oscar: Yeah yeah yeah. They did yeah.
Martin: And how did people react around you? Was that important?
Oscar: It wasn't really important to me but everyone sort of took a step back and thought, 'Whoa!' because I wasn't usually like that. I'm just sort of . . . But yeah it really surprised heaps of people so . . . But I didn't really do it for that I just did it because I didn't see any other way to stop this so I just . . . yeah.

Harry from Mountainview has a similar story to tell:

Harry: I used to fight all the time in year seven.
Martin: Why was that?
Harry: People didn't like me and they'd try to hit me and I'd react.
Martin: And when did things start to change?
Harry: When I fought back
Martin: Do you think if you hadn't fought back that would have been a big problem?
Harry: Yeah it would of been.

In these instances, Oscar and Harry have demonstrated their loyalty to hegemonic forms of masculinity and were thus welcomed (back) into the fold. A boy who is not prepared to engage in acts of physical violence in order to stand up for himself is a popular target for abuse in schools. Such abuse regularly contains comments about the boy's sexuality. In order to avoid such comments and abuse a boy, like Oscar, will have to demonstrate that he does not have an aversion to using the tools of hegemonic masculinity and consequently reinforces the validity and effectiveness of such behaviours.

Hegemonizing violent masculine behaviour thus takes work and boys/men are expected to continually assert the legitimacy of such behaviour. For instance, in a conversation about the sorts of things boys talk about among themselves, Joshua notes:

> *Joshua:* And if it was like something like fighting everyone's like you know 'Oh yeah I fight and all that,' proud of the fact that they fight.
> *Martin:* Why do you think they'd be so proud of the fact that they fight?
> *Joshua:* Oh because they get a chance to show off to everyone. Show everyone how strong they are . . . And their skills.

A number of the boys interviewed noted how boys like to talk about those things that confirmed their manhood, such as the fights they had been in, in contrast to their willingness to engage in discussions about emotional issues. Such topics are often off-limits for boys, and men (see Seidler 1994). For once the expression of boys' feelings represent a threat to dominant representations of hegemonic manhood, these boys often experience a subordinating process. It is this process that serves to maintain a masculine silence on issues of gender justice. Subordinating discourses work to ensure that the majority of men become complicit in dominant relations of power.

Subordinate masculinities

Connell's second category, subordinate masculinities, relates to those forms of manhood that occupy the bottom rungs of the masculine hierarchy. They are the boys above who are under constant threat from their peers for not having 'masculine' skills. For many of these boys, homophobic discourses work to position them outside the norms of 'real' masculinities, as the most notable grouping within the category of 'subordinate masculinities' are gays. However, it is not only gays who are adversely affected by homophobic discourses. Homophobia is a discourse that is often implicated in the subordination of particular non-homosexual masculinities. For as Connell (1995a: 79) points out many men/boys who may be heterosexual experience oppression on the basis of their particular representations of masculinity (see also Walker 1988; Martino 1997). Homophobia is omnipresent in the subordination of many boys' lives and at the same time it serves as a means of policing the boundaries of hegemonic masculinity (Epstein 1997).

Fracturing the protective coating of hegemonic masculinity requires men to articulate their concerns about the way in which pressures on men to conform to an idealized image of masculinity is dangerous for both men and women. This means men have to engage in a 'feminine' activity: the sharing of feelings. This is fraught with problems for some boys in some social contexts. For instance, one grade nine boy (Peter) from Tamville stated:

> I've never been like that you know shared my feelings or anything . . . it is hard for men to do it because, they'll say, 'Ooo, what is he? Is he a bit queer?' or something else . . . Or 'Is he a bit of a fag or something?' Some shit like that you know . . . I don't think, like in our society, you like you gotta be, for men, you gotta be like you gotta be like you can't be like a little queer. Like a little shy you know like a little softie sort of thing. You can't be like that. Or people start sussing you out. 'Ahh, shit this fella looks a bit suss stay away from him.' . . . You know, like that and it's, and like I don't know, it's just a lot, and a lot of pressure's on and stuff and you, I don't know. Oh yeah, and it just wears down the pressure of stuff like that. Men shut their feelings away . . . and yeah you'll get called a 'girl' 'cause you see that's what girls mainly do.

Or as a grade nine boy, Joshua, put it, boys who expressed their feelings in class would 'probably be called a "wuss" or a "gaybo"'. A community worker (Richard) involved in the Mountainview programme indicates some of the dangers that boys can face as a consequence of attracting the 'wuss' tag:

> In asking boys to confront things we often don't pay enough attention to safety, to the extent that we need to recognize things like rape as a mechanism of male socialization. I know of boys penetrated with penises and objects because they were 'wusses', they were effeminate. I'm not saying many boys are actively conscious about this possibility, but I think they are subliminally conscious of fear, and about not attracting attention to their level of conceptualization of themselves . . .

Homophobia thus becomes central to men's complicity in maintaining existing gendered relations of power. Kimmel (1994: 131) describes homophobia as 'the fear that other men will unmask us, emasculate us, reveal to us and the world that we do not measure up, that we are not real men.' Kimmel argues that men are ashamed of this fear, and thus:

> Shame leads to silence – the silences that keep other people believing that we actually approve of the things that are done to women, to minorities, to gays and lesbians in our culture. The frightened silences as we scurry past a woman being hassled by men on the street. That furtive silence when men make sexist or racist jokes in a bar. That clammy-handed silence when guys in the office make gay-bashing jokes. Our fears are the sources of our silences, and men's silence is what keeps the system running.
>
> (Kimmel 1994: 131)

Homophobic pressures thus serve as a means by which men can be made complicit in maintaining unjust gendered relations of power. In Chapter 1 the dangers that boys face from homophobic discourses were indicated. Homophobia is one of the most powerful weapons used to protect the patriarchal gender order from men's efforts to weaken it. It produces a terror that ensures boys' and men's complicity in the perpetuation of societal violence.

Complicit masculinities

Complicit masculinity is a pervasive form of masculinity, which is typified by the majority of boys and men who, while not meeting the criteria of hegemonic status or demonstrating the worst excesses of hegemonic masculinity, do little to challenge the patriarchal gender order, thereby enjoying its many rewards. For many such boys and men some feminist issues and concerns are recognized as being legitimate; however, others are often negated. Oscar for instance, comments:

> a lot of the feminist issues are really very trivial very silly I believe. I mean things like a manhole cover being a person hole cover and all this sort of stuff. Being politically correct. I think it's a bit trivial. But in terms of jobs and that yeah I think they've got a case and men are put off by them sort of coming into that, yeah.

Harry from Mountainview comments that, while women have a legitimate complaint about their lack of representation in government, 'they go overboard on women's rights and stuff.' Many such boys draw on men's rights or men's liberation type rhetoric in order to dismiss feminist demands for a more socially just gender order. For instance, Will states:

> it's almost gone full circle now, instead of equalling up the situation we've over equalled it, if you like and well some people may be discriminated against who usually, who in the past, would have had the power.

And Luke, who refers to feminists as 'feminazis', argues that:

> Women have taken it too far. You can't even joke anymore. I saw a sheet the other day called 'Male Bashing.' I laughed at some of it. If it had been about women it would've been called sexual harassment.

Men and boys who perform forms of complicit masculinity are often opposed to male violence against women, and sometimes against other men/boys. However, this does not usually translate into any concrete rejection of the existing gender order. In some instances it takes the form of protecting women from 'other' men. And, in others there is a denial of violence.

For example, for some of these boys, there is little evidence of sexual harassment in their schools,

> *Martin:* If you, if you felt strongly about things like sexual harassment, do you think you could talk to your friends about that? Say, 'I think sexual harassment is wrong.'
> *Than:* Ah I don't really care about that . . . Yeah it doesn't really happen much around me.

For some it is simply a case of boys 'mucking around.' Bryce, a Tamville grade nine boy, for example, is one of the boys who doesn't think many boys engage in sexual harassment at the school: 'I don't really reckon . . . and if they do it's sort of just playfully. Not really full on pick. "I'll fight you. Punch the living daylights out of you." I just think it's playful what they do.' And another grade nine boy, Joshua, said:

> Oh everyone's pretty you know all right with that sexual harassment because we don't really do it. Because you know everyone here's, you know, pretty close together. We're all friends and everything . . . Because everyone just you know doesn't look at it like sexual harassment. Just looks at it like you're mucking around.

This 'playfulness' was also part of the behaviour between boys, as explained by James:

> But nothing serious goes on at this school . . . Ah you know there's just people like Will B. and Harry C. cops a lot because his Mum works at this school. Um so just people that drive Holdens, people that drive Fords you know you like you just give them a bit of a bagging from time to time . . . But it's all right. Nothing ever gets serious and everyone always knows you're joking . . . and it's always made sure that everyone knows you're joking . . . Like if you found out like that you'd actually hurt someone's feelings you'd usually go up afterwards and say, 'Sorry mate, I didn't really mean it you know just having a bit of fun.'

Interestingly one of the boys who is named by James is the Harry above who had to fight his way into an acceptable manhood. Clearly, this playful teasing has not been a fun experience for him (see Kehily and Nayak (1997) for a discussion of the role of humour in the regulation of masculinities in schools). A similar pattern was evident among the grade 11s at Tamville, as exemplified by Julian:

> I've . . . you know I've called my mates poofters and that. You know it doesn't mean nothing. It doesn't mean they are a poofter but it just . . . it's just a joke. That's all we consider it. And it never goes any further than that you know it just. Like that Ian he gets a bit of flak.

Because he just does things everybody else doesn't do and they just make fun of him . . . Ah they . . . they're going on about him going to the gay Mardi Gras. (Laughter) You know. Mainly Issac. You know that's it (laughter). It just happens. It's just all part of growing up. It's always going to happen.

During the course of an interview, the Ian referred to by Julian, broke down and cried about the teasing he received from the other boys. And interestingly, the ways in which Ian responds to the challenges to his masculinity is to express a dislike of homosexuals and to aspire to be a 'policeman' or a 'fireman.' He wants 'some job with action instead of a boring job . . . Stuff like that. You risk your life to save people and stuff like that.' Ian's great desire is thus to be a 'real' man.

It is these three broad groupings of masculinity, hegemonic, subordinate and complicit masculinities, which are engaged in an internal politics of masculinity. Membership in these categories places men in positions that are able to receive some form of patriarchal reward. The last Connell category, marginalized masculinities, raises important issues in any consideration of issues of masculinity in particular, and gender in general. It is perhaps an important time to make note of these issues.

Marginalized masculinities

The concept of marginalized masculinities brings external factors, that is factors other than gender, into play in the politics of masculinity. Race and class, for instance, cannot be separated from the internal dynamics of this politics (Evans 1992; Goodall and Huggins 1992; Pyke 1996; Fine et al. 1997; Gardiner 1997; Sewell 1997, 1998; Power et al. 1998; Wright et al. 1998). This does not mean that they are absent in the previous categories where, for instance, men typifying an Australian hegemonic masculinity tend to be, although not necessarily, Anglo in origin. Rather, this category leads to an understanding of how the distribution of privilege is mediated through the impact of other social and political considerations pertaining to such factors as class and ethnicity. Thus, in some instances of marginalized masculinity the benefits of being male are not always easy to discern. The situation of Aboriginal men is the most starkly obvious example of this in the Australian context.

Aboriginal men as a social group (Young 1990: 42–8) are economically, socially and politically marginalized in relation to non-Aboriginal groupings. However, the high incidences of domestic violence within some Aboriginal communities (Burbank 1994; Ferrante et al. 1996) could be interpreted as indicating that gender relations operating in Aboriginal communities are a reflection of those operating within non-Aboriginal patriarchal society. And, thus, that while Aboriginal men are discriminated against by a colonial society, they in turn are a privileged group in relation to Aboriginal women. This, though, is not necessarily the case (Gardiner 1997). For instance, in relation to Aboriginal women's contact with early women's liberation movements, Heather Goodall and Jackie Huggins (1992: 402) note how the situation for Aboriginal women was different from their non-Aboriginal counterparts: 'Aboriginal women were better educated than Aboriginal men, and when they were employed, they worked in jobs with better status than Aboriginal men.' This is not to suggest that Aboriginal women have not suffered greatly within white colonial society, especially at the hands of white men. For instance, rape, forced sterilizations, removal of children, poorly paid employment have all been experiences of Aboriginal women (Goodall and Huggins 1992).

The point here is not to determine who is more oppressed, Aboriginal men or Aboriginal women. Nor is it to argue that Aboriginal men never act oppressively towards Aboriginal or non-Aboriginal women. Rather, it is that the oppressions of Aboriginal women and non-Aboriginal women are in some ways different, and the perpetration and complicity in both of these oppressions on the part of Aboriginal men and non-Aboriginal men is consequently different. This is important in any consideration of how men as a group benefit from the patriarchal gender order. For example, the high rates of Aboriginal men's imprisonment, deaths in custody, ill health and poverty make it difficult to identify how they are benefiting from the existing gender order. Thus, broad generalizations about all men and patriarchal privilege may beget a blindness to issues of colonialism and capitalism that have been so much a part of the violence imbuing the last two centuries of Australian history.

This blindness is usually a luxury of a dominant group (Kimmel 2000). This was typified in comments made during lessons and in the interviews with the boys from the two schools. Race and racism were important considerations for the boys at Tamville, while they were rarely raised by the boys at Mountainview. Unlike Mountainview, Tamville draws its school population from numerous cultural backgrounds and consequently racism became a major theme in many of the lessons that were conducted at the school.

For all of the Anglo boys their ethnicity was an unspoken. However, this was not the case for non-Anglo boys. For instance, Peter, a grade nine Aboriginal boy, commented in relation to what he perceived as success, that: 'I'd really like to do a lot of stuff for my people, for the Aboriginal society, and stuff like that. And I'd like to be a good role model to them and stuff and to everyone.'

A student from a Vietnamese background saw the biggest problem with regard to violence in Australia as having a racial dimension, which he linked to the existence of gangs. However, at the same time he saw them as being necessary for protection:

> *Than:* Like most Asian boys we have more gangs a lot more guys. Like
> I see like the Australian guys, they're more big that's why don't get
> picked on. They can act different, wear their hair long, dye their
> hair. I think we just act different because we are small and just go
> five to one or a lot on one.
> *Martin:* And what do you think some of the biggest problems are in
> terms of violence?
> *Than:* Gangs . . . There's stacks of gangs going around having fights . . .
> Men and women they don't actually like shoot each other. You
> know they don't actually do that. But gangs in Melbourne, Sydney
> they start a lot of fights.

Thus, for Than, the racialized violence that he experienced as part of his
day-to-day reality was far more significant than issues of gender and violence.
Like many marginalized men Than's ethnicity cannot be a forgotten factor.
This is not to say that in certain instances and contexts marginalized
masculinities cannot benefit from the existing gender order. Numerous
examples abound of non-Anglo and non-middle-class men who become
exemplars of hegemonic masculinity within the sporting and entertainment
arenas. However, marginality will always impact on the extent of these
benefits. One only has to think of the experience of Mandawuy Yunupingu
to see this. Yunupingu, the lead singer in the internationally recognized rock
band Yothu Yindi, in the same year as being named Australian of the Year,
1992, was denied service in a Melbourne cafe because he was Aboriginal.
   The discrimination meted out to Yunupingu demonstrates that, despite
his official recognition within his own community, the broader Australian
community and the international community, social practice attracts discourses that 'do race' (West and Fenstermaker 1995) on all Aboriginal
men. However, his high status positioning within Australian society enabled
media attention to be focused on this incident, and consequently permitted
liberal outrage at this act of racism. But, such experiences are surely com-
monplace occurrences for the majority of Aboriginal men, and women,
who do not have his social status, especially if they attempt to operate out
of 'normalized' Aboriginal subject positions. Gender cannot be experienced
in isolation from other factors. Gender, race and class, for instance, are all
experienced simultaneously (West and Fenstermaker 1995), although social
practice will at times foreground particular social groupings of which one is
a member.
   The case of O.J. Simpson in 1995 also provides a clear example of how
issues of class, gender and race can become enmeshed in social practice.
Simpson epitomized a sporting hegemonic masculinity within the United
States (see Burstyn 1999: 163). He was a skilled professional football player.
He was rich and he was famous. And, he was Black. All these factors came
into play after he was accused of killing his estranged white wife after a

history of domestic violence. The cost of his defence would have been far beyond the reach of working-class men in the United States. He appears, according to various witnesses at his trial, to have been a violent man towards his wife. The Los Angeles police involved in his arrest and subsequent charging were proved to be racist. Popular support for and against Simpson's innocence was often grounded in conceptions of the importance of the factors of class, gender and race in his trial and subsequent acquittal.

He was sometimes cast as a rich man whose acquittal was guaranteed as a consequence of being able to hire the best legal defence force in the country. At othertimes, he was portrayed as a violent man and, it was argued, should be recognized as such. And in still other instances, he was described as a victim of a racist society which, during his trial, was playing out its mythical constructions of Black men as dangers to white women. It is not important here as to which of these viewpoints are/were right. The issue is that gender not only intersects with issues such as class, but often merges to the point where if one pulls apart the threads of gender, race and class within any picture there is a danger that the tapestry will fall apart. Thus, as Hey *et al.* (1998: 140) have stated, 'We need, in short, a form of language that allows us to think through 'more than one difference at once.' For in any discussion of masculinity, issues of race and class, along with other issues such as sexuality, age and physical abilities cannot be ignored.

This does not mean it is impossible to talk about a generalizable patriarchal gender order. A worldwide patriarchal gender order is evidenced by the near monopoly men hold on, among other things, wealth, the means of production, decision-making structures, the repressive state apparatuses (for example the police and army, to borrow a term from Althusser 1972), valued knowledge and status. However, this is not a monolithic political structure. Difference creates tears and ruptures throughout the fabric of this system of power relations. Not all boys and men benefit in the same degree from this order. And, not all girls and women are excluded from some of its benefits. Nor is it uncontested as a legitimate system.

Conclusion

This contestation may occur through the education system. I am arguing throughout this book that the brutality of existing gender arrangements has been normalized within various institutional frameworks through the construction of 'normalized' masculine and feminine subjectivities. Thus, transformation of the patriarchal gender order will require the disruption of normalizing discourses working through these various sites. This book takes the contemporary secondary school as its site for transformative work. Schooling cannot be separated from the sexualized violence that permeates societal relations. It is clear that schools are a major social site within which masculinities and femininities are formed and contested. Thus, schools can serve as sites where the association of masculinity with violence can be deconstructed and an 'exit politics' constructed.

The construction of an 'exit politics' within schools will necessitate an engagement with normalizing processes and the social organization of masculinity. A problematization of the construction of masculinity, the meanings it produces and its relationship to the production of femininities and 'other' masculinities is a requirement of such concerns. However, this problematization faces many difficulties. These relate to the expectations and responsibilities that are placed on both schools and individual boys within those schools.

Gendering processes are widespread. Schools are only one of many of a society's institutions that reinforce notions of inherent differences between females and males. A significant body of research demonstrates how gendering processes begin from birth and are well and truly in train by the time a child reaches primary school age (Danby and Baker 1998). Thus, it may appear that by the time a person has reached the level of a secondary school education the gendering process has been completed. However, this is far from painting a complete picture of gendering processes. Gendering processes are never finished. They begin at birth and end at death. Further-more, these processes are neither monolithic nor totalizing. Gaps and spaces occur within the feminizing and masculinizing processes operating through-out a person's life. These gaps and spaces provide opportunities for new and non/less dominant/subordinate subject positions to be made available to males and females. School teachers who treat the gendering processes of their students as having been completed are perilously close to becoming complicit in perpetuating, or at least condoning, the violence that has been an integral part of Western national political projects. However, teachers cannot simply expect their students to change without providing frameworks of support.

It is possible that schools, at best, can be reshaped through discourses that are disruptive of the existing gender order or, at least, some spaces for such discourses can be created. However, in the latter instance, it needs to be considered whether or not it is reasonable to expect that boys, at that level of schooling, can come to challenge entrenched attitudes. For instance: do schools provide safe enough environments for those boys who want to engage with an exit politics; and, are attempts to 'change' boys laying the blame for masculinized violence at the feet of individual subjects without recognizing the institutional framework of violence? These dangers mean that there has to be some overall attention to the ways in which existing school practices are legitimated and can be disrupted.

The chapters which make up the remainder of this book focus on the potential role of schooling in disrupting the existing social organization of masculinity, and hence also the patriarchal gender order. The following chapters thus provide an indication of various points within the educational discursive framework through which challenges to boys' normalized behaviours can be introduced into the schooling process. These processes relate to school curricula and pedagogy.

Strategies for schools

The following activities will enable you and your colleagues to develop a sense of the ways in which violence is regarded in your school. They serve to negate assumptions that there is one true way of being a boy. They will also enable you to develop some insights into the ways in which particular boys are feeling about their relationships with others in the school. By completing these activities you should be able to develop a picture of the social organization of masculinities within your school and of the ways in which violence is integrated into this picture.

- Consider how 'normal' behaviour for males and females is constructed. Collect a range of birthday cards, advertisements from different teenage magazines and toy catalogues (mothers' day and fathers' day catalogues, TV ads and music videos are also useful resources). List some of the common messages about gender being suggested through these resources. How are these messages transmitted through other practices? Discuss whether the prevalence of these messages suggests that gender is a social construction or if these messages are just reflecting what is 'natural'. (This can also be a useful activity to conduct with students.) List the ways in which these messages are reinforced through aspects of the schooling process. Think about the extent to which both girls and boys in your school actually live up to these images.
- Talk to boys about violence. What role does violence play in their lives? When have they experienced violence? When have they used violence? How do they feel about the use of violence? In particular, how do they feel about violence against girls, against gays and lesbians, and against each other? Find out if they think boys are more violent than girls? How do they feel about girls who are violent? Collate your research under a heading 'Boys' different attitudes towards violence in this school' and classify the different responses, noting how prevalent each type of response is.
- Talk to the girls in the school. What role does violence play in their lives? Do they ever experience harassment from boys? In what situations? From what kinds of boys? How often? How seriously do they think teachers take these issues? What do they think should be done about it? Collate the girls' responses and compare and contrast with boys' attitudes.

- Think about the boys in your school/class. Divide them into groups according to particular characteristics. What characteristics did you choose? Can these groups be arranged hierarchically? What are some of the hierarchies? On what contexts do these depend?
- Select one of these groups of boys and put yourself in their place. In role discuss with others how you feel you are treated by teachers, by other boys and by girls; how you feel about the school, its teachers and other students; how you feel about the other groups of boys; what you value and don't value in life; what you like to do for fun and why; how you feel about gays and lesbians and people of other races/ethnicities; and how you feel about violence as a means of solving conflicts. Do not caricaturize these boys!
- Consider the social organization of masculinities within your school. Place each of these groups of boys under one of the following headings: hegemonic, subordinate, complicit or marginalized (some groups may fall under more than one heading – if so discuss why this is the case). Create a diagrammatic representation of this organization of masculinities and of the attitudes towards violence that are displayed by these groups.

As a result of your research and discussions, make a list of priorities that the school needs to focus on in relation to violence issues.

Note

1 (Pro)feminist and (pro)feminism are used to signify both feminist and profeminist and feminism and profeminism.

chapter three

Boyswork programmes and the curriculum

while schooling is a site for the reproduction of gender relations, it is also a site for intervention and change.

(Gilbert and Taylor 1991: 5)

Introduction

In the previous chapters of this book it was argued that the links between violence and masculinity have been socially, culturally and historically constructed. In the remaining chapters I want to examine some of the ways in which schools can intervene in those gendering processes that normalize the links between masculinity and violence. However, any attempts by teachers, administrators or policy makers to engage in such disruptive practices will have to contend with the effects of a conservative reading of the 'what about the boys?' discourse. A dominant effect of this discourse is to construct boys and men as an oppressed group (for critiques of this see Epstein *et al.* 1998; Lingard and Douglas 1999; Francis 2000; Lesko 2000; Martino and Meyenn 2001). Such a construction makes the implementation of work with boys on gender and violence issues difficult in that boys often approach this work from an anti-feminist perspective. At the same time, though, the 'what about the boys?' debate has opened up some spaces to challenge dominant gendered relations of power within schools (Mills and Lingard 1997b; Lingard 1998).

The 'what about the boys?' discourse does not always work in ways that obviously shore up men's access to priviliges. In some schools there have been responses to the boys' debate from a (pro)feminist perspective. This has particularly been the case with the issue of gender and violence. The popular anxiety about boys and their behaviour has opened up some spaces in which the 'what about the boys' concern can be linked to the construction of masculinities in particular, and to the construction of gender in general. The remaining chapters of this book examine various issues that arose from the implementation of programmes for boys, that sought to utilize this space in two Australian State High Schools.

Attempts to provide boys with an understanding of issues of masculinity and violence are becoming increasingly popular in schools. However, these programmes and pedagogical approaches, known by the neologism of 'boyswork' (Martinez 1994), do not find their way into the curricula and structures of schools unproblematically (Dunn 1995). Pedagogical matters, which include the staffing of boyswork programmes, are taken up in the next chapter. Problematics connected with the curriculum are explored in this chapter. These relate to the nature of the curriculum and the ways in which concerns about gender and violence issues usually enter the school, that is as short-term programmes to be implemented through personal development type subjects such as Human Relationships Education (HRE) in Australia and Personal and Social Education (PSE) in the UK.

Differentiating between the curriculum and pedagogy is somewhat arbitrary, because the concepts and their practice are inextricably linked (Grundy 1994; Weiner 1994). This is particularly problematic when considering notions of the hidden curriculum (see Bowles and Gintis 1976; Henry *et al.* 1988: ch. 3; Lynch 1989). The term 'hidden curriculum' usually refers to the powerful normalizing processes that are at play in schools. For instance, the ways in which students learn to interact with authority, accept or reject particular gender positions, to negotiate conflict and/or to accept or reject particular forms of knowledge as truth are all aspects of what has come to be known as the hidden curriculum. Integral to the hidden curriculum is, thus, the ways teachers teach and how they relate to students. It should also be noted, though, that this curriculum is taught and implemented by students as well as teachers, and is consequently bound up with the regime of the school. Hence, various configurations of, and conflicts within, schools' gender regimes will impact on the availability of particular gender positions for students (and teachers) within particular schools. However, the hidden curriculum should not be regarded in conspiratorial terms. The hidden curriculum in a school is far from unified, and tensions and struggles over meaning are very much a feature of this aspect of schooling (see Mills 1996, 1997c).

The concept of the hidden curriculum is important in highlighting the significance of what students learn outside of the content found in the formal school curriculum. Hence, a whole school approach to issues of gender and violence is the most effective way of dealing with such issues (see Gilbert and Gilbert 1998: 239–41). Such an approach would examine curricula, pedagogy, relationships between teachers and students, students and students, teachers and teachers, and the various structures within the school, such as behaviour management strategies and school assemblies. However, a whole school approach to the problem of gendered violence is not always possible. In many instances, a concern about this problem finds its way into schools through particular areas of the formal school curriculum; although it may not remain there and in some instances has the potential to seep into other areas of school practice. Thus, a distinction is used here between curriculum and pedagogy in order to facilitate discussion of some of the issues involved in implementing 'boyswork' programmes in schools; and the term 'curriculum' is used strategically to mean the formal school curriculum.

The business of school curricula is often focused around academic achievements and outcomes. Teaching about issues of gender and violence usually take a backseat to this 'real business' of schools. Hence the focal point of 'what about the boys?' discussions has regularly been related to school results. The focus on the curriculum in this chapter is as a point of entry for gender and violence issues into schools. The school curriculum is a major site for this entry. Foster (1994) has argued that the curriculum needs to be reformed at an epistemological level. This would entail a reconfiguring of valued knowledges and a consideration of how such knowledges contribute to, or work against, a more gender just society. Such a reconfiguration is critical in the long term. However, there are currently options within the school curriculum, both in Australia and in other Western nations, which provide spaces for teachers to implement strategies and to cover content that problematizes issues of masculinity, sexuality and gender and violence. This can be seen in, for instance, the English curriculum (Martino 1995, 1998; Misson 1995); social science curricula (Lee 1996; Colleary 1998; Moore 1999); the science curriculum (Letts IV 1998); and music (Sapon-Shevin 1998) and at the whole school level (see Patrick and Sanders 1994; Curriculum and Gender Equity Policy Unit 1995; see also Letts IV and Sears 1998). However, as governments worldwide seek to exert greater control over the curriculum, as with the National Curriculum in England and Wales, these options are becoming more limited.

Hence, all too often this work is left to personal development type subjects, such as HRE or PSE, as was the case with the two schools mentioned in this book. These subjects are often devalued within the school curriculum. For many of the students interviewed in the two case study schools, HRE was not a subject that was placed high on their list of priorities. That students do not take this subject seriously is not the only problem with implementing short-term programmes through HRE and PSE. They are also subjects to which many teachers do not devote a great deal of time and thought. Time is a major pressure that teachers face in schools. Such subjects are usually non-assessable; are often not attached to any clearly defined subject department; and there is little accountability in terms of the amount or types of content teachers cover in their lessons. Thus, at times these subjects can be delivered in an ad hoc manner. However, at the same time, there are many dedicated teachers assigned to HRE/PSE-style subjects who have a commitment to many of the philosophies inherent in programmes such as those considered here. Furthermore, because of the way the curriculum is structured, such subjects might provide the only opportunity in many schools for gender and violence issues to be covered by boys.

However, even with committed teachers and students who take HRE/PSE seriously, there are still problems with such programmes. Dunn (1995) argues that one of the main problems is the hope that it will provide a 'quick fix-it solution' to an existing long-term problem. No such solutions exist. This is stressed in a position paper on gender and violence distributed by the Queensland Department of Education's Equity Unit, which states that: '"One-shot" programs or programs for individual groups of students are ineffective because they do not take into consideration the ways in which gender, violence and power relations are consistently and continually constructed by the "texts" of schooling and other societal institutions' (Equity Unit 1997: 8; see also Kenway and Fitzclarence 1997). This is often the case. However, while short-term programmes that seek to problematize masculinity will not in themselves provide students with new ways of looking at the world, they are not without merit. It is possible that they can provide a basis on which more long-term solutions can be built. They have the potential to provide a springboard from which students can come to question issues of gender and power. Furthermore, they can also help to 'normalize' attitudes and beliefs that are marginalized in the cultures to which the students belong.

The curriculum and boyswork programmes

One area of schooling that serves to reinforce dominant gender identities while at the same time providing opportunities for challenging such identities is the curriculum. The curriculum is a crucial participant in the gendering processes of a school (Haywood and Mac an Ghaill 1996). It is engaged in the production and control of culture through its hierarchization of knowledges. The school curriculum is thus hegemonized (Connell 1993; Paechter 2000) and consequently gendered. For instance, boys who are seeking an academic future tend to select a science based curriculum; academic girls, a humanities type programme; for boys, non-academic alternatives tend to be technical/woodwork/metalwork type subjects; and non-academic alternatives for girls consist of home economics or service industry based subjects (Smit 1992: 25; Teese et al. 1995). There is an obvious problem here in that girls' lack of access to valued 'knowledges' limits their options to enter into the public world dominated by men. However, the ways in which school subjects reinforce and construct gendered subjectivities is also integral to the maintenance of existing gendered relations of power (see, for example, Randall 1987; Walkerdine 1988; Parker 1996; Opie 1998; Povey 1998; Scaife 1998; Skelton 1998; Paechter 2000).

Curriculum documents are therefore more than just texts. They are part of a struggle over meaning and represent a power-knowledge nexus. For instance, some of the recent innovations in the formal curriculum, suggest that the current curriculum is a social product produced through the dominance of market-led discourses. Thus it could be argued that schools are responding to the demands of perceived economic crises and the demands of industry to address what is often regarded as a lack in students' abilities to cope with the expectations of the workforce. These responses include returning to the basics, developing work experience programmes and creating links, in Australia, with Technical and Further Education institutions (TAFEs). Changes to the curriculum are never neutral in the interests that the curriculum comes to serve (Apple 1988). In this instance, the vocationalization of the curriculum does not so much serve the interests of social justice but of the capitalist economy. For as Junor (1991) has argued:

> the employer pressure for 'basic skills' is really a pressure to restrict the types of material that students read and write. What are being defined as 'work skills' are in fact behaviours such as discipline, respect for authority, and individual competitiveness, as opposed to attitudes of questioning or of group solidarity. In schools vocationalism is a device for social control.
>
> (Junor 1991: 184)

The curriculum is thus a powerful force in the production of power relations. As such, the curriculum is not static but is constantly reconfigured to meet the demands of competing interests. For as Apple (1988: 201) has argued 'the curriculum does not stand alone, but is the social product of contending forces.' The current context within which boys' programmes are entering into schools is one within which there is a struggle of meaning over the relationship between boys and schooling. It is feminist discourses and men's rights and therapeutic style discourses that are the principal contending forces in this struggle. Boyswork programmes need to be seen in this context.

The dominant discourses in this struggle are unfortunately those represented by the position that boys are the new victims in schools. It is thus possible to identify a push for boyswork programmes to be introduced into schools, which are based on this premise (Mills and Lingard 1997a, b). A number of these programmes demonstrate a philosophy that has become known as mythopoetic, or masculinity therapy (see Connell 1995a: 206–12). The most well-known advocates of this men's politics are Robert Bly in the United States and Stephen Biddulph in Australia. Recent contributors to this stable of boys' advocates include Gurian (1999), Kindlon and Thompson (1999) and Pollack (1999). These men argue that boys (and men) experience significant oppressions because they are male. They point to, among other things, high rates of risk-taking activities, suicides, school suspensions, imprisonment, poor literacy and other communication skills among males compared with females as evidence of the oppressive nature of the male role. (Interestingly, as Yates 2000: 307, points out such spokespeople for men do not seem to take much notice of the statistics that refer to mathematics rather than literacy, welfare recipients rather than alcoholism, political office rather than imprisonment, and so on.)

Thus, many of the boys' programmes that enter school through a mythopoetic discourse are grounded in therapeutic politics which emphasize developing boys' self-esteem and communication skills (Kenway *et al.* 1997a, b). For instance, Gurian, who does work with schools emphasizes the problems boys face in schools as a result of the demands of traditional masculinity. There is a clear 'victim envy' underlying his book. The book clearly overstates the gains made by feminism in reshaping the education system. He argues that the feminis(t)ation of education has seen boys' interests become subservient to those of girls. It is worth quoting him at length here:

> We who care about the education of all our children now stand at the threshold of a new era, one in which we can say: 'Here are the ways girls are shortchanged. Tell me how boys are shortchanged. Let's work together to fix both.' If we do not work together – if we do not start from a point of view of equity – repairs made to female education will cause terrible problems in male education. That is what we face today. We have stressed so formidably the improvement of the lives of our girls that we have neglected the educational world of our boys. According to the latest National Education Assessment and the Educational Testing Service Gender Study – perhaps the two most comprehensive educational assessments available – *female indicators are up, and male indicators are dropping, dropping not to a point of parity with female but to a point of disparity.*
>
> (Gurian 1999: 179, original emphasis)

The sentiments expressed here that feminism has gone too far is a populist one. It is a claim made regularly by a number of boys in this book.

This belief has led many to argue that the education system needs to develop pedagogical practices which meet the needs of boys as well as those of girls (Gurian 1999; Kindlon and Thompson 1999; Pollack 1999). For instance, Gurian (1999) claims:

> So much of what males face in the classroom is a result of being normal boys in a setting that is not trained to handle many of our normal boys. On top of that, most educators are not trained specifically to handle the somewhat high–testosterone, male-brain, impulsive, and aggressive boys. These boys enter the classroom crying out

for discipline, direction focus, assistance and care. Some of them just don't get it and have to leave labeled, shamed, scared, scarred.

(Gurian 1999: 185)

This of course flies in the face of many feminist studies, which indicate that the most popular teaching methods are those that favour boys (Randall 1987; Stanworth 1987) and that boys dominate teacher attention in the classroom (Sadker and Sadker 1994). It also pays little attention to feminist concerns about how some more child-centred philosophies of education can work against women and girls in schools (Walkerdine 1989).

Some of these commentators are not unaware of the gendering processes operating within Western societies' institutions. For instance, Pollack (1999) talks of the 'boy code', which society and institutions such as schools impose. Apart from his use here of role theory, which ignores issues of power and privilege, this does not contradict some of the concerns (pro)feminists have about dominant constructions of masculinity, including the role of schools in that construction. However, there are some blindspots in his arguments. For example, he fails to see how this 'boy code' operates in ways that reinforce men's privileged positioning within most Western societies. For him boys, and men, are the victims of an uncaring society. For instance, this is the introductory paragraph to his book:

Boys today are in serious trouble, including many who seem 'normal' and to be doing just fine. Confused by society's mixed messages about what's expected of them as boys, and later as men, many feel a sadness and disconnection they cannot even name. New research shows that boys are faring less well in school than they did in the past and in comparison to girls, that many boys have remarkably fragile self-esteem, and that the rates of both depression and suicide in boys are frighteningly on the rise. Many of our sons are currently in a desperate crisis.

(Pollack 1999: xxi)

What many of these commentators do is demonstrate the siege mentality that many men exhibit due to the impact of feminism on all areas of life (Kenway 1995; Gilbert and Gilbert 1998). The defensiveness of these men serves to shift the blame for men's inability to verbally express emotions from masculinizing discourses to feminism. There is a recognition by some of these men that girls and women face problems in schools. However, issues of boys' 'disadvantages' are harnessed to launch a claim that boys' issues are as equally a matter of social justice as are those of girls. There are many problems with this. For example, there is the danger that issues of privilege, oppression and domination are subsumed under a concern about gender roles. Furthermore, making boys' welfare a social justice issue may encourage the diversion of funds away from girls' social justice programmes. Little consideration is given by these men's liberationists to the extent to which schools and education systems already devote huge amounts of resources to boys in the way of behaviour management issues, remedial help and counselling (Foster 1994: 5). On the contrary, the claim is that schools devote a disproportionate amount of funds in a favourable manner to girls and that the curriculum is often shaped around the interests of feminism.

The attention that the curriculum attracts in relation to bringing about changes in social relations is testament to the political opportunities it presents. The curriculum does not necessarily have to only serve dominant interests. The contestatory and political nature of the curriculum has made it an attractive target for programmes seeking to problematize normalized relations of power. This is not to deny that other factors are important, but simply to emphasize that the curriculum can be an important entry point for gender and violence considerations. For instance, Askew and Ross (1988: xii) argue: 'the position of girls will not really change fundamentally until the underlying nature of the school as an institution changes . . . However, the curriculum is the level which is most accessible for teachers to change.'

How the curriculum is utilized to bring about changes in, for instance, gender relations can be problematic. The curriculum represents the official knowledge of the school, thus the inclusion of certain knowledges into the curriculum has the effect of stating that these knowledges are worthwhile. However, as mentioned above, not all knowledge in the school curriculum is allocated equal value. Apple (1988: 192) has argued that the curriculum 'takes particular social forms and embodies certain interests which are themselves the outcomes of continuous struggles within and among dominant and subordinate groups.'

The inclusion in the school curriculum of gender and violence programmes specifically designed for boys can be seen as the product of such a struggle. Feminists, with the support at times of profeminist men, have argued quite forcefully that issues of masculinity and violence need to be on the agenda in schools. These demands have been overwhelmingly legitimated through numerous studies in schools (for example, Morgan *et al.* 1988; Milligan *et al.* 1992; O'Connor 1992; Sadker and Sadker 1994; Collins *et al.* 1996). The increasing demand for (pro)feminist boys' programmes in schools can be seen as a response to these legitimating demands. It is interesting to note that John Dunn, who was involved in the construction of the Personal Development Plan for Boys, in the Australian Capital Territory (ACT), comments:

> requests for help have changed over the years . . . Teachers are now interested in running such programs, not to appease the 'What about the boys!' cry but because school communities, even rural communities, are seeing a need to do something about boys' disruptive behaviour and the effect that it is having on both girls' and boys' learning.
> (Dunn 1995: 57)

This is not the experience of some of those working in the former Queensland Department of Education's Gender Equity Unit. For instance, Julie, a principal policy officer with this unit commented in 1996 that:

> I guess here in the last two or three months there's been a real growth in the number of phone calls, we're getting phone calls on a daily basis now ... The sorts of things schools are talking about most frequently are boys' academic achievements or this perceived fall in boys' academic achievement ... boys' reluctance to be involved in leadership programs in schools, or in leadership roles and behaviour issues. But it is the behaviour issues which ... I need to remind them about, when they ring me, you know, 'Are you also concerned about boys' behaviour?', 'Oh, yes. Yes. That too.' Two things that they are really focused on most, most enthusiastically and energetically, are the achievement and the leadership issues.
>
> In some cases it's a real concern about the problems that boys are creating in schools for others and often the notion of boys as victims is secondary to the idea that boys are going to become victims because they are not accessing the curriculum appropriately or they are not performing and achieving appropriately. But in some schools there is a very strong, a very strong concern about boys and suicide, boys and health, boys and violence, boys as victims of violence. One of the strongest themes is boys and loss of self-esteem and I think that is an unspoken, an unarticulated concern about boys' diminishing status in the community.

However, while such concerns do appear to be dominant in Queensland, as in many other Western societies, they are not totalizing. Some (pro)feminist programmes are finding their way into Queensland schools.

These programmes and strategies include the Curriculum and Gender Equity Policy Unit's (1995) *No Fear* kits; the Queensland Department of Education's (1994) school kit *Enough's Enough*; David Denborough's (1995) programme, based on Sydney's Men Against Sexual Assault's programme, 'Step by step: Developing respectful and effective ways of working with young men to reduce violence';[1] Brook Friedman's (1995) *Boys-Talk: A Program for Young Men about Masculinity, Non-Violence and Relationships*; and Salisbury and Jackson's (1996) *Challenging Macho Values*. The first two of these are not designed specifically for boys; however, they can be adapted to meet the needs of boys-only classes. The approaches utilized within these resources are based on the premises that there are multiple masculinities; that these masculinities are positioned against each other within various relations of power; that boys/men are not discriminated against as boys/men; and that gender justice requires that boys' and men's complicity in the oppression of girls and women be treated as a social justice issue. Boys' programmes built on such presumptions have the ability to bring into question many of the dominant assumptions that underpin existing gender injustices. However, these programmes typically find their way onto the school agenda through the HRE/PSE curriculum. This particular entrance into the curriculum can have a constraining effect on the effectiveness of such programmes.

The usage of the HRE/PSE curriculum to broach issues of masculinity and violence may compound the disregard many boys feel towards issues raised in boys' programmes. HRE/PSE's concerns with, among other things, emotions, relationships and sex education construct it as a feminized, and hence devalued, subject. It is thus not a subject that many boys take seriously. Furthermore, the non-assessable knowledge that it presents within an assessment driven culture serves to devalue its content even further, thus placing it among the least respected subjects within the school curriculum. There is no getting away from the masculinist values that are ever present within school structures. It is for this reason that programmes such as the *No Fear* kit (Curriculum and Gender Equity Policy Unit 1995) and Gender and Violence Position Paper (Equity Unit, Queensland Department of Education 1997) emphasize the need for gender and violence programmes to take a whole school approach. However, this is not always possible in the existing political climate in many schools. Thus, other means have to be found.

HRE/PSE: A short-term solution

A vast number of the gender and violence programmes that find their way into schools, as was the case with the programmes considered in this book, are of the one-off variety. Schools seek to address a number of social issues through additions to the regular school curriculum, for example: driver education, first aid, sexual health, drug and alcohol education *and* gender and violence education. Thus, gender and violence education is usually implemented as an add-on through HRE and PSE. This is a major failing of schools which seek to improve gender relations among members of their school community. As Connell (1993: 15) has stated in regard to social justice, matters of gender justice should not be an add-on but fundamental to good educational practice.

This was a concern of a number of teachers from the two schools. For instance Rebecca from Tamville remarked:

> *Rebecca:* Like take the eight-week programme on it's own, they're (the students) less likely to shift if they don't get the message reinforced. If it's not seen as being supported by the school. If they don't work together themselves and you know they're probably not terribly good at doing that.

Martin: What can schools do to support kids making those shifts?

Rebecca: We can do a lot of things and we can change the way in which we relate with them as teachers because I mean this still is gendered violence . . . We perpetrate that as well. Probably we are not anything like what some of the students are but that does happen. Again having it embedded in the curriculum so that they look at the same issues again and again in different ways. Yes, that would help. Oh I don't know whether I mentioned it as well but I think you know not having it as just a one-off programme as well I think would help kids to see that the school's serious about it.

Rebecca's point that students may perceive it to be tokenistic when it is only covered in a one-off programme is important. Schools do need to give credibility to such programmes by reinforcing and modelling non-violent forms of conflict resolution (Kenway and Fitzclarence 1997: 125). This credibility is further damaged when the only programmes provided are presented through one of the marginalized areas of the curriculum. This can be a problem in relation to having the issues treated seriously within schools. A senior policy officer, Julie, with the Queensland Department of Education's Gender Equity Unit stated in relation to this:

and I suppose in some ways HRE is the thing we have always had a problem with in terms of looking at these issues as part of the curriculum. HRE is so marginal and our preferred method of working has been for some time to work through the core curriculum and not through the marginal curriculum.

A similar sentiment was expressed by a number of the teachers who would have preferred to see gender and violence programmes being part of the broader curriculum. Donna, from Mountainview, in response to the question of whether or not the HRE curriculum is an appropriate place for gender and violence issues commented:

Donna: Well it probably is, but then I'm not too much in favour of HRE being a separate entity anyway. I come from the idea that it should be covered by every teacher in each lesson. But however if we have to have it as a separate lesson I think this is the place to do it.

Martin: And do you think kids take HRE seriously?

Donna: No, not in the main. The more perceptive ones probably do but certainly most of them in the main they would not. They see it as a lesson that is non-examinable and non-assessable and therefore there is very little relevance to them personally.

The comments made by students are an indication of how students perceive HRE and are thus an indication of the problems associated with attempts to implement programmes through the HRE curriculum. For instance, the following comments were made by students in relation to whether or not students valued HRE at Mountainview:

> *Will:* Not at all (laughter). Not at all . . . throughout the years we haven't really got in many discussions so maybe it's too difficult for the teachers. They're probably not qualified to do all the stuff but we just watch these out of date movies and instead of looking at the issues we just look at the characters in it: 'Ah he's from *Home and Away*,' or 'Gee this is corny,' and so I don't think it works at all. Not at this school anyway . . . I mean when I look to HRE every week I just think a blank lesson. I've studied in a lot of them and when we're in holiday mode for a period I'd say you wouldn't get the best attention out of us.

Oscar, from the same class, provides support for Will's opinion:

> *Martin:* Do people take HRE seriously?
>
> *Oscar:* Ah not usually no. Like because we're just covering the same things over and over they just tend to turn out, just like a free period. Do whatever we want.

On the whole the grade 11 students at Tamville had a more serious approach to HRE. For instance, Ben commented that 'It's just sort of like another class.' Although there are still misconceptions about what constitutes the HRE curriculum. Sean for example remarked: 'Some people think HRE . . . as soon as it comes up . . . they think oh it's a bit of a joke, all you talk about is sex . . . and stuff like that.'

For a number of grade nine students the subject HRE was often equated with the gender and violence programme we had been running, there was no distinction made between the subject and the programme.

> *Martin:* Is HRE taken seriously by students?
>
> *Peter:* Ahh yeah. I take it seriously and stuff because like I don't, I try not to like speak foul or dirty around girls or anything like that. And be careful what you say around them because they could get offended easily.

This is perhaps not the main thrust of HRE, however Peter does demonstrate that his understanding of HRE is that it has a gender dimension to it. Than, sees the lessons of HRE, which he also associates with the recently completed gender and violence programme, as not being relevant to him:

> *Martin:* Do you take HRE seriously?
>
> *Than:* Ah not really . . . It doesn't help me much. So I don't get into that situation . . . It depends on the person whether they're being picked on or something they might be interested in that. Some guys like they're quite known that they're quite strong see and then they

know that they won't be picked on see. So that's why they don't really take it seriously.

While many students do not have a high regard for HRE, this does not mean it is ineffective. Rebecca from Tamville, who was the grade nine class's regular science and HRE teacher, in response to a question relating to how successful the programmes were with her class, states: '(Laughter) Not very. (Laughter)' However, she continues to say:

> Not very. But I mean I find that with teaching in all sorts of respects. That you, a little bit of an input or a little bit of change is worth it. So I do think that 70 minutes for eight weeks in terms of teaching that's a fair commitment and so they've had that sort of an exposure . . . I don't know whether you're getting at where it needs to be, more embedded in the curriculum, which I personally think it has, it does need to be, and eight weeks in the school is nothing really on what we ought to be able to do. But I mean we do, there are things that we are doing at Tamville already . . . I think there is more that can be done with schools and that . . . could be part of an integrated approach to the issue.

HRE did have its supporters, for example Simon, a teacher at Tamville, sees it as something special: 'I think (HRE's) a good position for it because it makes the kids alert that this is something special and that human relationships vary. You know I think, I think that's a good, a good place for it.'

Victoria, the HRE coordinator at Tamville, takes a pragmatic view to introducing gender and violence issues into education through the HRE curriculum. She recognizes the difficulty of embedding something in the curriculum; her views on this would, I am sure, resonate with those educators who held significant hope for other whole-school initiatives, such as the 'language across the curriculum' programmes of the 1980s:

> I think there are other places that it can be done, but I don't think it does. Because when you, when you have people who talk about integrating these things into other subject areas, it's been my experience that the minute you talk about integrating it into something else it gets lost . . . And so people will pay lip service to doing it, but when it comes down to the nitty-gritties, especially when you are dealing with a whole lot of staff . . . And that is the kind of thing that worries the life out of me because you can't just guarantee that you are going to get those teachers to do it. And I mean with the best intentions in the world too, because you've got teachers who say, 'Yes it's a worthwhile thing to do.' But they might not do it because they don't feel comfortable with it. Or they don't have the training in it. Or they are worried about the time constraints with other things and so it just gets left behind because it is lower and lower on their priorities all the time.

Yeah. So for that reason HRE . . . might be the only chance you get to do it. Might be the only chance you are ever going to get to raise those issues.

The guidance officer at Mountainview, Sarah, expressed a similar view:

We talked about this before, some people think it should be, you know, in all the different subject areas. I have a really strong concern regarding that because I think that it might disappear . . . I guess I'd still go for having specialist teachers for HRE just like you have specialist teachers for any other curriculum area and it's a curriculum area in it's own right perhaps.

However, Sarah also commented that the HRE programmes could be supported by an across the curriculum approach to gender and violence issues.

Even though teachers saw the programmes as important, they recognized that they were not going to bring about major changes in the students' attitudes and behaviours. For as Simon states, 'Well you're not . . . going to create miracles in an eight-week programme.' Most of the teachers interviewed were in agreement with this. For example Victoria remarked: 'If you are going to modify anything that's happening it's a slow process and that's the sad thing actually, that you are not going to see a lot of changes just, just in a few weeks or even, or even in a year.'

They cited numerous examples of the forces arraigned against them in the enormousness of the task of changing attitudes. Simon was quite emphatic about this:

You know because there's tremendous pressure for violence. You've just got to look at any TV show. I watched the last 20 minutes with my daughter the other night of Melrose Place and I think there were two infidelities, a suicide, you know, a fight and a fraud, a swindle. You know. Well look at the crap that they're getting . . . And all those cases they're about unequal distributions of power in relationships. You know that's the overarching theme of this crass modern world.

The impossibility of schools working outside of existing relations of power within the broader community is recognized in the Federal *Sticks and Stones: Report on Violence in Australian Schools*. The report states that: 'It is unrealistic to draw a line at the school gate and suggest that what happens inside that boundary is the school's business, and what happens outside that boundary is the community's responsibility' (House of Representatives Standing Committee on Employment, Education and Training 1994: 1). One is reminded here of Bernstein's famous adage: 'Schools cannot compensate for society.' However, school can be a strategic site within which normalized constructions of gender can be disrupted (White and White

1986; Connell 1989; Haywood and Mac an Ghaill 1996). Those working within schools are not powerless to effect change.

Most of the teachers interviewed here argue that it is essential that something be done in schools to begin a process of change. Their views on the role of education would have fitted neatly with Bob Connell's (1989) argument that while factors such as family, employment and sexual relations are powerful influences on the formation of masculinities,

> schooling is the next most powerful influence across the board, and in some cases and some situations it is decisive. It may also be the most *strategic*, in the sense that the education system is the setting where an open debate about the democratisation of gender relations is most likely to happen, and can gain some purchase on practice.
>
> (Connell 1989: 301, original emphasis)

It is perhaps through the process of debate that changes can be initiated. For many of the teachers interviewed for this research, a significant aspect of the programmes was seen to be the raising of consciousness about, or a bringing into discourse of, alternative subject positions for males.

> *Victoria:* I think they (boys' programmes) raise consciousness more than anything else . . . You might get the kids who say, 'Oh what a load of rubbish' . . . , and carry on, but then in six months' time somebody else will have the same thing to say and the light bulb might go on for some of them and it says, 'Hey that's what that fellow said that other day, maybe there is something in this.' And so the second time they hear it they actually have a more positive reaction to it or they may actually do something about it. There might really be a change in behaviour. So you might not change a lot of behaviours. You hope you change some, but I think it raises consciousness about a lot of issues. And that's the thing I think is pretty important for a lot of these courses because if you don't have them, for a lot of kids and especially for a lot of the boys, they're never going to hear those points of view at all . . . They will never hear them unless somebody puts them in front of them in a structured course like this.

Thus, for many of the teachers here it was the future rather than the present that motivated their commitments to programmes such as these. The boys may not demonstrate an immediate rapport with the programmes. However, there is a strong hope that some of it will take effect in the future. For instance, Simon remarked:

> You know you're going to make them think . . . And it's not for them now it's for their future. That's why the programme is important. When they're 21 or 22 or when they . . . when they come home late at

night and get angry with their wife they'll restrain themselves from belting her . . . We're looking for the long term aren't we . . . Not just the short-term playground behaviour. That's how I see it anyway. I really do. I think that's why I think it's important. To change . . . to decrease the violence in our violent society. To show them that violence isn't an answer. But not necessarily in their, you know, in their school life but in their . . . all their life. That's why it's so important . . . I think that seed has been sown . . . You've had someone telling them for eight weeks it just isn't on. It's not the right way. There's better ways to do it. Now they're going to make mistakes in their lives as we all do. But at least they know now that there's someone . . . there's another view and that violent behaviour isn't a legitimate . . . or isn't a productive form of behaviour in the long run and I think that's where we're looking for it.

However, and fortunately, Rebecca noticed some recent positive changes in her grade nine class. There also appear to be other positive spin-offs from the programme. For instance, Simon made the following observation:

You know like Than and another boy in year nine, Vang were having a kick-boxing contest out on the oval the other day when I was on playground duty. They weren't actually hitting each other but it could have had that potential. There was about 50 or 60 kids gathering . . . you know when a fight happens in a school they start gathering around and so on and I didn't say anything about the programme I just walked over and they saw me and they both stopped. See kids need that sort of circuit breaker sometimes.

Victoria also commented later that some of the grade 11 students had been asking about when they could have HRE/PSE again. (The grade 11 classes do not have HRE/PSE as a regular class at Tamville. HRE has to share its time slot with a variety of other school-based programmes, for example study skills.) However, perhaps it was at Mountainview where the programme appears to have had the greatest impact. It is worth giving some specific attention to some of the events that occurred at Mountainview during the course of the programme (see Mills 1997a).

Mountainview snapshot

The Mountainview programme, which was introduced through the HRE curriculum, had grown out of teachers' concerns about the behaviours of grade 12 boys. The school's guidance officer along with a small group of teachers, in consultation with the State Department's Gender Equity Unit, had decided to implement separate gender and violence programmes for female and male grade 12 students. The boys were divided into two groups. The first and larger group, of approximately 25 students, consisted of those who were considered to be the most likely to respond to the programme in a positive manner. The second and smaller group, approximately eight students, consisted of those who it was considered by the school would most benefit from a small group approach. This last group was facilitated by a male community psychologist, Richard, and the other by a male teacher from Mountainview and me.

It is the larger group of boys that I am concerned with here. In the early part of the programme many of the boys were very loud and vocal in their claims that the 'gender regime' (Connell 1987) of the school served the interests of girls, and hence was an unjust arrangement. Many of the boys clearly saw themselves as victims of feminism and demonstrated what Eva Cox has referred to as 'a competing victim syndrome' (Cox 1996: 221; see also Cox 1997). This is a claim that is acquiring significant currency in popular discourse in relation to the wider 'gender order' (Connell 1987). For instance, the arguments that men are becoming 'tomorrow's second sex' (Men: Tomorrow's second sex 1996) and that male power is a myth (Farrell 1993) were views articulated by many of the boys at Mountainview.

In the first session it was claimed by a large section of the class that boys were the most discriminated group in the school. They pointed to the fact that no boys held positions of responsibility in the school. One boy, James, commented later:

> at the start of the year when you came in . . . the boys had been bumped out for school captain and two girls had gotten it . . . when the guys received so many . . . so much of a high percentage of the student vote . . . that the guys were really having a bad opinion of the girls and that did cause a lot of conflict at this school . . . That really did. Just the fact that the boys felt unrepresented. They felt left out. Unneeded. I heard a parent say, she had two young boys . . . she said that, 'If that's the way that males are treated at Mountainview State High School, I will not be sending my children up there.'

This feeling of injustice was similar to that being displayed by some of the boys in the study carried out by Kenway et al. (1997b: 25). The perceived discrimination that the Mountainview boys were facing was reflected in a list the boys drew up of the most powerful groups in the school. They positioned grade 8 boys as the least powerful and the grade 12 girls as the most powerful groups among the student body. Thus, the victim politics of mythopoetic and men's rights claims were impossible to sidestep and had to be confronted head-on.

This was easier said than done. The resistances we met from the boys were significant, even though this group of boys was considered to be the group who would be most responsive to the issues. Some of them commented later that they had done programmes like this so many times before that it had been boring. One (Luke) for instance stated:

> Last year we had a programme for just boys. We'd been told that we were a problem group of boys. Someone special had been brought in for a day to work for us. Then we heard that two people were coming in to do the same thing again this year and we thought 'Here we go again!'

The depth of feeling in the room and the anger that was directed at women from the first session, and at a later date also at gays, would seem to indicate that more than boredom was at play.

One student, James, did attribute this resentment to other sources:

> I think that a lot of people our age associate these sorts of issues with gay and being gay and all the rest of it. So I think they were afraid of that sort of area and just as a result resent the programme I guess.

If, among these boys, homosexuality was associated with being supportive of feminist aims or of gay rights, many of them went to great lengths to demonstrate their heterosexuality.

Some argued emphatically that they were the victims of feminism, and a number of activities elicited angry responses about feminists, often referred to in the increasingly popular term as 'feminazis'. One student stated, after a newspaper activity examining the positioning of men and women in news stories, that the dominance of men in the public sphere was 'natural'. According to this student, the reversal of the 'natural state of affairs' at the school was because there were too many feminists in the school and that the girls at the school were protected by the administration. Thus, in the 'real world', as opposed to the 'non-real world' of school, girls would find it difficult to succeed because of their inferiority. This boy had significant support from his classmates.

The anger towards women and gays was clearly evident in an activity that allowed students to make comments and ask questions anonymously. Some of these comments and questions included: 'Boys will be boys, and girls will have all the power'; 'What right do gays have to have rights?', 'Women want to be equal to men at work. Why do they want things over men?'; 'Why do women want equal rights with regard to work etc. but still want ladies first'; 'Why does a feminist act like a Nazi?'; 'Why should women be treated equally?'; and 'If they're banning semi-autos why not ban fags?' This last comment/question was a reflection of the rhetoric of the gun lobby's responses to the anti-gun laws being proposed by the Federal government after the Port Arthur massacre. A number of boys drew on the homophobic and misogynist aspects of the gun lobby arguments in order to define their perceptions of being a 'real' man. (See Connell 1995a: 212–16 for a discussion of gun lobby style masculinity politics in the United States.)

Interestingly, however, as time went on a number of boys began privately to express their concerns with the way things were progressing in class and began to offer suggestions about how we could improve the programme. During the course of one lesson, a student responded to the activity by stating quite emphatically and eloquently that the issues were not irrelevant, but that they had covered them so many times before that it had become monotonous. This was reflected in some of the anonymous comments at the end of the lesson: 'We have heard all this before and though we might not act like it we know the right thing' and 'You're the one who thinks there is a problem. We know all the right answers to all the questions. It's just that we are sick of doing this type of thing. You're so easy to make things difficult for.'

At this point we decided to abandon the planned programme, to put our doubts aside and to work with the assumption that many of them found the issues relevant. In the lesson following these suggestions we asked them to think of some ways in which the issues of gender and violence could be tackled within the school. If they knew there was a problem, what could they do about it? After substantial dialogue, one boy suggested that they could implement a similar programme to the one we had been providing to them with the grade eight boys. A number of the grade 12 boys argued that the school administration would never let them work with grade eights. However, approximately half of the group volunteered to do this work if the administration agreed. Some of these boys had been those most vocal in their criticisms of the programme.

Contrary to the boys' expectations, when this idea was taken to the school administration they were very supportive. The grade 12 boys were provided with time off school to attend a day long in-service style programme and were invited to attend the year eight camp to run a session with the boys there. During the course of this in-service the year 12 students were provided with a theoretical background to constructivist theories of gender (given by Julie, the senior policy officer from the Department of Education's Gender Equity Unit), with the opportunity to trial and select some activities they could do with the grade eight boys, and with time to express their hopes and fears about doing this work.

Some problems did occur with the implementation of the grade eight programme. The camp was cancelled due to a lack of interest on the part of the grade eights, and the activities had to be done at school. These activities, which were largely drawn from Salisbury and Jackson (1996), were not implemented in what would probably be considered an optimal manner. Those grade 12 students who were adequately prepared did well with their groups of grade eights. However, some of them rushed through the programme too quickly, leaving them with little to do with the grade eights in the remaining allocated time; some of the grade eight students' responses to the grade 12 boys made aspects of their programme a little difficult to implement (a little poetic justice!); and due to reasons such as these there was perhaps a little more teacher intervention than had been intended. However, what is important here is that many of the grade 12 boys at Mountainview who had been very antagonistic towards issues of gender equity were prepared to engage, even if only momentarily, with what Connell (1995a) has referred to as an 'exit politics': that is, a masculinity politics which brings into question the legitimacy of dominant ways of performing masculinity.

Connell (1995a: 224) says that such a politics is likely to be episodic. This would appear to be the case at Mountainview High. Many of the boys who chose to work in the grade eight programme were concerned about issues of sexual harassment and male violence towards women. They wanted to see change, and be part of that change. However, at the same time many of these boys still attributed behavioural differences between males and females to 'nature', and some while recognizing the legitimacy of various feminist claims trivialized others, and in some instances argued that 'many feminists go too far.' These latter attitudes reflect aspects of reactionary masculine politics, but the boys' willingness to engage in change shows how such politics are not always as monolithic as they seem. Thus, while these boys at times prop up the existing gender order, they also demonstrated that they can work within the cracks and fissures of dominant masculine practice, thereby undermining its stability. They provided substance to Connell's (1994: 5, original emphasis) claim, as mentioned in the Introduction, that: 'Support for women's emancipation is always a *possible* stance for men.'

Opportunities to demonstrate this support have paradoxically been opened up through the 'what about the boys?' backlash. The work done at Mountainview High represents an attempt to engage with this debate. However, it has done this not by treating boys as victims, and hence seeking to make the school more 'boy friendly' (Fletcher 1995a; Pollack 1999), but by examining the effects of dominant representations of masculinity for girls and boys. The boys who engaged with this programme demonstrated to themselves and others that while at times they might feel that they are powerless victims, they are also able to be active agents who can take on the responsibility of working with other boys to problematize masculinity.

The opportunities opened up through the Mountainview programme also point, using the work of Bourdieu (for example, Bourdieu and Wacquant 1992; Bourdieu 1998), to the importance of the particular social fields in which people operate.[2] Bourdieu, argues that social fields operate in similar ways to markets or strategic games (see Carrington *et al.* 2000). Within every social field various forms of *capital* – economic, social, cultural, and symbolic – are differentially valued. As a result, fields can be understood as dynamic 'social worlds' in which, as the result of people's store of various capitals and skill at deploying each capital appropriately, individuals are differentially positioned. Bourdieu explains this relationship in the following way:

At each moment, it is the state of the relations of force between players that defines the structure of the field. We can picture each player as having in front of her a pile of tokens of different colors, each color corresponding to a given species of capital she holds, so that her relative force in the game, her position in the space of play, and also her strategic orientation toward the game . . . the moves that she makes, more or less risky or cautious, subversive or conservative, depend both on the total number of tokens and on the composition of the piles of tokens she retains, that is, on the volume and structure of her capital.

(Bourdieu and Wacquant 1992: 99)

In the social context of the Mountainview programme the capital, or token, recognized by many of the players as holding the most value was a specific masculine discourse that was identified and valued by the teachers within the HRE programme. This discourse was one that valorized a range of counter-hegemonic masculinities. However, for many of the boys, this was not a valued discourse, indeed accepting and utilizing such a discourse within the classroom was likely to have had negative consequences. However, once the social field was rearticulated in such a way that knowledge of the content of the course was likely to have a pay off in relation to being given greater responsibility, to being treated like an adult who had something to offer the younger students and being given time off school to be 'in-serviced', many of the students demonstrated a much greater awareness of the benefits associated with this counter-hegemonic discourse. Thus, in the Mountainview programme, the changing relationship between the students and the intent of the school's programme occurred as a result of students ascertaining some rewards for making strategic changes in their game plan. This points to the need for those working in schools to pay attention to the broader social context into which their work takes place and perhaps of addressing the question of, 'What is in it for the boys?'

Conclusion

The experiences at Mountainview demonstrate that even though it might be preferable to have a whole school approach to gender and violence issues, one-off programmes implemented through the HRE curriculum do have the ability to bring about change. However, the events there also indicate that such issues cannot stay within the confines of the personal education curriculum, but need to become part of the broader school community. The potential of the outcomes from the HRE programme at Mountainview to bring about alterations in the gendered relations of power at the school hinge on the success of the grade 12 boys to continue their work with the younger boys outside of the official curriculum. HRE has served as a starting point for introducing gender and violence as a social justice concern into the lives of a number of boys in the school. It must not be the endpoint as well.

The use of HRE is therefore a question of strategy. It is one accessible point of entry into schools for discourses that can disrupt the legitimacy of masculine hegemonic arrangements. It is not necessarily an optimum means of addressing gender issues. However, it has important implications. The inclusion of gender and violence programmes anywhere in the curriculum helps to disrupt any pretensions that might exist about the neutrality of the school curriculum. It indicates that schools are prepared to take some responsibility for a social problem. However, in doing this it is important that the dominant construction of masculinity, and the consequent effects of such a construction, is treated as a social justice issue. That is, it is important not to pathologize incidents of violence. Violent incidents are not the product of a sick individual, but of a sick society.

Some 'boyswork' programmes, which are based on a mythopoetic approach, do critique some aspects of Western societies' dominant masculinizing processes. However, they have to be questioned about the assumptions and social constructs they legitimize. Such approaches focus on the emotions of boys without examining the social role of emotion (Kenway *et al.* 1997b: 22). Advocates of this type of education for boys focus their attention on how the traditional ways in which men and boys respond emotionally to various situations are damaging to themselves as well as to others. One of the assumptions implicit in this approach is that if boys learn to express their 'innermost' feelings then they will cause less harm to themselves and others. There is little talk in this approach of gender relations and their social organization, rather there seems to be a belief that by encouraging boys to be more expressive this will of necessity limit their oppressive behaviours.

Many programmes constructed in this mould emphasize the importance of a male leader. Hence, they argue for male teachers to conduct these programmes and stress that it is important to encourage fathers to take an interest in their sons. This desire to provide boys with male role models has the attraction of having males shoulder the major responsibility for promoting non-sexist education. The danger occurs when such arguments are based on the premise that men can teach these issues to boys better than women. This issue is taken up in the next chapter. However, it should be stressed here that whenever homo-social environments are created there is always the danger that oppressive behaviours will go unchallenged. Profeminist programmes must be accountable to feminism. Accountability is the glue that holds the 'pro' and the 'feminism' of profeminism together.

The danger of therapeutic anti-feminist programmes slipping into schools is very real. However, the discourse of 'what about the boys' championed by men's rights activists and mythopoets has, by putting masculinity on the agenda of schools, also enabled the problematization of hegemonic masculinity and its relationship to other masculinities and femininities to occur within schools. In problematizing hegemonic discourses it needs to be understood though that, while not totalizing, hegemonic masculine discourses hold a powerful position within Western societies. The adoption of such an understanding will help to acknowledge the small gains that are made through the introduction of such programmes. Thus, any attempt on the part of boys to disrupt these discourses has to be seen as a significant step towards promoting gender justice. As Simon states: 'It's a pretty big thing. A pretty big ask for kids, for children. But when they become adults hopefully they'll . . . some of them will see that there's a different way.'

Changing the dominant construction of masculinity is a big ask. And, as mentioned in Chapter 2 by Richard, the community worker and counsellor, and by the boys themselves, there are risks for boys in transgressing normalized boundaries. Schools must not expect too much change on the part of boys without seeking to change the support structures offered by schools for such changes.

Thus school administrations will play a major role in determining the success of such programmes. It should be stressed here that the support of the school administration at Mountainview was significant in providing in-service time (and finances) for teachers and students. The sense of importance that the administration allocated to this programme was not lost on the boys involved in preparing to work with the grade eight boys. The extent to which this programme continues to operate will be largely determined by the support it is given by the Mountainview administration. It is also important that the school does not rely on such programmes to bring about change. The boys' programmes being conducted through HRE courses need to be seen as an introductory step, not as an end in themselves. For as Dunn (1995: 58) has argued, 'schools should operate in such a way as to make discrete boys' programs unnecessary in the long term'.

Altering the structures of schools and initiatives sponsored by a school administration are critical in creating more gender-just schools. However, this is not to underestimate the power of teachers to bring about change in their schools even where there is little administration support, and even in some instances where there is administration antagonism, towards the issues (Mills 1996, 1997c). The importance of teachers and teaching is taken up in the next chapter, which explores some of the pedagogical dynamics and dilemmas that result from the introduction and implementation of boyswork programmes into the curriculum.

Strategies for schools

There are no quick fix solutions to the problems of violence in school. Changes will have to be introduced into the structures of schools, into the curriculum and teaching strategies over a lengthy period of time in order to effect significant improvements in the ways in which boys engage in violent practices. The activities suggested here are designed to encourage thoughts about the ways in which the curriculum can be a strategic site for beginning this work.

- Consider the curriculum content in a variety of subject areas. How can these curricula incorporate content that challenges dominant assumptions about gender, and in particular about boys' use of violence as a legitimate means of solving conflicts? Can these subjects introduce content that deals with issues of homophobia and anti-lesbianism and misogyny?
- How can boys and girls be encouraged into non-traditional areas? How can this be done in ways that do not devalue those subjects in which girls have traditionally performed well? What can be done to ensure that boys and girls who move into non-traditional areas are not harassed?
- If work with boys is going to be primarily through personal development type subjects, schools will need to make sure that they are respected, thorough and challenging in their approach to this issue. How can this be done? How do students see this subject? How do teachers treat their work in this subject? How are teachers selected to teach this subject?
- A copy of Salisbury and Jackson's (1996) *Challenging Macho Values: Practical Ways of Working with Adolescent Boys* is an essential resource for working with boys. Which activities in this book are suitable for the boys in your school? Can any of these be incorporated into the current work being conducted in a range of curriculum areas?
- Is it possible to involve students in planning strategies to introduce anti-violence work into schools? Which students? How?
- How can the momentum for change be maintained? What does the school need to do to ensure that concerns about gender and violence in the school are nothing more than a passing fad? Can concerns about these issues be written into school policies and other documents in order to legitimate them as official concerns of the school.
- Record any decisions that are made in relation to any of the above discussions. Determine a meeting time to discuss the implementation of particular strategies. Ensure that suggestions for improvement and inhibitors to change are recorded along with detailed accounts of what worked well.

Notes

1 A later edition of this is published in McLean, Carey and White (1996), the 1995 version is used throughout this book.
2 I am grateful to Vicky Carrington for this observation.

chapter four

Implementing change:
a question of pedagogy?

The popular notion of 'empowerment' . . . is all but meaningless in the context of groups who are already overempowered, leaving us with the patent absurdity of 'empowering men to disempower themselves.'

(Redman 1996: 170)

For men and boys, who experience the subjective powerlessness that goes with being a small cog in an overpowering machine, it is very difficult to see that they are, in fact, part of a dominant group.

(McLean 1996: 71)

Introduction

The preceding chapter discussed the ways in which one-off (pro)feminist anti-violence programmes implemented through a Human Relationships Education (HRE) curriculum, while having many drawbacks, have the potential to yield some long-term benefits for schools and for students. In this chapter, pedagogical issues related to the implementation of these types of programmes will be considered. The appropriateness of teachers, as opposed to members of community organizations, implementing programmes and the sex of the teachers or community workers implementing the programmes are issues examined in the first part of the chapter.

The focus in the latter section is on approaches to pedagogical practices. Distinguishing between pedagogy and curriculum, as mentioned in the previous chapter, is problematic. It assumes a formal definition of the curriculum: that is, it creates a notion that a curriculum is simply a text that can be 'properly' implemented through the correct selection of pedagogical techniques and it negates the ways in which pedagogical practices are implicated in the construction of particular knowledges. Thus, while for discussion purposes this chapter focuses on pedagogical considerations of the who and the how, curricular considerations of the where and the what of boyswork programmes, raised in the previous chapter, are never far away. Matters curriculum clearly impact on matters pedagogical.

Unlike most topics within the formal school curriculum, which are taught by teachers from within the school, boys' programmes are often taught by people external to the school. It is frequently assumed that those who specialize in the delivery of such programmes have both more knowledge of the issues and also more time to prepare resources than do teachers within the school. However, because the outsider is not a member of the school community, the long-term benefits of their involvement are likely to be limited. Other complex issues, which can arise when schools draw on outside people, relate to the abilities of the outsider to teach. Closely tied to the outsider–insider dynamic of presenters is the issue of the sex of the presenter(s). This taps into the recent debate about men and the teaching profession covered in the popular press (see, for example, Aldred and Butler 1996; Merymant 1996; Griffith 1997a: 19, b: 2; O'Chee 1997b, d). There is currently a major push to have more males enter the field of teaching. One of the dominant arguments here is that boys need more male role models. This is often founded on either the belief that the feminized domain of schools has meant that boys have not acquired the discipline necessary to control their disruptive behaviour or the interrelated belief that the education of boys is a form of men's business. Those who argue for more male teachers on these grounds, that is that men either should have or do have more authority or influence when it comes to educating boys, are reinforcing gendered power relations. Unfortunately there are a number of men writing in the field of boys' schooling who work from such a perspective (for example, Biddulph 1995, 1997; Fletcher 1995a, b; Gurian 1999; Pollack 1999).

However, some men, myself included, do argue that males need to be working with boys on gender issues from a profeminist perspective. Such a perspective is based on the premise that it is men's responsibility to tackle those issues which are the source of their own privilege as well as those of other males. A profeminist politics does not seek to exclude women from gender programmes, and indeed argues that it is crucial that boys (and men) listen to girls and women about their views on gender issues. This does not mean that there is no place for the construction of temporary homo-social environments within which boys can come to discuss those issues that concern them. However, any attempt to silence women's and girls' contributions to debates on gender and violence will serve to preserve dominant relations of power. Men working with boys in schools need to be accountable to feminists. A lack of accountability is likely to lead to situations where women's and girls' interests become submerged beneath those of men and boys.

In the second part of this chapter pedagogical practices are considered, with a particular focus on critical pedagogy. Critical pedagogy seeks to provide an outline for teaching practices that promote a more just society. However, in many ways elements of this approach will resonate with therapeutic approaches to boys' education. In particular the notion of 'empowerment' is a problematic concept utilized in this literature when applied to the education of boys in a gender and violence programme. Many of the problems associated with critical pedagogy are exacerbated when the teacher is a man. It is suggested here that a more appropriate programme for boys will be grounded in notions of respect rather than empowerment. Such an approach is more conducive to a profeminist masculinity politics than is critical pedagogy, especially when the teachers are men.

Unfortunately though, there are not many men working in schools who identify with a profeminist politics. Thus, while it is important that men take on the responsibility of implementing profeminist gender and violence programmes in schools, there is often a lack of willing male staff to take on such programmes (Dunn 1995). This perhaps means that women will still be bearing the brunt of getting these programmes off the ground. It is probably not coincidental that the guidance officer responsible for initiating Mountainview's programme was female, that the Tamville HRE coordinator who invited Men Against Sexual Assault into the school was female, or that the gender equity officer who was also instrumental in the setting up of the Mountainview programme was female. In each of these instances the women involved have looked beyond their school to staff these programmes.

Male teachers

The staffing of boys' programmes is a major gender issue. Men do need to take responsibility for the organization and implementation of gender initiatives and thus they should be present in gender and violence programmes. However, there can be problems with this. The reasons underpinning men's involvement are all-important. It is crucial that men are not reinforcing dominant constructions of masculinities in their deliveries of these programmes. Unfortunately, this is the case with many of those men who offer to do boyswork in schools. This presents a number of problems for schools wanting to implement gender and violence work in schools.

In many schools it is difficult to find male teachers who are prepared to take on the responsibility of working in these types of programmes. Thus, unless schools draw on outside agencies to implement them, it is female teachers who are bearing the weight of introducing gender and violence programmes for boys into their schools. For a number of the women teachers interviewed here there was a feeling of uncertainty about their knowledge of issues facing boys. For example, Sarah explained:

I've always felt that it needs to be (males). When I was sort of a fly on the wall last year when Richard came in and worked with those boys for those sessions Craig was also there in the mornings but I was there for the whole sessions . . . there's a lot I don't know about boys' or male culture . . . I don't know if I skewed the results on those . . . on those sessions, being a female, but it was really quite valuable for me because there is a lot I didn't know. So I think if you were a female working within that area, I think you would just have to be really sure and know that you felt that you really understood all the issues and things and I definitely don't . . . yet. I guess . . . I used to come from a place where I thought it should only be males and that's one hundred percent males. Like I guess I can see that you know if a female feels comfortable doing it and feels that you know she understands the issues coming in for portions of it but I still think it needs to be owned. At this point in time anyways.

Donna made a similar comment:

Well I thought about that . . . for this school at this time I really think that it's better having men working with the boys. That doesn't mean to say that it should happen every time. Occasionally I thought that such and such wouldn't happen or so and so would not have said that had a woman been in the room. But that might have defeated the purpose so I was prepared just to see how it went and for this purpose at this time, I think it was better having men and no women.

This degree of uncertainty by the women is interesting. Neither woman seemed to be prepared to state definitively that it should be only males conducting these programmes. It has often been asked by feminists whether men can be trusted to deal with gender issues without the presence of women (Hagan 1992). This is quite understandable given the politics of some of the men who argue for the need for more male teachers (see in particular Biddulph 1997). Furthermore, it is also possible to point to the ways in which homo-social environments have often been used to reinvest males with patriarchal privileges, for example in the male dominated reproduction of managers. Donna's comment that she wonders whether 'so and so would not have said that had a woman been in the room' is a telling one (see Kenway and Fitzclarence 1997: 130; Kenway *et al.* 1997a: 25–7). Men getting together in all-male environments can have negative effects for women. This has been demonstrated by the homo-social practices of the men's mythopoetic movement, both in Australia and elsewhere (Kenway *et al.* 1997a, b; Mills and Lingard 1997b).

Mythopoetic politics are coming to dominate much of this 'what about the boys?' discourse (see Mills and Lingard 1997a; Mills 2000a; Roulston and Mills 2000). Central to this politics is a perceived need for boys to be initiated into responsible manhood by older men. This concern is taken up in the refrain calling for more male teachers (Biddulph 1997; Pollack 1999; Gurian 1999; Kindlon and Thompson 1999 – the concern about the lack of male teachers in the education of boys is of course not new, see for example Sadker and Sadker 1994). For instance, in the UK *The Times*, in an article with the headline 'Boys need a father figure to do well' (1999: 7), reports on a study which suggests that 'Teenage boys without a strong father figure are more likely to suffer from depression, display anti-social behaviour and do badly at school'. The *Times Educational Supplement* (*TES*) reports on research that suggests primary school boys in Welsh schools progressed faster with male teachers (Budge 1998). The *TES* also reports on the concerns of Ralph Tabberer, the chief executive of the Teacher Training Authority, that there is a relationship between the low levels of male primary teachers and boys' supposed underachievement in the 2000 A level and GCSE results (Mansell 2000). The *Scotsman* (*sic*) in asking the question 'Should we put manhood on the national curriculum for boys?' provides a detailed account of the UK Men's Movement's proposal for schools to provide wilderness boys' only camps within which boys can be initiated into the world of men under the tutelage of a male role model (Spowart 1999). Similar concerns about boys' lack of role models have been articulated in Australia. Brisbane's *Courier Mail* and *Sunday Mail* have regularly featured articles with headlines reflecting concerns about a lack of male teachers, for example: 'It's goodbye Mr. Chips: Guys give our schools a miss' (Griffith 1997a); 'No panic, guys, kindies need you – lecturer' (O'Chee 1997b); and 'Even fewer men on the roll'(O'Chee 1997d). There are numerous reasons given as to why the teaching profession has become 'feminized'. However, a feature that is raised over and over again relates to fears associated with sexual harassment and paedophilia allegations. This concern is also reflected in newspaper headlines such as: 'Suspicious minds set against men in schools' (Cole 1999); 'Sex fears deter male teachers' (Griffith 1997b); 'Sex traps for men teachers' (Griffith 1997c); 'Sex-charge fears put men on the outer' (O'Chee 1997a); 'Male teacher's sex claim nightmare' (Griffith 1997d).

This obsession with the possibility of false accusations being levelled against male teachers serves to discredit many of the achievements of feminists that have enabled sexual harassment and child abuse to be put on the education agenda within schools. The notion that feminism has corrupted the education agenda can also be found in other reasons given as to why some males either leave or reject teaching. For instance, an article entitled 'Feminism, race talk upset Brett' (1997) is about a young man who liked the idea of teaching but dropped out of his university course because 'the course was starting to portray ideas that were more to do with political correctness. They came from the PC direction'. Again feminism is blamed for turning men into today's 'second sex'.

The concerns about male teachers in the media are reflected in the attitudes towards the issue being taken in Queensland (as elsewhere, see Weiner *et al.* 1997: 628) by various Education Ministers. For instance, Griffith (1997a: 19) reports that the Queensland Government spent Aus. $80,000 in a campaign in 1996 to encourage more young men into teaching (this included a video featuring a popular professional rugby league identity!). The then Education Minister, Bob Quinn, argued that this was necessary due to the lack of male role models to which young boys had access because of the dominance of females in primary school teaching and the rise in single parent families (Maher 1996). He claimed that this 'lack' contributed to poor outcomes for boys, and the likelihood of them becoming involved in juvenile crime or committing suicide. Interestingly, Quinn regularly used the notion of 'gender equity' in his calls for more male teachers. For instance in March 1997, in response to the release of statistics, which indicated that the amount of males applying for teaching courses had increased, O'Chee (1997c: 3) wrote: 'Education Minister, Bob Quinn, yesterday welcomed the increase, saying it was a small step towards gender equality in teaching.' This usage of social justice language is demonstrative of a masculinity politics which utilizes the language of social justice to legitimize claims that, while a gender equity agenda for girls might have once been necessary, the pendulum has swung too far and boys and men are now a disadvantaged group. The next Queensland education minister also demonstrated a similar sentiment (Lawrence 1999). The issue of male teachers has thus become a core feature of attempts to improve the lot of boys in schools.

However, having men implement gender and violence programmes does carry an important message to students. Boys do need to be made aware that it is a legitimate activity for men to take a stand on these issues. As Victoria, the HRE coordinator from Tamville, stated:

> I think it is really important for them to see males doing it because then they are actually seeing another guy saying 'Yes, this is possible.' And because some of the males in their lives are role models for their behaviour it is important that they see someone who has a different sort of behaviour to what that stereotypical behaviour is.

The issue of authority is important here. It is sometimes argued that boys will listen to men about these issues more than they will women. The argument suggests that women articulating the same concerns that men do in these programmes are written off by the boys as feminists who distort the reality of existing gender relations. However, some argue, it is often a little harder for these boys, although far from being impossible, to position men in such a way. Simon, a teacher from Tamville, argues that it is important that males implement these programmes with the younger boys for this reason:

For the males . . . for the boys it is. Yeah I do. I do because it has more credibility for a male to say, 'Hey, I'm you know I don't think violence is an answer,' than having a woman say that to them. Especially the year nine level. I think that possibly in the senior school it mightn't be so critical. Like Sarah could do it . . . You know no problem. Probably Sarah could probably do it with the boys there too, but I think the personnel you select is pretty critical.

This is a dilemma for programmes in schools. Bowing to arguments that boys will listen to men better than women reinforces existing gender relations of power where men are constructed as authority figures. However, at the same time it is important that boys come to see the issues as important, and the question has to be asked as to whether a 'by any means' approach is appropriate.

This dilemma though is often a luxury for schools, as finding suitable male staff to be involved in such programmes is not always easy. A number of the female teachers commented on how difficult it is to find male teachers to take up these issues. For example, Sarah said:

many men perceive that they will lose their power base rather than gain in so many other ways. Possibly because of this perceived threat. Possibly also because (male) teachers may not take the time to understand and agree with the connection between gender, violence and teacher management. At the moment actually teachers come and go, like at the moment in this school there seems to be only one male teacher that's actually wanting to be involved in anything sort of extra-curricular I guess, if you can call it that. It's not really, but outside of the actual curriculum, curriculum areas, and that's Craig at the moment. A couple of years ago there were I think two teachers, two male teachers that would have . . . But even this year I mean I think the energy just sort of goes up and goes down. At the moment there's . . . if this hadn't been happening and I guess if I hadn't been sort of pushing it, as I feel I have been pushing it, I don't know that it would've happened. I doubt that it would.

Donna from the same school commented:

I don't know too many men who would leap to it . . . it's quite a difficult thing for men to do and handle and I suspect it would be fairly difficult to get men to do it. I was pleased that we had outsiders come in and support our male staff.

The issue of a lack of male teachers was significant for Mountainview High School. They were feeling quite positive about the successful ways in which the programmes had developed, and had thus planned to implement a similar one with the year 11s, leading into grade 12. However, the plans had to be shelved because Craig, the teacher who had worked in the grade 12 programme, had been granted long service leave for the last term of the year. This created a situation where there were no male staff members prepared to take on this responsibility.

The situation is perhaps a little different at Tamville, which is a much larger school. Simon does not think it would be difficult to find male teachers at Tamville who would take on the responsibility of dealing with such issues:

> I think in this school you'd find a group of teachers who'd be prepared to. You know we've got . . . in the school we've got HRE teachers who are males and, and the sexual harassment coordinators, half are male and half female. Like you've got a group of people who are really concerned and caring and concerned about this sort of issue. But I think, I think you . . . if you do it you've got to make it something . . . you know you've got to make it . . . at least initially . . . a special sort of programme.

Victoria supported this:

> I think that every school has a problem trying to find the male teachers who have some commitment to it. We have been a little bit luckier than some schools here because we've got people who are good at working in that field and who feel comfortable with it. But by and large a lot of them aren't. And I know other schools where they have no male teachers taking HRE classes at all and there must be a gap in credibility then when they don't see any men talking about those sorts of issues.

The important point here is perhaps not that women could or should not conduct these programmes, but whether they should have to.

There was general agreement among most of the teachers that women were quite capable of teaching these programmes. For instance:

> *Victoria:* I think women can, ah qualify, I think that some women can do some of it. And do it well because we've all seen those kinds of things.

> *Rebecca:* Mmm . . . For me I think the understanding the person, who is working with the kids, has is more important. Certainly boys may be less inclined to take the word on a particular issue from a woman but . . . there are ways around that . . . But a good understanding and a well-designed course I think could be run by men or women. Or maybe two together.

The work of Dianne Reay (1990) with primary school boys in England is testament to the very positive and successful ways in which women can work with boys on gender projects. However, it does need to be recognized that the resentment which faces those attempting to implement such programmes may be greater for women than for men. For instance, the boys at Mountainview were already articulating an anti-feminist language when the programme was first introduced. This may have made it more difficult for a woman to present ideas without some of the boys utilizing their 'feminazi' discourse. The potential for antagonism to women is suggested in some of the comments made by boys from the different classes. Oscar, a grade 12 Mountainview student, commented:

> I reckon it would be just as easy to discuss it (with women teachers) but you wouldn't get the feedback. Because you'd get a lot more mucking around just to sort of . . . just because the female teacher is there you'd get a lot more kids mucking around I guess. Just to put off the female teachers. There's some kids just like that.

Jordan, a grade nine Tamville boy, said 'And if there was a girl or a woman there they would probably mess around more.'

Interestingly some of the boys recognize that some of the comments they made in class would have been offensive to women (see also Kenway *et al.* 1997a: 25–7). For instance Bryce noted:

> *Bryce:* A female teacher might get pretty offended about some of the stuff we say.
> *Martin:* Like what?
> *Bryce:* I don't know about girls and stuff. About how you treat some of them so that's probably why it's good to have males.

What is significant here is that Bryce makes it sound as if the homo-social environments being created for these programmes provide spaces where boys can articulate anti-feminist or anti-female comments without raising the ire of women. This is obviously one of the big concerns feminists have about males working together without some form of accountability to feminists. Bryce was asked about this:

> *Martin:* And do you think that male teachers would challenge you as well about those things?
> *Bryce:* Oh I do think the male teachers would bring up the point except for it's just probably a lot easier for other, for you to discuss that point with another male. I don't know maybe. Some people would probably find it easier with a female but I don't know.

For a number of the boys there was a sense that women would not understand their points of view and that this could lead to discomfort for the boys. For instance, Bill states 'Yeah I think it's better than females because I think some guys get a bit embarrassed when they're with females.' Peter comments:

like it's best to have a man because a man can like sort of knows what a boy's nature is about but women's women, I don't mean to sound like a Nazi or anything like that or sexist or anything, but women understand girls better and stuff and men understand boys better, and stuff like that.

It is interesting that Peter has recognized that there is perhaps a problem with essentialist notions of gender. Peter, at various times goes to great pains to not be 'sexist' or a 'Nazi'. However, what he taps into here is the social dimension of gender. There are things that women do not understand about the ways in which some discourses impact on men's gender construction, as there are those that men do not understand in relation to female gender constructions. One problem though is that Peter has an understanding of the programme, which suggests it dealt with men's issues rather than relationships between males and females and males and males. For those boys who had similar views to Peter, this did not mean they did not want to listen to women. In response to a question about whether gender and violence programmes are best presented by males or females, Paul answered:

Paul: Both I reckon.
Martin: Why both?
Paul: Because then you can have both views.

Paul was not alone in his views. Other students, some of whom did not seem to be concerned at all about the sex of those conducting such programmes, were interested in hearing different views. For example:

Ben: I think it is good with a male teaching the male group. But in some cases it would be good to have a female perspective but I think guys, males running males' groups is a good idea. More open and similar experiences like having similar, I don't know, beliefs I guess you'd say.

Issac: Females could do it just as well.
Martin: Would there be any benefits to having males doing it or benefits to having females do it?
Issac: You could relate more if it was just like males. You could probably you know talk about certain things that you wouldn't want to talk about in front of a female.
Martin: And what would be the benefits of having a female doing it?
Issac: Her views on the subject. Because we had that other teacher in here and she had her points and they were good as well.

It is interesting to note here that Issac was one of the boys who seemed most comfortable with the issues. He spoke during lessons about a gay man he worked with, and often made anti-homophobic statements during classes. In the anonymous comments made in the shoebox activity at the end of two lessons when Victoria had joined this class, comments were made about how good it was to hear women's views on these topics.

In one of the sessions at Mountainview, Craig was absent and a female relief teacher joined the class. A few boys made some very positive comments about this lesson in the interviews.

> *Martin:* Do you think that boys in those classes would listen to a female teacher doing those issues?
> *Harry:* No I don't think it would make much difference. You know the day we had Ms Brown in there she . . . they listened more to her.

> *Luke:* One of the best lessons we had was when Ms Brown was in the room, when we did that going from side to side of the room. It's good to hear what women have to say. They may find it difficult to do it all the time with the teasing, but I think women could do it.

The issue of boys' reactions to women who deliver these types of programme is a significant one. It is critical that boys do not perceive men's involvement in these programmes as a consequence of men's greater ability to control classroom behaviours. Such an interpretation serves to reinforce dominant constructions of masculinity. Thus, it is important that men consider how they will exercise their authority over the class in ways that do not valorize hegemonic masculine practices. However, it ought to be recognized that in some situations men will probably need to use what might seem to be authoritarian pedagogical approaches. For, in some instances seemingly democratic pedagogical approaches can have oppressive consequences for others (see for example Walkerdine 1989). At Tamville, this came out in a discussion with one grade nine boy with a Vietnamese background (Than). For him the sex of the teacher was not important. He had other priorities: 'It doesn't make a difference I don't think . . . I think it's better done by a person that they don't talk a lot or they don't muck around or something.' For Than the major issue is discipline. He had very firm ideas on appropriate behaviour and the discipline necessary for maintaining that behaviour.

Another, and often interrelated issue is that of bringing people into schools from outside the teaching profession to run such programmes. For many who are advocating work with boys in schools, as mentioned above, there is a strong push to have this work done by men. Hence, where there are few male teachers prepared to do this work within a particular school, outsiders are often called in. The argument put forward is often similar to the one offered by Gurian (1999: 193): 'The very presence of the male in the class increases a boy's emotional and psychosocial education.'

However, the argument that 'any man' in a classroom works well for boys is trite (see Roulston and Mills 2000). This is especially the case when dealing with gender and violence issues. Concerns about the sorts of people who are being asked into schools has caused the Queensland Department of Education to develop protocols for schools working with outside agencies. Such protocols may of course work both for and against the introduction of (pro)feminist educators. However, there does appear to be some need to consider who is invited into schools. Julie, a senior policy officer with the Queensland Department of Education's Gender Equity Unit, who has been working on the issues of protocols, states in relation to men's rights organizations who slip into schools under the 'what about the boys?' banner:

> developing the issue of the protocols is so important . . . We were at a presentation at an entirely different school a couple of years ago where they were running a gender equity programme for all of their year ten boys and girls, which looked at a whole range of issues. And the people that they actually got in for the girls' programme were mostly people from the Gender Equity Unit and other people from the Department who have worked in this area. But when we looked at who they had for the parallel programme that they were running for boys they actually did have someone from the Lone Fathers' Association, who delivered this amazing sort of men's rights diatribe, and army recruiting officers and a whole range of sort of quite bizarre groups, given the context of the day they were supposed to be running. So that was one of the other issues you know, we are really concerned that the school actually gives something of a consistent message to the kids and doesn't actually simply provide a platform for all kinds of weird and wonderful points of view under the banner of gender equity or boys' programmes.

It is unfortunate that those who are most regularly invited into schools are the people about whom schools concerned with promoting a (pro)feminist agenda need to be most careful. Many of these men articulate a conservative reading of the 'what about the boys' discourse, even though on the surface they appear to have a social justice agenda. For example, both Biddulph and Gurian acknowledge a commitment to gender equity and social justice programmes for girls. Biddulph (1995: 32) states: 'Feminism elevates women from a long subservience. It's important and must continue.' And, in his more recent *Raising Boys*, Biddulph (1997: vi) begins with 'An important note'. In this note he announces that: 'In writing a book about boys and their special needs, I wish in no way to take away from the efforts being made everywhere to advance women and girls.' And Gurian (1999) states that:

> As I present this material, I offer the following caveat: Always we must come to center, wherein we know that *both* girls and boys suffer in different ways that need our various, not our singular, responses. If

you advocate for adolescent boys, I plead with you not to help the pendulum swing against girls.

(Gurian 1999: 180, original emphasis)

However, under closer scrutiny their anti-feminist colours usually become obvious.

Despite problems associated with the politics associated with some organizations and some consultants on 'boys' issues, outside agencies can often be important in being able to provide support to schools in their endeavours to provide students with a broad curriculum, as many schools do not have sufficient staff with the expertise to adequately cover the issues that are currently being placed on the educational agenda. Furthermore, some issues do not have the full support of staff and thus outside agencies can be used to fill gaps in the staff consensus. One issue that appears to be particularly difficult to tackle 'in-house' is gender, violence and masculinity. One of the perceived problems here is that teachers have little knowledge of this area. For instance, Julie continues:

The schools do need to be addressing the issues themselves, but there are often resources . . . one of the issues about schools trying to address these things themselves is that it is very difficult to get any school to the point where there is a consensus amongst the entire staff and because that's the case those other agencies are going to be brought into the school in any case. And it seems to us strategic to try and have some kind of framework within which they can be evaluated and their place in the curriculum can actually be assessed. And that I guess is the basis on which we were going ahead and also because a lot of those . . . I mean there are agencies in the community we think have the potential to offer an enormous amount to schools and we wanted to look at whether or not it was possible to find a way to give priority and to give some sort of status, or some sort of preferential status to those agencies . . . whose policies and practices coincided with the policies of the Department

This perception about teachers' lack of knowledge in this area is also articulated at times by some of the students:

Sam: I think it's good because the outsiders probably know more about it than the teachers. Like they've been doing it for longer.

Peter: Oh well it's, I think it's best if people . . . from outside the school come in and talk to us about it. You know, who's learnt about it more and stuff like that . . . And because like insiders, oh yeah like Mrs Young she's, ah I like her a lot, but she, like everyone knows her as a science teacher and not as an harassment officer and they don't take her for serious . . . Just take it for granted, 'Ah, you're a science teacher you can't tell us you know this stuff.' Simple little things like that.

That students are sometimes too close to their teachers to deal with this issue is also picked up by Victoria at Tamville:

> kids in the school get to regarding their teachers as parents in a way and your Mum never knows anything, so your teacher never knows anything, and so I think that getting someone else in who has a bit, bit of different credibility might get a bit more respect for their views. 'Might' is the operative word, but they might get a bit more respect for their views.

The notion of 'comfortability' is relevant for many of the students, for example Bryce said, 'you know teachers might go say stuff in their staff room.' This concern that teachers might talk in the staffroom is a significant one. It represents an understanding of the power that is given to a teacher by a student once they reveal aspects of their personal lives to them. This issue of student voice is taken up later in this chapter.

The majority of those students who were interviewed felt that it was better for outsiders to come into schools to run these programmes. Of course it has to be borne in mind that I was doing the interviews and students may well have been wanting to provide me with the 'right' answers (see Reay 1990; Carrington *et al.* 2000). One issue which surfaced a few times was that students become familiar with their teachers in a particular role, and thus find it difficult to switch into a mode where they may be expected to deal with emotions and feelings.

> *Paul:* Oh yeah people from outside. Because teachers like most teachers here I don't like.
> *Martin:* Why's that?
> *Paul:* I just don't like them. Like, some of the teachers I like, but most of them you couldn't really talk to.

James is quite forceful in his position on teachers and these programmes:

> *James:* I don't even think the teachers should be in the room. Because that was creating a lot of problems.
> *Martin:* Why do you think that was?
> *James:* I don't know people are just a lot more reluctant to open up in front of teachers, and teachers that they know that they are going to be taught by or are being taught by. So it just I don't know it just sort of changes the atmosphere completely.

Harry also thinks it is better to have people coming in from outside the school: 'Because they get taught by the teachers all through school. People from outside have a bigger . . . greater influence on them.'

The teachers at Mountainview supported these views. Sarah commented:

Definitely. For example you and Richard and Heath come in with different perspectives, a lot of energy. It's just nice that you are able to come in and you seem to have the motivation, commitment and don't have all the other baggage. Like for example I do or somebody else might have and able to just devote that time. In that way, yes. Also the fact that generally people like . . . Richard or whoever are able to specialize in a particular area at the time, which means that you have expertise at that point that is just far greater and I think that's very worthwhile. I also think that it's good for students who get used to you know teachers and so on, I think it's very valuable for them to get to meet somebody from the outside world every so often.

This sentiment was shared with Donna, the deputy principal from Mountainview High:

Well it gives a lot of credibility to a course to have an outsider. The kids are very used to us and they react one way to teachers they're dealing with regularly but they react a different way to adults who they perceive as knowledgeable or coming in with new . . . different skills or different techniques and I think that they felt it is important . . . having outsiders come in . . . it was good for this course to have outsiders and I think it achieved the purpose of giving more credibility to it.

However, a number of the students felt that teachers were not necessarily bound by their roles as teacher, and that outsiders would not necessarily be more appropriate than a teacher:

Martin: Do you think that these programmes are better run by outsiders or by teachers in the school?

Jeff: That would depend on the actual outsider. If the outsider is a very conversational sort of person and mixes well and can really . . . can get people talking, flicks a switch and flicks the right one.

Julian: I don't think it could really matter all that much. I suppose some teachers would be all right at it. But there'd be some that would be . . . you know . . . 'We're telling you, we're not asking you.' That's the ones that wouldn't be any good at it . . . And then that's when you have the people from outside come in and do them . . . But I think you know teachers'd make . . . like some of the smarties, the troublemakers, you know not to act that way . . . if you have someone else that's not a teacher who comes in and does it well then I think kids understand more.

The issue of student behaviour is an important one here. Many of the people who come into schools to implement these programmes are not trained teachers. Some of them have very good teaching skills. However, some do have difficulties with 'behaviour management' (as of course do some experienced teachers). This can be crucial in implementing programmes that work to challenge many of the students' established ways of looking at the world. Thus, some students, such as Than, prefer to be taught by a teacher: 'I think it's better with a teacher. It's more strict. Because some guys they just muck around. They don't just look into it. They don't look at the thing carefully they just muck around and laugh all the time you know.'

The teachers from Mountainview were far less concerned about outsiders coming into the school than their Tamville counterparts. Rebecca from Tamville, as other teachers at Tamville, would like to see a greater role for teachers in these programmes:

> I think I would prefer to see it embedded in the curriculum, integrated in the school and by experts (laughter), which I'd prefer to be teachers just from the point of view that I do think we've got skills and we can do things in the classroom well and so you'd get the best out of the programme. But I do think there's a place for people coming from other agencies in a course like that because they've got a lot to share. A lot of understanding a lot of experience to share. So perhaps I would be looking for a mix of the two.

> *Simon:* I can see benefits of both. But irrespective they've got to be . . . it really has to be done with a trained teacher.

This desire on the part of the teachers grew out of their aim to see programmes such as this thought through and developed according to the students' needs. There was a recognition that teaching is a skilled activity. It requires skills not only in being able to impart information, but also in being able to facilitate discussions and being able to ward off 'trouble' or defuse tense situations. Teaching situations are likely to be more tense and more explosive when they involve disrupting boys' valued ways of being, as is likely to occur in gender and violence programmes (see Kenway *et al.* 1997a, b). Thought needs to go into the ways in which boys are 'taught' about gender and violence issues.

In the construction and design of the programmes used at both Tamville and Mountainview many of the principles of critical pedagogy had been adopted because of the commitment advocates of critical pedagogy have towards notions of justice (see Smyth 1987; Giroux and McLaren 1989; Giroux and Simon 1989; Giroux 1992, 1994; Kanpol 1994; McLaren 1994). However, during the course of the programme it became apparent from both experience and by engaging with feminist criticisms of critical pedagogy (see in particular the edited collection by Luke and Gore 1992 and

Gore 1993) that there are a number of gendered problematics with this pedagogical approach. When critical pedagogy is considered for use in gender and violence programmes for boys, new twists emerge on some of these criticisms. These are worth noting here.

A note on critical pedagogy and boys

Critical pedagogy provides an approach to education that seeks to implicate teachers in processes which challenge dominant relations of power founded on unjust practices. However, some of the processes and principles advocated by critical theorists demonstrate a gender blindness. In particular feminists have focused on critical pedagogy's use of notions such as 'authority', 'reason', 'authentic voice' and 'empowerment'. These aspects of critical pedagogy, when applied to the teaching of boys, provide further gendered problematics.

The concept of 'authority' raises important issues when considering how to implement gender and violence programmes with boys. Kanpol (1994) states, in relation to the critical pedagogical approach to teaching, that:

> Teacher authority will be negotiated with students. That is, within the confines of their bureaucratically granted authority, teachers will create a classroom climate that allows open deliberation of teacher-student relationships. Teacher-student relationships will become dialogical and not remain distant and aloof.
>
> (Kanpol 1994: 49)

The negotiation of this authority was deemed necessary in the boys' programmes in order to avoid authoritarian didactic teaching strategies that valorize power and control. Such methods would have been particularly inappropriate because in both schools the presenters were men, and we wanted to avoid situations whereby masculine assertions of authority were recognized as being valid ways of obtaining one's will. The situation may of course be different if the presenter is a woman. For instance, as Diane Reay (1990: 271) comments in relation to primary school teachers working with boys: 'Progressive, as opposed to didactic methods of teaching, too often subsume the primary school teacher's expertise within her role as facilitator of children's learning, and in doing so can subscribe to traditional stereotypes of male superiority and female incompetence.' This problem is taken up in a number of other studies (see for example Walkerdine 1989). Even in boys' only classes with a male teacher, child-centered approaches to learning may not work in the best interests of some students. For instance, a number of students at Mountainview and Tamville wanted the classroom to be more ordered than it was, and recognized the potential for a laissez-faire approach (which is sometimes the product of intentions to create a child-centred learning environment) to produce an oppressive atmosphere in the classroom. For example, Than, as previously stated, thinks 'it's better with a teacher. It's more strict.' However, authoritarian methods do not work with students either. For as Julian also commented earlier, teachers who have an approach summed up in the following statement: 'We're telling you, we're not asking you' are the types of teachers who 'wouldn't be any good at it.'

This presents a dilemma. On the one hand many of the traditional authoritarian forms of teacher–student interaction are based on values that reinforce the legitimacy of masculinized forms of control, on the other hand more nurturing strategies do not always work to contain oppressive relations of power within a classroom. Critical pedagogy seemed to offer ways around this dilemma, although we were aware that control can be effected by more insidious means (Foucault 1977, 1981). However, such a pedagogical approach also has a number of problems associated with it.

Critical pedagogy has been identified by a number of feminists as a masculinist discourse (Luke and Gore 1992; Gore 1993; Matthews 1994). For instance, its emphasis on critique and action, it is argued, presupposes a rational masculine subject. Historically, critique and action 'have been the prerogatives of men empowered to inscribe and exchange critique and action in the formal public discourse of policy and law, in academic text, cultural (film, TV) text, the editorial page, or the corporate memo' (Luke 1992: 29). Within critique and action propositions there is an appeal to reason. Reason is an enlightenment concept, which identifies a rational subject who is able to influence the public sphere. This subject is male. Reason further suggests that there is one Truth. Thus, operating from a critical pedagogy perspective implies that the teacher has this Truth, and therefore has been emancipated from the constraints that face lesser-emancipated beings, such as students (Ellsworth 1992). In so doing, this approach reinforces the rationalist values, such as reason, associated with hegemonic masculinity.

Reason operates in a binary relationship to emotion. Reason is masculinized and emotion feminized (see Seidler 1994; Morgan 1996). Hence, critical pedagogy's emphasis on reason as a means of effecting social change devalues emotion and subsequently the feminine. One of the significant aspects of the programmes at the two schools was to try and provide space for emotions to surface and to explore the ways in which males deal with emotional issues. For as Kenway *et al.* (1997b: 20) have stated about boys, 'their emotional experiences of malehood and of schooling are central to their responses to gender reform' (see also Kenway *et al.* 1997a: ch. 5). Thus, critical pedagogy's valorization of the voice of reason, at the expense of the voice of emotion, may well serve to negate the significance of boys' emotional attachment to particular forms of masculinity.

This is not necessarily the intention of critical pedagogy. For many of the advocates of critical pedagogy regard it as a pedagogical process that can be employed as a means of tackling injustice. For example, Kanpol (1994: 27) states that:

> Critical pedagogy is a cultural-political tool that takes seriously the notion of human differences, particularly as these differences relate to race, class and gender. In its most radical sense, critical pedagogy seeks to unoppress the oppressed and unite people in a shared language of critique, struggle, and hope to end various forms of human suffering.

In this process critical pedagogues often seek to incorporate student (reasonable and emotional) voices into the teaching process. However, this too can be problematic. For instance, Luke (1992) claims, in relation to the teaching of girls, that:

> Granting voice to girls in the public sphere of the democratic classroom is an add-on tactic of incorporation . . . For, without a rewriting of the masculine public subject, women end up doubly inscribed in marginal public positions and in 'natural' caretaking positions in the private.
> (Luke 1992: 32)

What does this mean for the teaching of boys? There are obvious problems if the teacher is female. For example, male voices are privileged over the female voice in the room and if it is a case of boys learning to express their feelings and emotions women yet again are constructed as the nurturers of boys/men. However, the context with a male teacher is different. For example, boys learn to negotiate and to share their emotions and feelings with other men. However, it would be ridiculous to suggest that this will inevitably lead to greater gender justice. There is little evidence to suggest that boys/men with good negotiating skills and who are able to share their feelings are unlikely to oppress women. It might even be suggested that such men could become more competent in their oppression of women. Oppression does not always have a violent face (Foucault 1977, 1981).

Luke's claim that the attention to student voice is 'a tactic of incorporation' applies to boys as well as girls. For instance, Ellsworth (1992: 98) claims that: 'Strategies such as student empowerment and dialogue give the illusion of equality while in fact leaving the authoritarian nature of the teacher/student relationship intact.' Reay (1990) considered the dangers of this in her work with boys. She states: 'Initially I found my role an uneasy one, primarily because of the policing component implicit in producing compliant, responsible adherents of the school discipline policy' (Reay 1990: 270). Attempts to empower students through providing a forum for their voices are fraught with difficulties (Ellsworth 1992; Orner 1992; Kramer-Dahl 1996).

It is especially so if student voices are regarded as authentic. For as Orner (1992) argues, such a construction of the student voice is grounded in essentialism and ignores the multiplicity of voices with which people speak. Ellsworth (1992) comments on this:

the particularities of historical context, personal biography, and subjectivities split between the conscious and unconscious will necessarily render each expression of student voice partial and predicated on the absence and marginalization of alternative voices. It is impossible to speak from all voices at once, or from any one, without a trace of the others being present and interruptive.

(Ellsworth 1992: 103)

One of the aims of the programmes for boys was to provide them with some understanding of how subjectivities are constructed, and how there are multiple selves and how dominant representations of masculinity serve the interests of social injustice. Any attempt to identify a true self works against this teaching objective, for the notion of an 'authentic voice' implies the existence of an 'authentic self'. Underpinning much of the theory utilized in the boys' programmes researched for this book were assumptions about the historical, social and cultural ways in which masculinized identities are constructed. Thus, the search for an authentic student voice is better replaced by a search for the contradictory voices that construct students' selves and then deconstruct those voices within a context. For example, this can be done by having the boys explore the ways in which they behave in different contexts; by considering the effects of that behaviour on them and on others; and by hypothesizing about the effects of 'different' behaviours in particular contexts.

Rejecting the concept of an 'authentic voice' also helps the boys to understand the contradictory voices with which they engage with gender and violence programmes. One interesting aspect of this contradiction can be the ways in which boys 'comply' with gender programmes in class but not out of the class setting. This contradiction is noted by Reay (1990) following the distribution of a questionnaire to the boys with whom she had been working. This questionnaire examined their attitudes to the programme:

There were no negative comments about the girls not, I am sure, because all the boys had ceased to be sexist. Rather, I feel they had learned something girls learn more readily – to please the teacher. I do not intend to mock them or myself. I genuinely believe, over the year, a relationship of trust and mutual respect had been built up and, as a consequence, the boys were attuned to my needs and sensitive to my feelings in a way they had not been during the autumn term . . . Some, I am sure meant what they wrote. For others, the exercise was much more a process of providing Diane with the answers she wanted.

(Reay 1990: 279)

The contradictory ways in which boys sometimes approach gender and violence issues were also present in the Mountainview programme. One example occurred during the training session provided to the boys who were planning to work with the grade eight boys. One boy who was very articulate about his concerns regarding gender discrimination and who had spoken about the programme to a gathering of educators at the Queensland Governor's residence, made a big point of retelling a sexist story that he had recently heard. This story suggested that feminists sometimes overreact to particular situations. There could have been many reasons for this story, for instance that he just thought it was funny and not sexist; that he wanted to demonstrate that he was still 'one of the boys'; that he wanted to protect masculine privilege from disruptive demands of feminism; or a combination of these. Neither of the voices he used at the Governor's residence nor at the training venue was more authentic than the other. Each has to be interpreted in the social context within which it was heard.

The concept of empowerment is another problematic concept utilized in the critical pedagogy literature (Ellsworth 1992). It is particularly problematic when it relates to the education of boys. Gender equity programmes for girls have often had the 'empowerment' of girls as a central focus. So too have approaches to education that seek to challenge various dominant relations of power. In many ways such approaches make sense when they are being deployed in situations where it is in the students' own interests to challenge those relations of power. Thus, for instance, the concept of empowerment, while problematic for a number of other reasons (Ellsworth 1992; Gore 1992), can legitimately be an important aspect of gender equity programmes for girls. It makes sense to strive to empower girls to resist the oppressions they face, because it is in their interests to challenge existing gendered relations of power. However, such an approach makes less sense when applied to boys.

(Pro)feminist boys' programmes are based on a premise which suggests that the current gendered relations of power favour boys' interests over those of girls. Thus, unlike programmes for girls, boys' programmes are asking the participants to work against their own interests. It would, therefore, seem to be a little paradoxical to be seeking to empower boys in these programmes, for this would amount to an attempt to empower boys to disempower themselves (see Redman 1996). Most boys are aware that (pro)feminist programmes are not about empowering boys. It is this that often precipitates boys' poor behaviour and also makes programmes advocated by men, such as Biddulph and Pollack, which seek to empower boys in order to improve their social positioning within society, more compelling to boys and to those who feel that feminism has made victims of boys.

Despite the existence of oppressions that boys face for reasons other than their gender, empowerment seems to be an inappropriate goal when conducting gender programmes with boys. Such an approach would seem to fit more clearly with that articulated by advocates for therapeutic-type programmes for boys, rather than a (pro)feminist one. It is worth quoting Biddulph here on this:

> What we must do now is make comparable changes in the empowerment of men to those that have begun to happen for women. Most men (and certainly most able and thoughtful men) not only welcomed feminism – many of us grew up envying it, admiring it and working to further its aims. Therein lies the problem. If the most significant social movement of the time is one which does not involve you at all (and in fact excludes you by virtue of some dangly things between your legs), then you are in trouble! What are you supposed to do? The Men's Movement of the Nineties isn't a reaction to the Woman's Movement. **It's the Women's Movement's missing half.**
>
>   (Biddulph 1995: 25, original emphasis)

The notion of empowerment used by Biddulph here implies that boys are trapped within gender roles, rather than engaged in an active negotiation and contestation with gendering discourses. To argue that feminism does not involve men is ludicrous. Feminism has long demanded that men change (Kenway 1996: 447). However, the changes that feminism have asked for are those which involve men giving up their privileged position within gender relations. These do not appear to be those with which Biddulph, and those like him, are concerned. Instead his idea of empowering men would seem to be a means of protecting men's privileges from feminist criticisms.

Other problems also exist with the notion of empowerment. It presupposes that some voices tell the Truth more than others do. It also presupposes that it is the teacher who speaks with such a voice. Thus, there is an implication that the enlightened teacher (perhaps someone like Biddulph) is to be the person who will set the gender-trapped student free. Ellsworth (1992: 98) comments on critical pedagogy in relation to this point:

> The literature explores only one reason for expecting the teacher to 're-learn' an object of study through the student's less adequate understanding, and that is to enable the teacher to devise more effective strategies for bringing the student 'up' to the teacher's level of understanding.

Thus, power is treated as a quality that can be imparted by an empowered person to enable another to be enlightened about a desirable state of affairs (Gore 1992: 56). This also serves to position students in gender and violence programmes as 'the problem'. It does not take account of the teacher's own complicity (especially when the teacher is a man) in maintaining gendered relations of power or of the systemic way in which these relations of power are (re)produced. McLean (1997) makes a very useful comment on this point:

Such approaches are still based on the assumption that adults have all the answers, and that we are capable of giving them to young people. Instead we need to acknowledge that we are part of the problem. Finding answers means first of all looking at ourselves, our assumptions, and the effects we are having on others. The only way we are able to do this is by forming respectful partnerships with the young people we are wanting to help, and being open to the feedback they may be willing to give us.

(McLean 1997: 63)

One of the grade nine students from Tamville, Peter, provides an insightful comment on how students sometimes regard teachers' attempts to moralize about the Truth: 'you can't say, ah, yeah "Violence is wrong" and that because like a lot of us . . . we grow up we like we . . . violence comes in contact with us every day.' This does not mean that teachers should not try to provide students with alternative ways of reading existing relations of power. Rather, it means as Gore (1992: 63) states:

In attempts to empower others we need to acknowledge that our agency has limits, that we might 'get it wrong' in assuming we know what would be empowering for others, and that no matter what our aims or how we go about 'empowering', our efforts will be partial and inconsistent.

Programmes and activities, such as those described by David Denborough (1995, 1996) and Salisbury and Jackson (1996), go a long way towards making this acknowledgement. It is an acknowledgement that takes into account not only the ways in which boys and men are privileged within gendered relations of power, but also the ways in which boys are oppressed within relations of power constructed on the basis of age. Underpinning work founded on this acknowledgement will therefore be an attempt to construct, as suggested by McLean above, respectful relationships with boys in these programmes. I thus argue in the following section that 'respect' ought to be a key feature of programmes in schools that seek to engage boys in schools with an 'exit politics' (Connell 1995a: 220–4).

Towards a respectful pedagogy

The ways in which gender and violence programmes are to be implemented with boys in schools raise numerous problems in relation to pedagogical strategies. The privileged position from which boys operate *as* boys makes the implementation strategies used with girls on gender projects seem inappropriate. Gender equity programmes for girls are usually constructed on the premise that existing gender relations of power work against the interests of women and girls. This means girls' programmes seek to uncover ways in which girls can resist the oppressions they face. Hence, it is in the interests of girls to take on board much of what is contained within such programmes (this is not to deny that powerful hegemonic processes work to ensure that girls comply with dominant constructions of femininity). The converse is the case for boys. (Pro)feminist gender programmes for boys are based on the premise that men and boys are privileged within these same relations of power. Thus, programmes for boys that are based on social justice intentions, rather than masculine style therapies, ask many boys to work against their own interests. This, of course, does not make them overly attractive to a great number of boys. Pedagogical strategies used in boys' programmes need to take this into consideration.

One of the problems of programmes aimed at encouraging boys to engage with an exit politics is that large numbers of boys do not feel privileged. Anti-feminist discourses have been partly to blame for this. However, this situation cannot solely be attributed to the construction of a 'false consciousness'. These discourses do provide a means by which some boys and men can make sense of their lives in the current social context. Many men, and most boys because of their age, experience some type of oppression. What backlash discourses have done has been to gather all of these oppressions together and to conceive of them as a totality derived from a form of gender discrimination. (Pro)feminists working in schools with boys on gender and violence issues will need to address the different ways in which boys are oppressed and to demonstrate how these oppressions are not the product of feminism but of other factors. This means acknowledging the different forms of pain that boys face, while at the same time preventing the source of this pain being identified as feminism. During this process boys need to be given the tools to make sense of the world in ways different from that encouraged by backlash discourses. This is not likely to be an easy task.

Attempts to engage boys with a profeminist masculine politics run into two interrelated and significant stumbling blocks. First, there is little attraction for boys in arguments which suggest that they should consider giving up privileges and the desire to be powerful actors in the social order. Second, the existing social organization of masculinity has ensured that vast numbers of boys in schools feel neither powerful nor privileged. Thus, boys in such programmes are often faced with what they consider to be a contradictory problem: they are being asked to give up a social positioning, which they feel they do not have. Effective boyswork programmes will need to clarify this apparent contradiction.

A (pro)feminist approach to boys' education ought to begin from the premise that in contemporary Western societies boys are members of a privileged group. However, it also needs to recognize that this is not how large numbers of boys feel. For as McLean (1996: 19) has stated: 'One of the central paradoxes of masculinity is that while men, as a group, clearly hold the reins of power, the majority of men experience themselves as powerless.' Many factors work to produce this sense of powerlessness among boys. This powerlessness is not always derived from their identity as a male. For instance, boys experience powerlessness as young people. The hierarchical nature of schools and the positioning of youth in society often work to ensure that young people have little influence in the day-to-day running of their lives. In schools boys, like girls, have every move monitored and they are under constant surveillance as they are expected to conform to the dictates of the education system (Foucault 1977). Society generally constructs youth as irresponsible and of needing to be kept under tight controls. In these instances boys experience oppression not as males but as young males.

A significant source of this powerlessness also stems from the ways in which various forms of masculinity are socially organized. In this organization most boys are happy being boys; they recognize the status that goes with being a man in today's society – hence the use of the term 'girl' or 'woman' as an insult to be deployed against other men and boys. However, a number of factors impact on males to produce hierarchized masculine relationships. In schools, as elsewhere, these factors relate to the extent to which boys can measure up to criteria designated by hegemonic masculinity and its mediation by factors such as class, race/ethnicity, sexuality and age.

Few boys or men can meet the standards constructed as the 'ideal'. Hegemonic versions of masculinity require the performance of particular physical and emotional attributes, characterized by such things as toughness, stoicism and stamina. However, even these attributes are not always enough to guarantee that a man or boy will not experience any form of oppression. For, it is only a few men who are privileged in every sense, that is not only are they male, but also white, middle class, middle aged, heterosexual and able bodied. As Kimmel (1994) has said in relation to American men:

> we've constructed the rules of manhood so that only the tiniest fraction of men come to believe that they are the biggest of wheels, the sturdiest of oaks, the most virulent repudiators of femininity, the most daring and aggressive. We've managed to disempower the overwhelming majority of American men by other means – such as discriminating on the basis of race, class, ethnicity, age or sexual preference.
>
> (Kimmel 1994: 138)

The important point here though is that while most men experience oppression of some form or other they do not experience it because they are men, but because they are particular types of men. The way in which men distribute the patriarchal dividend among themselves thus works to make some boys feel powerless.

The current moment in which masculinity politics are situated is also a contributor to boys' feelings of impotence. For instance, a sense of powerlessness may arise from the oppressive social, cultural, historical and economic conditions that are being produced by a restructured globalized economy. Such an economy is characterized by high youth unemployment and an increase in demand for 'feminized' service sector occupations (Walby 1997). These changing conditions have served to create a perception that many traditional masculine values are being replaced by 'feminized values'. Pat Mahoney (1998) has noted how this presents a difficult challenge for educators:

> on the one hand, in terms of the demands of the labour market, the problem for some boys seems to be that they are not more like girls. It would follow that some masculinities need to change. On the other hand any attempt to critique or transform such masculinities strikes at the heart of the gender regime from which men earn the patriarchal dividend (Connell 1995a: 41).
>
> (Mahony 1998: 47)

Thus, while both boys and girls face many uncertainties in the current social and economic climate, for boys these uncertainties have produced a sense that their privileged positioning, their taken for granted status, in the world is under threat.

Consequently, for many boys the uncertainties they face after school, their experiences of being a young person and of being oppressed on axes other than gender, and confrontations with internal masculinity politics contribute to a contradictory experience of power (Kaufman 1994). Understanding men's contradictory experiences of power is perhaps the key to engaging boys with a profeminist politics. However, acknowledging that there are costs in living up to the masculine ideal is not an easy tasks for boys.

Many boys want to construct themselves as powerful, that is as men who will have the potential to make their mark on the world. There is little status in constructing oneself as a victim. Rather, the status comes from demonstrating a power that has the potential to make others victims (see Chapter 1). Julie, a policy officer with the Queensland Department of Education's Gender Equity Unit, commented on this:

> I think one of the issues, one of the major issues, is that boys have no experience in our culture of looking at masculinity as problematic and of looking at . . . costs or negatives or difficulties associated with being male and a large part of the way that all boys construct their masculinity, no matter what kind of masculinity it is, within that framework of 'my version being the best possible of all versions' of masculinity that could exist. So I think there is that issue. I mean when you start to talk about this stuff to girls it's very easy for girls to identify ways in which they are disadvantaged as a result of being female no matter what their class most girls can find some common ground with each other. But

boys find it very difficult I think to admit that there is anything that is a penalty about being male and extremely difficult to identify any common ground with each other in terms of experiences of negative consequences.

The difficulty in admitting that there are problems associated with being a man may well grow out of the unwillingness to admit that one has failed to acquire the attributes and social status associated with hegemonic masculinity. Ignoring these problems and the uncertainties and pain that they produce will not improve gender relations.

It is important to acknowledge that men and boys experience pain in their lives. However, the pain that many boys feel should not be highlighted at the expense of dealing with issues of power. As Kaufman (1994) has argued power and pain are not separate issues, but interrelated. The pain that boys often feel is the price that some boys pay in order to ensure that patriarchal privileges for males as a 'social group' are maintained. It is, as noted in earlier chapters, a price some boys are prepared to pay in order to gain societal respect. However, there needs to be some discussion about who wins and who loses from the pains and anxieties produced in some boys' pursuit of manly status.

Acknowledging that men and boys experience pain is not the same as asserting that men are an oppressed group (Clatterbaugh 1996). However, this construction has been an attractive way for boys and men to make sense of boys' situations in schools and has consequently opened the way for men's backlash politics to become accessible to those concerned about the well-being of boys. Backlash politics thrive on notions of men's lack of power and men's fear of losing positions of privilege within gendered relations of power. Programmes grounded in these politics tend to focus on, among other things, improving the self-esteem of boys and on minimizing boys' pain without considering the wider patterns of gender relations. In some instances, boys' positioning within society is explained by constructing boys as facing similar oppressions to those faced by girls in earlier times. These approaches to the education of boys are thus usually based on premises that pit boys' interests against those of girls', and more specifically against feminism. In some instances they even draw on the language of feminism to describe men's perceived oppression, hence, ironically, using feminist discourses against feminism. It is perhaps no surprise that men such as Warren Farrell, who in the 1970s were supporters of women's liberation movements, have employed the same liberation discourses to examine the problems of men. Men's liberation discourses provide an avenue for men to pour out their pains and to rail against a system that they believe has caused them so much suffering. Thus, in many instances they acknowledge the danger of some masculinizing practices, such as sport, for both men and those to whom they are close (Pollack 1999). However, at the same time they argue that the oppression of men is synonymous with that faced by women.

Such a stand not only denies the social realities of girls and women, but also contributes to the notion that feminism is irrelevant to men and that similar resources which have been provided to women now need to be contributed to men's issues. The construction of this competition, in which feminists are denoted as the villains, enables men concerned about their pain to identify a causal relationship between the successes of the feminist movement and this pain. Mythopoetic therapeutic approaches to the education of boys do little to challenge this presumption. This presumption enables boys to construct themselves as victims of feminism and thus to attribute a blame to an oppressor, which leaves hegemonic masculinizing practices unproblematic. Indeed the construction of feminism as the enemy enables boys to portray themselves as fighters for men's liberation. This hegemonic representation of a heroic warrior masculinity has found its niche in much of the men's mythopoetic literature. The dangers of this approach to the education of boys, for girls, women and 'othered' boys and men, are obvious. For example, the construction of men as warriors of any sort opens the door to legitimizing violent masculinities.

However, there are ways in which men can respond to the existence of men's pains and anxieties without seeking to contain feminist demands. Such responses require not looking back to some mythical past in order to resurrect a distant esoteric masculinity, but looking forward to creating more positive, sensitive and just ways of being men. In order to create these opportunities the existing social, political and economic environments that boys inhabit need to be acknowledged. Thus, as Friedman (1995), who is concerned that boys' programmes be delivered in a respectful manner, suggests such programmes should 'start from where the student is at' (1995: 15). This is perhaps more difficult than it seems. Boys in schools have not been unaffected by a masculinist reading of the 'what about the boys?' discourse. Thus, many boys see themselves as victims of feminism. Paradoxically, however, many also seek to construct themselves as powerful agents in the world.

Teachers delivering gender and violence programmes with boys will have to deal with the reality that a number of boys are unlikely to be willing participants. For as McLean (1997: 61) has argued: 'The power of masculine meaning systems ensures that men tend to hear even the most gentle criticism as an attack, and this is strongly reinforced by the mainstream media's continued portrayal of feminism in cliched, confrontational terms.' In order to avoid coercive practices, some implementers of boys' programmes only deliver their programmes to students who have not been coerced into participating (Denborough 1995, 1996). This is one way of heading off resistances to the programme, and the attempt to respect students' 'rights' is commendable. However, in only working with volunteers opportunities can be missed. For example, as mentioned in the previous chapter, many of the Mountainview grade 12 boys who in the early days of their programme were very disruptive and resistant to its aims were later instrumental in constructing a similar programme for the grade eight boys in their school. Indeed, their work with the grade eights was stimulated out of hostility to their own programme. At the same time, though, it is important not to contribute to the sense of powerlessness many boys feel, or to contribute to their antagonism towards feminism by taking an authoritarian approach to the teaching of these issues or by ignoring the issues that many boys face. Furthermore, as young males they cannot be held fully accountable for existing gendered relations of power. For as Denborough (1995) has indicated:

> Education of the young is always seen as the first response to any global problem. I suspect this is not because it is the most effective means of social change, but because it is the easiest. Often such a perspective abdicates adults' responsibilities for change, and is used to justify the lecturing of young people about the 'correct' ways of living. In many cases, such an approach simply makes young people feel more powerless, and is a perpetuation of injustice.
>
> (Denborough 1995: 78)

Denborough suggests that an approach which takes account of boys' privileged positioning in the world while recognizing the systemic nature of gendered violence is one that is founded on respect. I agree with this. Boys need to be made aware of the advantages that they accrue as a part of being a male, and of the increased patriarchal dividend they will receive once they become men. However, a politics of blame needs to be avoided. Such an approach will surely work to immobilize boys who already feel powerless. Respectful practices will work to demonstrate that men have a collective responsibility to tackle issues of gender injustice. This means that the male teachers working in these programmes will have to acknowledge their own complicity in maintaining the existing gender order and that other involved teachers will have to make themselves as vulnerable as they are expecting the boys to make themselves.

The preparedness of male teachers to listen and respond to feminism in ways that demonstrate their respect for feminism while also treating the students with respect will serve to transmit to students the teachers' concerns with justice. Justice needs to be a central concern of the ways in which teachers implement these programmes. The notion of justice can quite clearly be linked to a concern with 'reciprocal respect' (Yeatman 1995b: 202). Reciprocal respect in this instance means not denying the ways in which girls and women have been differently situated within existing gender relations and not ignoring the ways in which differences between men have served to create unjust relations of power in the social organization of masculinity. One of these unjust relations of power is founded on age. Teachers must remember this. However, male students will not always experience oppression because of their youth. They will one day be men. Creating a more just gender society will require that these men have the skills and tools with which to subvert the existing gender order.

Conclusion

This chapter has focused on pedagogical problems facing (pro)feminist boyswork programmes. These have included issues of male teachers and insider/outsider dynamics in schools. In each of these the spectre of men's rights and mythopoetic discourses have hovered around. Males do need to be involved in the anti-sexist education of boys. It is our responsibility. Men reap many privileges simply by being men; therefore it is up to men to challenge the legitimacy of this social arrangement. This is a social justice issue.

However, if men are working with boys as a means of inducting them into some form of 'true' masculinity (whether it be a mythopoetic or a men's rights formulation of a 'true' man) then the social justice aspects of masculinity politics are likely to become buried beneath concerns about the well-being of men. Social justice may even be turned on its head by arguments which claim that men are discriminated against too. This of course begs the question: 'By whom?' The implicit assumption is no doubt by women, or more specifically by feminists. This competition with women, which seeks to prove the substantial damages inflicted on men by an uncaring society, has the potential to derail much of the feminist gains made during the past three decades.

Unfortunately the politics of men such as Biddulph, Fletcher, Kindlon and Thompson, Gurian, and Pollack are often reflected in the work of men getting into schools under a 'what about the boys?' banner. The argument that boys are oppressed too is an attractive one for those not prepared to give up masculine privileges. Using the frequency and nature of boys' behavioural problems to justify their work with boys is attractive to school administrators, teachers and those anxious about their children's safety at school. Their claims that they are not opposed to equality for girls serves to alleviate the concerns of some who do not want to see the gains of feminism restricted by programmes for boys. However, unless these advocates for men pay attention to matters of justice, improvements in existing gender relations are unlikely.

The problem of mythopoetic and men's rights men coming into schools should not be a deterrent to bringing people in from outside the school to teach boys. There is much that feminist and profeminist community agencies and individuals can offer schools, especially given the increasing workloads of teachers in a schooling system constantly trying to do more with less.

Perhaps the screening process that is being advocated by the Queensland Department of Education's Gender Equity Unit is an appropriate means of ensuring that the damaging influences of such men as Pollack and Biddulph are kept out of schools. However, there is always the danger that screening processes may be used against (pro)feminist programmes. The conservative desire to keep 'politics' out of schools is far more likely to impact on feminists and profeminists who have a stated political agenda than it is on some mythopoetic programmes that have a 'therapeutic' agenda.

Consideration also needs to be given to the teaching skills of those coming into schools. There was recognition in both of the schools mentioned in this book that any programme that sought to influence the gendered behaviour of boys needed to be conducted over at least a period of one term. This meant that the presenters had to have some pedagogical skills in working with young people. It is possible that these skills can be developed 'on the job'. However, underpinning the development of these skills there has to be a pedagogical approach, which is founded on principles of respect.

Critical pedagogy is a form of teaching that seeks to do this. However, there are a number of problems with this approach, especially in relation to men teaching boys about gender and violence issues. Critical pedagogy's emphasis on negotiating authority is important in the sense that men using didactic forms of teaching serve to legitimate domination as a means of securing one's will. However, as we experienced, attempts to create non-oppressive environments in which boys' voices may be heard can provide spaces where homophobia and misogyny are difficult to contain. In these situations, critical pedagogy's aim of empowering students seems inappropriate. Indeed, empowerment in this sense fits more comfortably with a therapeutic politics than it does with a (pro)feminist politics. The goal of 'empowerment' is also problematic in that it implies that the student is the problem and that the teacher (or adult) has the means to fix them up. In this sense empowerment denies aspects of the power relationships operating between adults and young people, and the students' experiences of that and other power relationships. Recognizing this does not mean that boys should not be challenged about harmful attitudes and behaviours when they are expressed. However, nor does it mean that they should be treated as knowing nothing and the teacher everything. Respect recognizes the privileged position from which boys are situated within gendered relations *and* is aware of how boys may be oppressed on other axes of power.

Strategies for schools

Within a school there will be a range of experiences and skills when it comes to working on gender issues, especially in relation to boys and violence. It will be important to know what resources are within the school to assist in the work with boys in the school. This knowledge will enable a determination of what assistance will be needed from outside the school and what is available from within. Thought will also have to be given to the roles that male teachers within the school play in relation to challenging or reinforcing dominant constructions of masculinity.

- There are probably a range of skills and knowledges that exist among your colleagues. What are some of these? What other skills and knowledges are needed? Are there community organizations, education department officers, university academics or other interested parties who can be called on to offer advice or assistance to the group or to work with boys in your school?
- If you are going to use 'outsiders' in your work check their credentials. What are their views on feminism? Why do they think boys tend to be more violent than girls? What are their views on female teachers working with boys? How do they account for differences among boys?
- How can these 'outsiders' provide support, in the form of being a 'critical friend' to a school, which is lasting rather than simply delivering a one-off programme/lecture/workshop to either students or teachers.
- In working with boys, provide them with opportunities to explore the multiple ways of being a boy. How can individual teachers do this? Are some of the activities from the 'strategies for schools' sections of Chapters 1 and 2 useful here? What are the advantages/disadvantages of working with boys on their own? Are there times when it is useful to construct single sex classes? Should a male or female teacher take these lessons? What are girls going to be doing while boys are engaged in this work?
- Many boys who will be engaging in this work will feel either oppressed or powerless. Think about the particular boys you will be working with. Who is likely to feel this way? Why? Make a list of all of the reasons why a boy might feel that he is powerless in a system that favours boys. What does this mean for gender programmes encouraging boys to reject violence as a legitimate means of solving problems. Make a list of all the advantages that are likely to accrue to boys, girls, the school and community if boys as a group take up this position. What will you say to a boy who asks, 'What's in it for me?'?
- How will behaviour issues be addressed in these and other classes? Is it possible to correct behaviours without reinforcing 'might is right' approaches to conflict resolution?
- What about male teachers in the school? Are there male teachers who are prepared to engage in this kind of work who to date have not been involved? How can these teachers be incorporated into strategies designed to challenge boys' violent behaviours? Are there male teachers who are likely to inhibit change? What strategies can be employed to defuse their resistance?

- Start developing an action plan. What are the priority areas for challenging violence in the school? Who needs to be the focus of work on violence? What are some small steps which can be taken now? Where in the school should this work be initiated? Who will be conducting this work? When can this work be done? Where has this school been successful to date in its work with challenging violence in the school? What have been the inhibitors to change? What are some longer term aims that need to be developed? What projects can be set in place to satisfy some of these aims? Who will be responsible for particular tasks necessary to effect some of these long-term projects? Include within the plan a time frame that provides for reflections and evaluation of achievements and problems.

chapter / **five**

Conclusion: principles for action

In the past few years I have been invited into schools on a regular basis to speak to groups of teachers about boys. In some cases I have been asked to respond to the current panic about boys' academic results, in others about boys' behaviour and sometimes specifically about violence. In each instance I raise issues of homophobia and misogyny. I note how homophobic and misogynist discourses work to valorize forms of masculinity that cause boys to be problems to both themselves and others within the school. I also suggest that feminism offers some solutions to these 'problems'.

When I raise these issues I always know that some teachers are going to respond negatively. They want to hear about the ways in which boys have been made victims. They want to be informed about how the perceived gender imbalances favouring girls can be addressed. Many in this group argue that theories about the construction of gender deny the importance of biology in shaping boys' and girls' behaviours. It has even been stated that I am trying to turn boys into girls. This group of teachers are usually the ones who have come to the session expecting to have their views on the excesses of feminism reinforced. In most instances they go away disappointed.

There is always another group of teachers who respond quite differently. I often notice these teachers nodding their heads quite vigorously when I speak of gender construction and gender policing. These are the teachers who are only too well aware of the ways in which boys often utilize homophobic and misogynist abuse to control each other and to put down girls (and sometimes teachers). They are also the ones who want to hear about class and race issues. They know that there are boys in their classes who are doing well and girls who are not. They want questions of 'Which boys?' and 'Which girls?' addressed. And, they also want to talk about harassment, bullying and violence *and* boys.

However, one thing that some members of each group often have in common is that they want to be told what to do 'period one Monday morning' to solve the problem. This is, of course, one of the attractions of many of the current crop of boys' books. In many of these books there are concrete examples of what schools and teachers can do to improve the lives of boys. However, there are no definitive solutions or 'ten-point plans' to solve these issues. Changing gender patterns and relations is a long-term process that will require major cultural shifts. This is not an impossible task. Such cultural shifts can take place, and schools can be one important site where these shifts can be initiated and/or reinforced. Hence, in this last chapter, while I do not attempt to provide a quick fix solution to the problem of gender and violence in schools, I want to offer a number of principles that can be integrated into work in schools which will help to create the cultural shifts necessary to minimize boys' violences. These ten principles will hopefully satisfy some of the issues raised by the above two groups of teachers. They take into account the disadvantages some boys face and the harm that they do themselves, while at the same time there is a recognition of the extent to which boys oppress others.

1 Reject the competing victim syndrome

Any work being done with boys in schools will have to confront the existence of a backlash politics, which is shaping much of the gender agenda within schools. Backlash politics work to construct men as the victims of feminism. These politics work on the presumption that feminist agendas have been too successful, and that as a result boys and men are being oppressed by a society which now prioritizes the interests of girls and women over those of boys and men. This presumption is clearly fallacious. Many boys are doing very well at school. Many girls are not. Questions regarding which girls and which boys need to be asked. Issues of poverty and race/ethnicity also need to be addressed. Thus, for instance, those concerned about the ways in which academic achievements are distributed in their schools and the relationships of such with particular constructions of masculinity, will need to engage in thorough data collection, which disaggregates results on factors other than gender. Consideration should also be given to the post-school pathways of their students.

Such research will most likely demonstrate that backlash arguments about the claims of boys' underachievement have been vastly overstated, it will probably also reveal that there are disproportionate numbers of boys *and* girls from marginalized backgrounds not doing well at school. However, in some instances, for example in literacy, it will probably become apparent that as a group boys are doing less well than girls from similar socioeconomic and race/ethnic backgrounds. In many of these instances, gendering processes, or more precisely masculinizing processes, are intersecting with other factors such as class and ethnicity/race to produce a particular masculine relationship to schooling. These processes need to be understood in relation to boys' engagement with schooling. Questions like the following have to be asked: 'How do dominant masculinizing practices negatively impact on those boys who are performing them?'; 'How do these practices impact on others in the school?'; 'How are the impacts different for girls, boys, students from the non-dominant culture and so on?'; and 'Who benefits most from such practices?'

It is perhaps by asking questions such as these that dominant masculinizing processes, which harm both boys and others in their lives, can be addressed within a framework that does not draw on backlash arguments. Such a process will benefit both those boys who are experiencing school failure *and* also those boys and girls who are being hurt by the violent behaviours of some boys.

2 Work to understand boys' violences as a masculinity issue

In many of the concerns raised about violence in schools, masculinity as a problematic concept is seldom raised. This has to change. In many schools there are cultures where dominant masculinizing processes have a clear identifiable link with violence. Teachers and community workers conducting work with boys on violence issues need to have some understanding of the ways in which these processes operate to normalize boys' violences. Furthermore, recognition has to be given to how these violences are deployed in ways that shore up masculine privilege and create a hierarchy of masculinities. As such they should not be regarded as the playing out of individual pathological behaviours. Nor should such violences be seen as the product of boys' 'nature'. Instead boys' violence should be treated as systemic acts of injustice that preserve existing relations of power. Thus, work with boys on issues of gender and violence requires a focus on the ways in which violence, domination and oppression are implicated in the construction of an idealized masculinity.

This idealized, or hegemonic, representation of masculinity is signified by the traditional forms of work men and boys do, the popular sports they play, and the extent to which they can demonstrate power over women and other men. This construction of a homogenous natural masculinity works to delegitimize those forms of masculinity that do not conform to this ideal. Further, these signifiers of masculinity work to legitimate violence as a masculine property. Masculinity has been violenced and violence masculinized. The relationships between these signifiers of hegemonic masculinity and violence and the ways in which practices within schools reinforce this relationship need to be disrupted if there is going to be a significant reduction of the amounts of violence within schools.

3 Explore the social organization of masculinity operating within the gender regime of the school

The notion of men as a homogeneous category found in backlash, and other, discourses serves to deny the complex ways in which masculinities are hierarchized within a social organization of masculinity. Attempts to understand how this operates at the school level will entail an exploration of the pressures and costs boys face in terms of conforming to a particular representation of 'proper' masculine behaviour. Hegemonic masculinity is clearly related to a man's access to violence and other forms of coercive power. In the pursuit of such status, many boys have to pay a cost, a cost that may involve harming one's own body or damaging one's emotional well-being. In many instances it is a cost boys, and men, are often willing to pay in return for the privileges such status carries with it.

However, men who are able to measure up against the standards of hegemonic masculinity are not necessarily the most powerful nor the most privileged in society. Many of the men who acquire this status experience significant presures on other, non-gendered, axes of oppression, for example race/ethnicity and class. When the actual performance of an individualized violence is combined with particular class or racialized categories, such performances might act to signify, for example, working-class young men as 'savage'. It is perhaps no coincidence that disproportionate numbers of working-class boys can be found in detention rooms, in remedial reading rooms, in school football teams and on suspension lists.

Hence, while violence works on the one hand to signify men's superiority over women, in excess and when shaped through other lenses combined with gender, violence works to legitimize some men's positioning within a masculine hierarchy. Some men benefit more than other men do from gendered power relations. However, those who benefit least do not do so because they are simply men, but because they are being oppressed as a consequence of being particular types of men. Issues of race/ethnicity, class and sexuality and the ways in which these marginalize particular masculinities also need to be on the agenda. In recent times, matters of class and race/ethnicity have been largely washed away among concerns about boys in schools. Along with a concern about the education of girls, they need to be brought back into a much shaper focus, and in particular the ways in which they inflect gender need to be explored.

Some boys' complicity in maintaining the gender order also needs to be considered. These are the boys who are never violent, who often do not have the same social status within a school community as those performing hegemonic masculinities, but who are seldom the recipients of violence. In many ways such boys reap a greater share of the 'patriarchal dividend' than do many boys who perform hegemonic forms of masculinity. These boys often do not take the same risks to prove their manhood that are required of those boys performing hegemonic masculinities. Hence, they do not engage in behaviours that are likely to endanger their physical safety; they are less likely to be found in special needs classes; and are less likely to be suspended from school. Their behaviours seldom have a direct impact on girls or other boys. Although, in some instances, such boys can shore up their masculine privileges by pointing to the hypermasculine behaviours of some boys as proof that boys belong to the physically 'superior sex'. However, it is their silences about other boys' behaviours that is of most concern. Such silences clearly support a context that allows some boys' violences to thrive. These silences need to be understood.

Boys' silences about violence against girls and against other boys can have a number of sources. For instance, silence protects privilege. For many boys there are no rewards associated with challenging a regime which serves to demonstrate the superiority of their sex over that of females. Furthermore, as boys who do not experience violence, the existence of violence against 'other' boys also serves to demonstrate their more valued position within the existing social organization of masculinity. However, it is not only privilege that prevents some boys from speaking out against other boys' violences, but also fear. Boys speaking out against violence often make themselves traitors to their gender. The role of homophobia has to be acknowledged in the production of this fear.

4 Confront homophobia as a matter of priority

Homophobia is a key gender policing discourse which serves to ensure that not too many boys challenge the existing gender order. Many boys quoted throughout this book spoke of how it was only after having been involved in fights that their peers had accepted them. An active avoidance of such behaviours or speaking out against them has the potential to stigmatize a boy as 'gay'. Homophobia works to ensure that both heterosexual and homosexual boys who do not conform to the requirements of hegemonic masculinity always have the potential to be subordinated within the social organization of masculinity. The fear of this happening leads many boys to become complicit in maintaining existing gendered power relations. Consequently, as Epstein (1997: 113) has argued, 'misogyny and homophobia are not merely linked but are so closely intertwined as to be inseparable: misogyny is homophobic and homophobia is misogynist.'

Many in schools are often reluctant to tackle the issue of homophobia (see Epstein 1994; Boulden 1996; Mills 1996). However, if work with boys on rejecting violent masculine performances is to have any success at all then tackling homophobia has to be seen as a key strategy. The silences that many in schools try to enforce around this topic are a major barrier to counteracting hegemonic masculinizing processes. Homophobia is a very real presence in boys' lives. Most boys interviewed for this book stated how they would find it difficult to discuss with their friends many of the issues covered throughout the programmes. This difficulty arose from their fear of being thought gay. At the same time many of the same boys who would have liked to discuss the issues had a strong disliking of homosexuals. For anti-violence work with boys to have any great success, processes that acknowledge the presence of homophobia in schools and identify it as an unacceptable form of harassment have to be set in motion. This will require significant changes in the ways in which schools have tended to deal with homophobia. For as Julie, the principal policy officer with the Gender Equity Unit, points out:

> I think schools on the whole do not deal with the issue of homophobia at all . . . I think one of the reasons is that they don't register it for a start, and I think when they hear the sorts of homophobic things kids say the response is usually in terms of an attack upon the obscenity rather than on the fact that it is a denigration of an individual or a denigration of a group of people within a society. I think that there are a whole lot of people in schools who are homophobic themselves you know who . . . in schools the notion of, just as in the broader community, the notion of paedophilia and homosexuality is still a very common conflation . . . I think that teachers just don't, don't see how that language is involved in constructing gender and maintaining gender boundaries.

In dealing with issues of homophobia it cannot be left to adults to assume that boys can do this on their own. There needs to be an awareness in schools of the safety issues facing boys (and others) when they confront issues of masculinized violence and privileges. They are being asked to engage in behaviours that may have dangerous consequences for them. Thus, not only do structures within schools need to be set up which serve to identify homophobic practices as gendered harassment, but structures are also required to provide boys with support for adopting counter-hegemonic subject positions (such structures should, of course, also be set up in relation to anti-lesbianism). These structures are important for both girls and boys. Homophobia works to (re)produce unjust relations of power between the social groups of 'men' and 'women', and also between men.

5 Explore boys' sense of powerlessness within a context of privilege

The marginalization and subordination of many men and boys within the current social organization of masculinity ensures that many men and boys do not feel powerful despite the ways in which the gender order favours the social group of 'men'. Consequently, the focus on men's and boys' senses of powerlessness within many backlash discourses has served to ensure that these discourses strike a chord with substantial numbers of men (and some women). However, men feeling neither powerful nor privileged is not a new state of affairs. Historically, large numbers of boys and men have felt, and quite rightly so, oppressed or powerless. This, though, is not because of their sex, but because of their positioning within other relations of power. Power and privilege are determined by contexts. In those contexts where class, ethnicity/race, sexuality, age and physical abilities shape social and political interactions many men are not privileged. For instance, it is difficult to see how Aboriginal men in a colonial society such as Australia could be considered as privileged. However, their lack of privilege is derived from their positioning in society as Aboriginal men not simply because they are men. Attempts to understand this sense of powerlessness within a context of privilege need to be a core aspect of any work done with boys.

Exploring the complex ways in which various oppressions interlock and weave together is perhaps a useful starting point here. This will undermine backlash arguments, which tend to amalgamate all the oppressions men face as particular types of men under a gender discrimination banner. These oppressions are represented by statistics which denote, for example, rates of imprisonment, deaths in the workplace, suicides, literacy levels, murder victims and school suspensions. In the gathering together of these oppressions men are constructed as a unitary group who are all similarly disadvantaged. However, as argued throughout this book, if indicators denoting disadvantage are replaced be signifiers of privilege, for example, ownership of the means of production, membership of powerful organizations, representation in national and state governing bodies, and so on, to determine who is most privileged in society, it would become apparent that it is not women as a social group who are benefiting from men's experiences of oppression. Boys have to be made aware of this.

However, in creating this awareness students need to be treated with respect. This will mean rejecting a politics of blame where the agency of students is exaggerated to the point of ignoring the pressures facing them. In working with students in schools it is often too easy to identify them as the problem. The problem is bigger than the students (Denborough 1995: 79). There is thus, as Fitzclarence (1993) has argued, a need for a collective ownership of the behaviours, which represent the negative aspects of our culture. This is important. Adults in schools need to acknowledge their own complicity in maintaining existing gender relations. This is especially true for male teachers working on gender issues. Perhaps a way of doing this is to reflect on the times when we have stayed silent on issues of gender and violence because we were too scared, intimidated or embarrassed to say anything.

Reflections such as these can help male teachers acknowledge the fears and anxieties we face as adults in confronting these issues in certain contexts. Further, they will enable us to acknowledge our own privileges and the extent to which they are protected by the collective silences of men.

These acknowledgments will also assist us in treating boys with respect by considering how much harder it is for boys to 'step out of line' given the levels of homophobic abuse present in most schools; by not treating boys as *the* problem; and by recognizing the significance of creating a school context that is supportive of difference and involves students in the decision-making structures of the school.

6 Encourage male teachers to take responsibility for their privilege but do not exclude female teachers from the process of 'educating' boys on gender and violence issues

Dominant readings of the 'what about the boys?' discourse draw heavily on mythopoetic concerns that stress the need for male role models and for a more male-centred education system to improve boys' self-esteem. In this book I have stressed the importance of men owning up to the privileged positions from which they operate in gendered relations of power. As part of this owning up process I have suggested that men need to actively engage with a politics which seeks to undermine their privileged positions in the existing gender order. One aspect of that engagement, for male teachers, can be effected through working with boys on issues that problematize the relationship between hegemonic masculinity and violence. This is not because boys *need* men. My argument for men's involvement with boys on these issues springs not from a belief that women are less able than men to conduct such work, but from a belief that they should not have to.

However, while women should not have to do this work, there are some potential dangers associated with this type of work being done in homosocial environments. There is evidence to suggest that such environments are not conducive to boys or men challenging their own privileges, and there has often been a tendency in these situations for boys and men to solely focus on their own oppressions. Thus, in many instances there will be a need for male teachers working in such programmes to draw on the knowledges of their female colleagues. Boys need to hear girls' and female teachers' viewpoints on many of the issues associated with change. Men's struggles to create a more gender just world by working with boys on gender and violence issues are intertwined with women's struggles in this area. This should not be forgotten.

7 Be informed about any outside agencies before allowing them to work with boys on gender issues

Arguments relating to whether or not male teachers should conduct gender and violence programmes for boys are irrelevant in many schools. There is often a lack of male teachers in schools who are prepared to take on this task. In many cases this has led to schools interested in these issues drawing on people external to the school to conduct work in this area. This was the case at both Tamville and Mountainview. However, as indicated in this book, there are potential problems associated with such an approach.

One problem with drawing on outside agencies is the extent to which men conducting work in schools on masculinity issues are prepared to be accountable to feminists. Many of those who work in schools in this area, and whose work influences others' work in schools, see feminism as having little relevance to boys. In some cases this is quite explicit (Biddulph 1995, 1997; Fletcher 1995a), in others there is simply a silence about the relevance of feminism to work with boys (Pollack 1999). There is a danger that assumptions about the importance of men working with boys will lead schools into situations where they bring such men into the school to work with boys. This will do little to challenge existing gendered relations of power. A positive engagement with feminism is required by men working in schools in order to recognize the ways in which boys' and men's violence against girls, women and each other is an integral element in the policing of existing gendered relations of power. Hence, detailed outlines on the principles underpinning programmes provided by outside agencies should be obtained prior to them being invited into the school.

8 Don't rely on quick fix-it programmes

The introduction of (pro)feminist gender and violence programmes into schools does not occur without problems. It is not enough to assume that by introducing such programmes into the curriculum that the school is adequately dealing with the problem of gendered violence. There are no quick fix-it solutions to this problem. Schools' problems with gender-based violence are not of their own making; the construction of hegemonic representations of masculinity occur in numerous contexts, not just in schools. It would be foolhardy to think that an eight-week programme conducted through marginalized areas of the school curriculum is going to effect a significant disruption to the dominance of these representations of masculinity. These types of programmes can only introduce students to alternative discourses with which they might be able to make sense of their world.

In order to achieve more, schools will have to support students in engaging with an 'exit politics'. This will involve paying attention to change processes throughout the school. For instance, looking at the ways in which schools implement discipline strategies and the extent to which teachers' behaviours legitimate/disrupt existing gendered relations of power could be important steps in the process of devalorizing particular masculinities. In most instances, administrative support will be crucial in implementing significant changes. This does not mean that the process cannot start small. The manner in which the programme at Mountainview evolved, for example, where the principal and other school administrators were very supportive, points to some of the possibilities that can be opened up through personal development-type programmes. In this instance the programme went beyond the classroom and took on a life of its own. What was significant here was the way in which the school staff enabled the students to own the programme, thereby encouraging teachers and their students to momentarily engage with an exit politics.

9 *Any work done with boys in schools should be conducted within a framework that does not forget the importance of addressing vast inequalities and injustices in the lives of girls*

In much of the work being done with boys in schools there is little recognition given to the importance of doing gender equity work with girls. For instance, in relation to problematizing masculinity in the classroom, there needs to be a consideration of female students. In many countries and states the current curriculum is shaped around masculine interests, and female students are constantly being forced to participate in curriculum topics that have males as their focus. How, then, can masculinity be made an issue within the classroom without perpetuating this? A central feature of the patriarchal gender order has been the silencing of the voices of women/girls. Attempts to challenge hegemonic forms of masculinity through the curriculum will have to make spaces for women and girls to speak and to create opportunities for those voices to be heard.

There also needs to be a revaluing of gendered areas of the curriculum. This will mean emphasizing the value of currently feminized aspects of the curriculum, such as the social sciences and modern languages, for both girls and boys. This will serve to provide greater value to 'women's knowledges' and thus to value what girls do. In addition, the social skills and social critiques provided by this part of the curriculum will provide boys with useful skills and knowledges about their places in the world. It will provide many boys with some of the skills they need to operate successfully within a changing post-industrial society. Also, it will hopefully, but of course not necessarily, provide boys with an opportunity to challenge some of their dominant assumptions about masculinity.

The currently masculinized areas of the curriculum should be acknowledged as being the source of providing privileged post-school pathways. Any barriers to girls entering these areas of the curriculum because such access upsets boys' 'sense of entitlement' should be identified and challenged. Boys have to be made aware that nothing belongs to them simply because they are a boy. As part of this process, such areas of the curriculum need to integrate feminist understandings and critiques of their current structure and content bases. This will ensure that such subjects are made more 'girl friendly' and also that boys who avoid the more feminized areas of the curriculum are exposed to ideas and ways of seeing the world that do not always conform to dominant viewpoints.

10 Don't be afraid to use the word 'feminism'

Throughout many of the recent group of books on boys, feminism is seldom mentioned except in relation to the gains it has enabled girls to make in the education system. The same silences around the word often exist within schools, it is as if it was a 'dirty word'. This is evident in some situations where the term 'feminist' is used in a derogatory way to describe the actions of any woman who raises gender issues within a school (Gilbert and Gilbert 1998: 241). This is unfortunate. Feminisms have much to offer schools in the way of providing valuable insights into the lives of both girls and boys. Indeed, feminist work ought to underpin the approaches utilized with boys on gender and violence issues. The continued antipathy towards the word will only ensure that the interests of girls and boys are continually pitted against each other.

These ten principles can be integrated into any number of projects, programmes, practices and processes within a school. There is no blueprint for change. There is also no linear change pattern. Disrupting the relationships between masculinity and violence can begin anywhere within a school, for example, within the curriculum, through pedagogical reforms or structural changes and so on. The important thing is that such disruptions occur. For too long the relationships between masculinities and violence have gone unchallenged within too many schools. This has harmed many girls and women, and some boys. Greater gender justice in schools requires that this situation changes.

References

Aldred, D. and Butler, G. (1996) Men and young shun teaching, principals told, *Courier Mail*, 5 October.

Althusser, L. (1972) Ideology and ideological state apparatuses: 'Notes towards an investigation', in B. Costin (ed.) *Education: Structure and Society*. Harmondsworth: Penguin.

Altman, D. (1971) *Homosexual Oppression and Liberation*. New York: New York University Press.

Ang, I. (1995) I'm a feminist but . . . 'Other' women and postnational feminism, in B. Caine and R. Pringle (eds) *Transitions: New Australian Feminisms*. St Leonards: Allen & Unwin.

Apple, M. (1988) Social crisis and curriculum accords, *Education Theory*, 38(2): 191–201.

Apter, T. (1993) *Working Women Don't Have Wives: Professional Issues in the 1990's*. New York: St Martin's Press.

Arnot, M. (1984) How shall we educate our sons?, in R. Deem (ed.) *Co-education Reconsidered*. Milton Keynes: Open University Press.

Askew, S. and Ross, C. (1988) *Boys Don't Cry: Boys and Sexism in Education*. Milton Keynes: Open University Press.

Baird, J. (1999) Killing pranks in 7 schools, *Sydney Morning Herald*, 14 May.

Bart, P. and Moran, E. (1993) Introduction, in P. Bart and E. Moran (eds) *Violence Against Women: The Bloody Footprints*. Newbury Park: Sage.

Bartell, R. (1994) Victim of a victimless crime: Ritual and resistance, in D. Epstein (ed.) *Challenging Lesbian and Gay Inequalities in Education*. Buckingham: Open University Press.

Beasley, C. (1994) *Sexual Economyths: Conceiving a Feminist Economics*. New South Wales: Allen & Unwin.

Bhattacharyya, G. (1994) Offence is the best defence? – Pornography and racial violence, in C. Brant and Yun Lee Too (eds) *Rethinking Sexual Harassment*. London: Pluto Press.

Biddulph, S. (1995) *Manhood: An Action Plan for Changing Men's Lives*, 2nd edn. Sydney: Finch.

Biddulph, S. (1997) *Raising Boys*. Sydney: Finch.

Bloody toll world's worst (1996) *Courier Mail*, 29 April.

Bly, R. (1991) *Iron John: A Book about Men*. Dorset: Element.

Bordo, S. (1998) My father the feminist, in T. Digby (ed.) *Men Doing Feminism*. New York: Routledge.

Boulden, K. (1996) Keeping a straight face: Schools, students and homosexuality – Part 2, in L. Laskey and C. Beavis (eds) *Schooling and Sexualities: Teaching for a Positive Sexuality*. Geelong: Deakin University.

Bourdieu, P. (1998) *Practical Reason*. Cambridge: Polity Press.

Bourdieu, P. and Wacquant, L. (1992) *An Introduction to Reflexive Sociology*. Cambridge: Polity Press.

Bowles, S. and Gintis, H. (1976) *Schooling in Capitalist America: Educational Reform and the Contradictions of Economic Life*. London: Routledge & Kegan Paul.

Boys need a father figure to do well (1999) *The Times*, 12 November.

Braidotti, R. (1987) Envy: Or with your brains and my looks, in A. Jardine and P. Smith (eds) *Men in Feminism*. New York: Methuen.

Brant, C. and Yun Lee Too (1994) Introduction, in C. Brant and Yun Lee Too (eds), *Rethinking Sexual Harassment*. London: Pluto Press.

Brod, H. (1994) Some thoughts on some histories of some masculinities: Jews and other others, in H. Brod and M. Kaufman (eds) *Theorizing Masculinities*. Thousand Oaks, CA: Sage.

Browne, R. (1995) Schools and the construction of masculinity, in R. Browne and R. Fletcher (eds) *Boys in Schools: Addressing the Real Issues – Behaviour, Values and Relationships*. Sydney: Finch.

Brownmiller, S. (1976) *Against Our Will: Men, Women and Rape*. Harmondsworth: Penguin.

Bryson, L. (1987) Sport and the maintenance of masculine hegemony, *Women's Studies International Forum*, 10(4): 349–60.

Bryson, L. (1988) Women as welfare recipients: Women poverty and the state, in C. Baldock and B. Cass (eds) *Women, Social Welfare and the State*. Sydney: Allen & Unwin.

Buchbinder, D. (1994) *Masculinities and Identities*. Melbourne: Melbourne University Press.

Budge, D. (1998) Man's class 'helps boys', *Times Educational Supplement*, 20 February (www.tes.co.uk).

Burbank, V. (1994) *Fighting Women: Anger and Aggression in Aboriginal Australia*. Berkeley, CA: University of California Press.

Burstyn, V. (1999) *The Rites of Men: Manhood, Politics, and the Culture of Sport*. Toronto: University of Toronto Press.

Butler, J. (1996) The poof paradox: Homonegativity and silencing in three Hobart schools, in L. Laskey and C. Beavis (eds) *Schooling and Sexualities: Teaching for a Positive Sexuality*. Geelong: Deakin University.

Cannan, J. (1996) 'One thing leads to another': Drinking, fighting and working-class masculinities, in M. Mac an Ghaill (ed.) *Understanding Masculinities: Social Relations and Cultural Arenas*. Buckingham: Open University Press.

Cannan, J. and Griffin, C. (1990) The new men's studies: Part of the problem or part of the solution?, in J. Hearn and D. Morgan (eds) *Men, Masculinities and Social Theory*. London: Unwin Hyman.

Carrington, V., Mills, M. and Roulston, K. (2000) A feel for the game: Strategic deployments of masculinity, *Critical Pedagogy Networker*, 13(4): 1–11.

Chisholm, D. (1993) Violence against violence against women, in A. Kroker and M. Kroker (eds) *The Last Sex: Feminism and Outlaw Bodies*. New York: St Martin's Press.

Christian, H. (1994) *The Making of Anti-Sexist Men*. London: Routledge.

Clatterbaugh, K. (1996) Are men oppressed?, in L. May, R. Strikwerda and P. Hopkins (eds) *Rethinking Masculinity: Philosophical Explorations in Light of Feminism*, 2nd edn. Lanham: Rowman & Littlefield.

Cockburn, C. (1983) *Brothers: Male Dominance and Technological Change*. London: Pluto Press.

Cockburn, C. (1985) *The Machinery of Dominance*. London: Pluto Press.

Cole, M. (1999) Suspicious minds set against men in schools, *Courier Mail*, 6 July.

Collins, C., Batten, M., Ainley, J. and Getty, C. (1996) *Gender and School Education*. Canberra: Australian Council for Educational Research.

Collinson, D. and Hearn, J. (eds) (1996) *Men as Managers, Managers as Men*. London: Sage Publications.

Colleary, K. (1998) How teachers understand gay and lesbian content in the elementary social studies curriculum, in W. Letts IV and J. Sears (eds) *Queering Elementary Education: Advancing the Dialogue About Sexualities and Schooling*. Lanham: Rowman & Littlefield.

Comstock, G. (1991) *Violence Against Lesbian and Gay Men*. New York: Columbia University Press.

Connell, R. (1987) *Gender and Power: Society, the Person and Sexual Politics*. Sydney: Allen & Unwin.

Connell, R. (1989) Cool guys, swots and wimps: The interplay of masculinity and education, *Oxford Review of Education*, 15(3): 291–303.

Connell, R. (1990) An iron man: The body and some contradictions of hegemonic masculinity, in M. Messner and D. Sabo (eds) *Sport, Men and the Gender Order: Critical Feminist Perspectives*. Champaign, IL: Human Kinetics.

Connell, R. (1992) A very straight gay: Masculinity, homosexual experience, and the dynamics of gender, *American Sociological Review*, 57: 735–51.

Connell, R. (1993) *Schools and Social Justice*. Toronto: Our Schools/Our Selves Education Foundation.

Connell, R. (1994) The politics of changing men, paper presented at the Reproduktion und Wandel von Mannlichkeit conference, Munich, 27–8 September.

Connell, R. (1995a) *Masculinities*. St Leonards: Allen & Unwin.

Connell, R. (1995b) Politics of changing men, *Socialist Review*, 25(1): 135–59.

Connell, R. (1997) Gender politics for men, *International Journal of Sociology and Social Policy*, 17(1/2): 62–77.

Connell, R., Ashenden, D., Kessler, S. and Dowsett, G. (1982) *Making the Difference: Schools, Families and Social Division*. Sydney: George Allen & Unwin.

Cox, E. (1996) *Leading Women: Tactics for Making the Difference*. Sydney: Random House.

Cox, E. (1997) Boys and girls and the costs of gendered behaviour, in Gender Equity Taskforce for Ministerial Council for Employment, Education, Training and Youth Affairs *Gender Equity: A Framework for Australian Schools*. Canberra: Publications and Public Communication, Department of Urban Services, ACT Government.

Curriculum and Gender Equity Policy Unit (1995) *No Fear Kit*. Canberra: Commonwealth Department of Employment, Education and Training.

Dale, J. and Foster, P. (1986) *Feminists and State Welfare*. London: Routledge & Kegan Paul.

Daly, M. (1978) *Gyn/Ecology – The Metaethics of Radical Feminism*. Boston: Beacon Press.

Danby, S. and Baker, C. (1998) How to be masculine in the block area, *Childhood: A Global Journal of Child Research*, 5(2): 151–75.

Denborough, D. (1995) Step by step: Developing respectful and effective ways of working with young men to reduce violence, *Dulwich Centre Newsletter*, 2 and 3: 73–89.

Denborough, D. (1996) Step by step: Developing respectful and effective ways of working with young men to reduce violence, in C. McLean, M. Carey, and C. White (eds) *Men's Ways of Being*. Boulder, CO: Westview Press.

Disch, L. and Kane, M. (1996) When a looker is really a bitch: Lisa Olson, sport and the heterosexual matrix, *Signs: Journal of Women in Culture and Society*, 21(2): 278–308.

Donaldson, M. (1993) What is hegemonic masculinity?, *Theory and Society*, 22: 643–57.

Dunn, J. (1995) Gender awareness programs for boys: reflections on an ACT school-based program, *Unicorn*, 21(4): 55–62.

Dworkin, A. (1981) *Pornography: Men Possessing Women*. London: Women's Press.

Edwards, T. (1990) Beyond sex and gender: Masculinity, homosexuality and social theory, in J. Hearn and D. Morgan (eds) *Men, Masculinities and Social Theory*. London: Unwin Hyman.

Elliott, M. (ed.) (1991) *Bullying: A Practical Guide to Coping for Schools*. Essex: Longman.

Ellsworth, E. (1992) Why doesn't this feel empowering? Working through the repressive myths of critical pedagogy, in C. Luke and J. Gore (eds) *Feminisms and Critical Pedagogy*. New York: Routledge.

Epstein, D. (1994) Lesbian and gay equality within a whole school policy, in D. Epstein (ed.) *Challenging Lesbian and Gay Inequalities in Education*, p. 117. Buckingham: Open University Press.

Epstein, D. (1997) Boyz' own stories: Masculinities and sexualities in schools, *Gender and Education*, 9(1): 105–15.

Epstein, D. and Johnson, R. (1994) On the straight and narrow: The heterosexual presumption, homophobias and schools, in D. Epstein (ed.) *Challenging Lesbian and Gay Inequalities in Education*. Buckingham: Open University Press.

Epstein, D., Elwood, J., Hey, V. and Maw, J. (eds) (1998) *Failing Boys? Issues in Gender and Achievement*. Buckingham: Open University Press.

Equity Unit, Queensland Department Of Education (1997) Gender and violence position paper, Brisbane.

Evans, R. (1992) A gun in the oven: Masculinism and gendered violence, in K. Saunders and R. Evans (eds) *Gender Relations in Australia: Domination and Negotiation*. Sydney: Harcourt Brace Jovanovich.

Faludi, S. (1992) *Backlash: The Undeclared War Against Women*. London: Chatto & Windus.

Faludi, S. (1999) *Stiffed: The Betrayal of the Modern Man*. London: Chatto & Windus.

Farrell, W. (1993) *The Myth of Male Power: Why Men are the Disposable Sex*. New York: Simon & Schuster.

Feminism, race talk upset Brett (1997) *Sunday Mail*, 12 January.

Ferrante, A., Morgan, F., Indermaur, D. and Harding, R. (1996) *Measuring the Extent of Domestic Violence*. Annandale: The Hawkins Press.

Fine, M., Weis, L., Addelston, J. and Maruszas, J. (1997) In(secure) times: Constructing white working-class masculinities in the late 20th century, *Gender and Society*, 11(1): 52–68.

Fitzclarence, L. (1993) Violence in schools, *Education Links*, 46: 16–18.

Fitzclarence, L, Hickey, C. and Matthews, R. (1997) Getting changed for football: Challenging communities of practice, *Curriculum Perspectives*, 17(1): 69–73.

Flax, J. (1992) Beyond equality: gender, justice and difference, in G. Bock and S. James (eds) *Beyond Equality and Difference: Citizenship, Feminist Politics, and Female Subjectivity*. London: Routledge.

Fletcher, R. (1995a) Changing the lives of boys, in R. Browne and R. Fletcher (eds) *Boys in Schools: Addressing the Real Issues – Behaviour, Values and Relationships*. Sydney: Finch.

Fletcher, R. (1995b) Looking to fathers, in R. Browne and R. Fletcher (eds) *Boys in Schools: Addressing the Real Issues – Behaviour, Values and Relationships*. Sydney: Finch.

Flood, M. (1997a) *Frequently Asked Questions About Profeminist Men and Profeminist Men's Politics*. www.anu.edu.au/~a112465/pffag.html

Flood, M. (1997b) Homophobia and masculinities among young men. (Lessons in becoming a straight man), presentation to teachers, O'Connell Education Centre, Canberra, April 22.

Foster, V. (1994) What about the boys! The importance of the theory/policy/curriculum nexus in the education of girls and boys, *Education Links*, 48: 4–7.

Foucault, M. (1977) *Discipline and Punish: The Birth of the Prison*. London: Penguin.

Foucault, M. (1981) *The History of Sexuality, Volume One: An Introduction*. Harmondsworth: Penguin.

Francis, B. (1999) Lads, lasses and (New) Labour: 14–16-year-old students' responses to the 'laddish behaviour and boys' underachievement' debate, *British Journal of Sociology of Education*, 20(3): 354–71.

Francis, B. (2000) *Boys, Girls and Achievement: Addressing the Classroom Issues*. London: Taylor & Francis.

Freeman, P. (1997) *Ian Roberts: Finding Out*. Sydney: Random House.

Friedman, B. (1995) *Boys-Talk: A Program for Young Men about Masculinity, Non-Violence and Relationships*. Adelaide: Men Against Sexual Assault.

Gardiner, G. (1997) Aboriginal boys' business: A study of indigenous youth in Victoria in relation to educational participation and contact with the juvenile justice system, *Journal of Intercultural Studies*, 18(1): 49–61.

Gatens, M. (1983) A critique of the sex/gender distinction, *Intervention*, 15 (Special Issue): 143–61.

Gatens, M. (1996) *Imaginary Bodies: Ethics, Power and Corporeality*. London: Routledge.

Gilbert, P. and Taylor, S. (1991) *Fashioning the Feminine: Girls Popular Culture and Schooling*. North Sydney: Allen & Unwin.

Gilbert, R. and Gilbert, P. (1998) *Masculinity goes to School*. St Leonards: Allen & Unwin.

Gilbert, P., Gilbert, R. and Mcginty, S. (1995) Girls talk: Gender, disadvantage and schooling, unpublished report from 'Addressing the gender dimensions of educational disadvantage' study, a Gender Equity in Curriculum Reform Project, funded by the Department of Employment, Education and Training, School of Education, James Cook University of North Queensland.

Giroux, H. (1992) Resisting difference: Cultural studies and the discourse of critical pedagogy, in L. Grossberg, G. Nelson and P. Treichler (eds) *Cultural Studies*. New York: Routledge.

Giroux, H. (1994) Living dangerously: Identity politics and the new cultural racism, in H. Giroux and P. McLaren (eds) *Between Borders: Pedagogy and the Politics of Cultural Studies*. New York: Routledge.

Giroux, H. and Mclaren, P. (1989) (eds) *Critical Pedagogy, the State and Cultural Struggle*. New York: State University of New York.

Giroux, H. and Simon, R. (1989) Popular culture and critical pedagogy: Everyday life as a basis for curriculum knowledge, in H. Giroux and P. McLaren (eds) *Critical Pedagogy, the State and Cultural Struggle*. New York: State University of New York.

Goodall, H. and Huggins, J. (1992) Aboriginal women are everywhere: Contemporary struggles, in K. Saunders and R. Evans (eds) *Gender Relations in Australia: Domination and Negotiation*. Sydney: Harcourt Brace Jovanovich.

Gore, J. (1992) What we can do for you! What *can* 'we' do for 'you'? Struggling over empowerment in critical and feminist pedagogy, in C. Luke and J. Gore (eds) *Feminisms and Critical Pedagogy*. New York: Routledge.

Gore, J. (1993) *The Struggle for Pedagogies: Critical and Feminist Discourses as Regimes of Truth*. New York: Routledge.

Greer, G. (1971) *The Female Eunuch*. London: Paladin.

Griffin, S. (1979) *Rape: The Power of Consciousness*. San Francisco, CA: Harper & Row.

Griffin, S. (1981) *Pornography and Silence*. London: The Women's Press.

Griffith, C. (1997a) It's goodbye Mr. Chips: Guys give our schools a miss, *Sunday Mail*, 12 January.

Griffith, C. (1997b) Sex fears deter male teachers, *Sunday Mail*, 12 January.

Griffith, C. (1997c) Sex traps for men teachers, *Sunday Mail*, 26 January.

Griffith, C. (1997d) Male teacher's sex claim nightmare, *Sunday Mail*, 9 February.

Grosz, E. (1990) Conclusion: A note on essentialism and difference, in S. Gunew (ed.) *Feminist Knowledge: Critique and Construct*. London: Routledge.

Grosz, E. (1994) *Volatile Bodies: Towards a Corporeal Feminism*. St Leonards: Allen & Unwin.

Grosz, E. (1995) *Space, Time and Perversion: The Politics of Bodies*. St Leonards: Allen & Unwin.

Grundy, S. (1994) The curriculum and teaching, in E. Hatton (ed.) *Understanding Teaching: Curriculum and the Social Context of Teaching*. Sydney: Harcourt Brace.

Gunew, S. (1993) Feminism and the politics of irreducible differences: Multiculturalism/ethnicity/race, in S. Gunew and A. Yeatman (eds) *Feminism and the Politics of Difference*. St Leonards: Allen & Unwin.

Gurian, M. (1999) *A Fine Young Man: What Parents, Mentors, and Educators can do to Shape Adolescent Boys into Exceptional Men*. New York: Jeremy P. Tarcher/Putnam.

Hagan, K. (ed.) (1992) *Women Respond to the Men's Movement: A Feminist Collection*. San Francisco, CA: Harper.

Hagan, K. (1998) A good man is hard to bash: Confessions of an ex-man-hater, in S. Schacht and D. Ewing (eds) *Feminism and Men: Reconstructing Gender Relations*. New York: New York University Press.

Hanmer, J. (1990) Men, power and the exploitation of women, in J. Hearn and D. Morgan (eds) *Men, Masculinities and Social Theory*. London: Unwin Hyman.

Hanmer, J., Radford, J. and Stanko, E. (eds) (1989) *Women, Policing, and Male Violence: International Perspectives*. London: Routledge.

Harding, S. (ed.) (1993) *The 'Racial' Economy of Science: Toward a Democratic Future*, Bloomington, IN: Indiana University Press.

Harding, S. (1998) *Is Science Multicultural? Postcolnialisms, Feminisms and Epistomologies*, Bloomington, IN: Indiana University Press.

Hart, D. (1998) It happens all the time, you just don't take any notice, *International Journal of Inclusive Education*, 2(4): 327–40.

Haywood, C. and Mac an Ghaill, M. (1996) Schooling masculinities, in M. Mac an Ghaill (ed.) *Understanding Masculinities: Social Relations and Cultural Arenas*. Buckingham: Open University Press.

Hearn, J. (1998) *The Violences of Men*. London: Sage.

Hearn, J. and Collinson, D. (1994) Theorizing unities and differences between men and masculinities, in H. Brod and M. Kaufman (eds) *Theorizing Masculinities*. Thousand Oaks, CA: Sage.

Henry, M., Knight, J., Lingard, R. and Taylor, S. (1988) *Understanding Schooling: An Introductory Sociology of Australian Education*. London: Routledge.

Herbert, C. (1989) *Talking of Silence: The Sexual Harassment of Schoolgirls*. London: Falmer Press.

Hey, V., Leonard, D., Daniels, H. and Smith, M. (1998) Boys' underachievement, special needs practices and questions of equity, in D. Epstein, J. Elwood, V. Hey and J. Maw (eds) *Failing Boys? Issues in Gender and Achievement*. Buckingham: Open University Press.

Hinson, S. (1996) A practice focussed approach to addressing heterosexist violence in Australian schools, in L. Laskey and C. Beavis (eds) *Schooling and Sexualities: Teaching for a Positive Sexuality*. Geelong: Deakin University.

Hollway, W. (1996) Gender and power in organisations, in B. Fawcett, B. Featherstone, J. Hearn and C. Toft (eds) *Violence and Gender Relations: Theories and Interventions*. London: Sage.

Holly, L. (1985) Mary, Jane and Virginia Wolf: Ten-year-old girls talking, in G. Weiner (ed.) *Just a Bunch of Girls*. Milton Keynes: Open University Press.

Horsfall, J. (1991) *The Presence of the Past: Male Violence in the Family*. North Sydney: Allen & Unwin.

House of Representatives Standing Committee on Employment, Education and Training (1994) *Sticks and Stones: Report on Violence in Australian Schools*. Canberra: Australian Government Publishing Service.

Huggins, J. (1994) A contemporary view of Aboriginal women's relationship to the white women's movement, in N. Grieve and A. Burns (eds) *Australian Women: Contemporary Feminist Thought*. Melbourne: Oxford University Press.

Jackman, C. (1996) Understanding stats that don't figure, *Courier Mail*, 17 August.

Jardine, A. (1987) Men in feminism: Odor di uomo or compagnons de route?, in A. Jardine and P. Smith (eds) *Men in Feminism*. New York: Methuen.

Jardine, A. and Smith, P. (eds) (1987) *Men in Feminism*. New York: Methuen.

Jefferson, T. (1996) From little 'fairy boy' to the 'compleat destroyer': Subjectivity and transformation in the biography of Mike Tyson, in M. Mac an Ghaill, (ed.) *Understanding Masculinities: Social Relations and Cultural Arenas*. Buckingham: Open University Press.

Jones, C. (1985) Sexual tyranny: Male violence in a mixed secondary school, in G. Weiner (ed.) *Just a Bunch of Girls*. Milton Keynes: Open University Press.

Junor, A. (1991) Education: Producing or challenging inequality, in J. O'Leary and R. Sharp (eds) *Inequality in Australia: Slicing the Cake*. Melbourne: Heinemann.

Kanpol, B. (1994) *Critical Pedagogy: An Introduction*. Westport, CT: Begin & Garvey.

Kaufman, M. (1994) Men, feminism, and men's contradictory experiences of power, in H. Brod and M. Kaufman (eds) *Theorizing Masculinities*. Thousand Oaks, CA: Sage.

Kehily, M. and Nayak, A. (1997) 'Lads and laughter': Humour and the production of heterosexual hierarchies, *Gender and Education*, 9(1): 69–87.

Kelly, A. (1989) The construction of masculine science, in M. Arnot and G. Weiner (eds) *Gender and the Politics of Schooling*. London: Unwin Hyman.

Kelly, R. (1991) *The Gendered Economy: Work, Careers and Success*. Newbury Park, CA: Sage.

Kenway, J. (1995) Masculinities in schools: Under siege, on the defensive and under reconstruction? *Discourse: Studies in the Cultural Politics of Education*, 16(1): 59–79.

Kenway, J. (1996) Reasserting masculinity in Australian schools, *Women's Studies International Forum*, 19(4): 447–66.

Kenway, J. and Fitzclarence, L. (1997) Masculinity, violence and schooling: Challenging 'poisonous pedagogies', *Gender and Education*, 9(1): 117–33.

Kenway, J., Willis, S., Blackmore, J. and Rennie, L. (1997a) *Answering Back: Girls, Boys and Feminism in Schools*. St Leonards: Allen & Unwin.

Kenway, J., Willis, S., Blackmore, J. and Rennie, L. (1997b) Are boys victims of feminism in schools? Some answers from Australia, *International Journal of Inclusive Education*, 1(1): 19–35.

Kessler, S., Ashenden, D., Connell, R. and Dowsett, G. (1985) Gender relations in secondary schooling, *Sociology of Education*, 58(1): 34–48.

Kimmel, M. (1994) Masculinity as homophobia: Fear, shame, and silence in the construction of gender identity, in H. Brod and M. Kaufman (eds) *Theorizing Masculinities*. Thousand Oaks, CA: Sage.

Kimmel, M. (1996) *Manhood in America: A Cultural History*. New York: The Free Press.

Kimmel, M. (1998) Who's afraid of men doing feminism?, in T. Digby (ed.) *Men Doing Feminism*. New York: Routledge.

Kimmel, M. (2000) *The Gendered Society*. New York: Oxford University Press.

Kimmel, M. and Kaufman, M. (1995) Weekend warriors: The new men's movement, in M. Kimmel (ed.) *The Politics of Manhood: Profeminist Men Respond to the Mythopoetic Men's Movement (and the Mythopoetic Leaders Answer).* Philadelphia, PA: Temple University Press.

Kindlon, D. and Thompson, M. (1999) *Raising Cain: Protecting the Emotional Life of Boys.* London: Michael Joseph.

Kitzinger, C. (1994) Anti-lesbian harassment, in C. Brant and Yun Lee Too (eds) *Rethinking Sexual Harassment.* London: Pluto Press.

Kramer-Dahl, A. (1996) Reconsidering the notions of voice and experience in critical pedagogy, in C. Luke (ed.) *Feminisms and Pedagogies of Everyday Life.* Albany, NY: State University of New York.

Lawrence, E. (1999) Home troubles hurt boys most, *Sunday Mail,* 5 December.

Lee, A. (1996) *Gender, Literacy, Curriculum: Re-Writing School Geography.* London: Taylor & Francis.

Lesko, N. (ed.) (2000) *Masculinities at School.* Thousand Oaks, CA: Sage.

Letts IV, W. (1998) How to make 'boys' and 'girls' in the classroom: the heteronormative nature of elementary-school science, in W. Letts IV and J. Sears (eds) *Queering Elementary Educaton: Advancing the Dialogue About Sexualities and Schooling.* Lanham: Rowman & Littlefield.

Letts IV, W. and Sears, J. (1998) *Queering Elementary Education: Advancing the Dialogue About Sexualities and Schooling.* Lanham: Rowman & Littlefield.

Lightfoot, L. (1999) GCSE girls widen lead over boys, *Daily Telegraph,* 15 October 1999.

Lingard, B. (1998) Contextualising and utilising the 'what about the boys?' discourse in education. *Change: Transformations in Education* 1(2): 16–30.

Lingard, B. and Douglas, P. (1999) *Men Engaging Feminisms: Pro-Feminism, Backlashes and Schooling.* Buckingham: Open University Press.

Luke C. (1992) Feminist politics in radical pedagogy, in C. Luke and J. Gore (eds) *Feminisms and Critical Pedagogy.* New York: Routledge.

Luke, C. and Gore, J. (eds) (1992) *Feminisms and Critical Pedagogy.* New York: Routledge.

Lynch, K. (1989) *The Hidden Curriculum: Reproduction in Education, a Reappraisal.* London: Falmer.

Mac an Ghaill, M. (1994a) (In)visibility: Sexuality, race and masculinity in the school context, in D. Epstein (ed.) *Challenging Lesbian and Gay Inequalities in Education.* Buckingham: Open University Press.

Mac an Ghaill, M. (1994b) The making of Black English masculinities, in H. Brod and M. Kaufman (eds) *Theorizing Masculinities.* Thousand Oaks, CA: Sage.

Mac an Ghaill, M. (1994c) *The Making of Men: Masculinities, Sexualities and Schooling.* Buckingham: Open University Press.

MacDonald, E. (1991) *Shoot the Women First.* London: Fourth Estate.

McKay, J. and Middlemiss, I. (1995) 'Mate against mate, state against state': A case study of media constructions of hegemonic masculinity in Australian sport, *Masculinities,* 3(3), 28–45.

MacKinnon, C. (1989) *Towards a Feminist Theory of the State.* Cambridge: Harvard University Press.

McLaren, P. (1994) Multiculturalism and the postmodern critique: Towards a pedagogy of resistance and transformation, in H. Giroux and P. McLaren (eds)

Between Borders: Pedagogy and the Politics of Cultural Studies. New York: Routledge.

McLean, C. (1996) Boys and education in Australia, in C. McLean, M. Carey and C. White (eds) *Men's Ways of Being*. Boulder, CO: Westview Press.

McLean, C. (1997) Engaging with boys' experiences of masculinity: implications for gender reform in schools, *Curriculum Perspectives*, 17(1): 61–4.

McLean, C., Carey, M. and White, C. (eds) (1996) *Men's Ways of Being*. Boulder, CO: Westview Press.

Maher, S. (1996) Men wanted as teachers, *Sunday Mail*, 6 October.

Mahony, P. (1989) Sexual violence and mixed schools, in C. Jones and P. Mahony (eds) *Learning Our Lines: Sexuality and Social Control in Education*. London: Women's Press.

Mahony, P. (1998) Girls will be girls and boys will be first, in D. Epstein, J. Elwood, V. Hey and J. Maw (eds) *Failing Boys? Issues in Gender and Achievement*. Buckingham: Open University Press.

Mansell, W. (2000) More male teachers need to help boys, *Times Educational Supplement*, 8 September (www.tes.co.uk).

Marcus, S. (1992) Fighting bodies, fighting words: A theory and politics of rape prevention, in J. Butler and J. Scott (eds) *Feminists Theorise the Political*. New York: Routledge.

Marriott, D. (1996) Reading black masculinities, in M. Mac an Ghaill (ed.) *Understanding Masculinities: Social Relations and Cultural Arenas*. Buckingham: Open University Press.

Martinez, L. (1994) *Boyswork: Whose Work? The Changing Face of Gender Equity Programs in the 90s*. Brisbane: Queensland Department of Education.

Martino, W. (1995) Boys and literacy: Exploring the construction of hegemonic masculinities and the formation of literate capacities for boys in the English classroom, *English in Australia*, 112: 11–24.

Martino, W. (1997) 'A Bunch of arseholes': Exploring the politics of masculinity for adolescent boys in schools, *Social Alternatives*, 16(3): 39–43.

Martino, W. (1998) It's okay to be gay: interpreting straight thinking, in W. Letts IV and J. Sears (eds) *Queering Elementary Education: Advancing the Dialogue About Sexualities and Schooling*. Lanham: Rowman & Littlefield.

Martino, W. (1999) 'Cool boys', 'Party animals', 'Squids' and 'Poofters': Interrogating the dynamics and politics of adolescent masculinities in school, *British Journal of Sociology of Education*, 20(2): 239–63.

Martino, W. and Meyenn, B. (eds) (2001)'*What About the Boys?': Issues of Masculinity and Schooling*. Open University Press: Buckingham.

Matthews, J. (1984) *Good and Mad Women: The Historical Construction of Femininity in Twentieth-Century Australia*. Sydney: Allen & Unwin.

Matthews, J. (1994) . . . if radical education is to be anything more than radical pedagogy, *Discourse: Sudies in the Cultural Politics of Education*, 15(2): 60–72.

Men: Tomorrow's second sex (1996) *The Economist*, 28 September – 4 October: 23–8.

Merymant, E. (1996) Wanted: Male teachers, *Courier Mail*, 14 March.

Messner, M. (1990) Masculinities and athletic careers: Bonding and status differences, in M. Messner and D. Sabo (eds) *Sport, Men, and the Gender Order: Critical Feminist Perspectives*. Champaign, IL: Human Kinetics Books.

Messner, M. (1992) *Power at Play: Sports and the Problem of Masculinity*. Boston, MA: Beacon Press.

Messner, M. (1994) Sports and the politics of inequality, in M. Messner and D. Sabo (eds) *Sex, Violence and Power in Sports: Rethinking Masculinity*. Freedom: The Crossing Press.

Messner, M. (1997) *Politics of Masculinities: Men in Movements*. Thousand Oaks, CA: Sage.

Messner, M. and Sabo, D. (eds) (1990) *Sport, Men, and the Gender Order: Critical Feminist Perspectives*. Champaign: Human Kinetics Books.

Messner, M. and Sabo, D. (1994) *Sex, Violence and Power in Sports: Rethinking Masculinity*. Freedom: The Crossing Press.

Miller, T. (1998) Commodifying the male body, problematizing 'hegemonic masculinity', *Journal of Sport and Social Issues*, 22(4): 431–47.

Milligan, S., Thomson, K. and Ashenden And Associates (1992) *'Listening To Girls', A Report of the Consultancy Undertaken for the Review of the National Policy for the Education of Girls Conducted by the Australian Education Council, 1991*. Carlton: Curriculum Corporation.

Mills, M. (1995) Setting the gender agenda: Doing too much or doing too little, an administrative dilemma, in B. Limerick and B. Lingard (eds) *Gender and Changing Educational Management*. Rydalmere: Hodder Education.

Mills, M. (1996) 'Homophobia Kills': A disruptive moment in the educational politics of legitimation. *British Journal of Sociology of Education*, 17(3): 315–26.

Mills, M. (1997a) Boys and masculinities in schools, *Education Links*, 54: 22–4.

Mills, M. (1997b) Football, desire and the social organisation of masculinity, *Social Alternatives*, 16(1): 10–13.

Mills, M. (1997c) Towards a disruptive pedagogy: Creating spaces for student and teacher resistance to social injustice, *International Studies in the Sociology of Education*, 7(1): 35–55.

Mills, M. (2000) Issues in implementing boys' programmes in schools: Male teachers and empowerment, *Gender and Education*, 12(2): 221–38.

Mills, M. (2001) 'Pushing it to the max': Interrogating the risky business of being a boy, in W. Martino and B. Meyenn (eds) *'What about the Boys?': Issues of Masculinity and Schooling*, Buckingham: Open University Press.

Mills, M. and Lingard, B. (1997a) Masculinity politics, myths and boys' schooling: A review essay, *British Journal of Educational Studies*, 45(3): 276–92.

Mills, M. and Lingard, B. (1997b) Reclaiming the 'what about the boys?' discourse for gender justice in schools and society, *Social Alternatives*, 16(3): 51–4.

Mills, R. (1997) In public places: The trials of Aileen Wuornos and Tracey Wiggington, unpublished PhD thesis, Griffith University.

Misson, R. (1995) Dangerous lessons: Sexuality issues in the English classroom, *English in Australia*, 112: 25–32.

Moore, C. (1999) Understanding homophobia through teaching history: The development of Queensland's gay/lesbian/queer culture, *The History Teacher*, 37(2): 17–30.

Morgan, D. (1996) Learning to be a man: Dilemmas and contradictions of masculine experience, in C. Luke (ed.) *Feminisms and Pedagogies of Everyday Life*. Albany, NY: State University of New York.

Morgan, J., Maddock, A., Hunt, G. and Joy, M. (1988) *Sexual Harassment Between Students: A Report of Teachers' Attitudes and Experiences*. Northern Community Health Research Unit and Tea Tree Gully Community Health Service, South Australia.

Morris, M. (1987) In any event . . . , in A. Jardine and P. Smith (eds) *Men in Feminism*. New York: Methuen.

O'Chee, A. (1997a) Sex charge fears put men on the outer, *Courier Mail*, 28 January.

O'Chee, A. (1997b) No panic, guys, kindies need you – lecturer, *Courier Mail*, 20 February.

O'Chee, A. (1997c) More males apply to be teachers, *Courier Mail*, 3 March.

O'Chee, A. (1997d) Even fewer men on the roll, *Courier Mail*, 27 November.

O'Connor, D-M. (1992) *'Boys Will Be . . .' A Report on the Survey of Year 9 Males and Their Attitudes to Forced Sex*. Brisbane: Domestic Violence Resource Centre.

Opie, C. (1998) Whose turn next? Gender issues in information technology, in A. Clark and E. Millard (eds) *Gender in the Secondary Curriculum: Balancing the Books*. London: Routledge.

Orner, M. (1992) Interrupting the calls for student voice in 'liberatory' education: A feminist poststructuralist perspective, in C. Luke and J. Gore (eds) *Feminisms and Critical Pedagogy*. New York: Routledge.

Paechter, C. (2000) *Changing School Subjects*. Buckingham: Open University Press.

Parker, A. (1996) The construction of masculinity within boys' physical education, *Gender and Education*, 8(2): 141–57.

Patrick, P. and Saunders, S. (1994) Lesbian and gay issues in the curriculum, in D. Epstein (ed.) *Challenging Lesbian and Gay Inequalities in Education*. Buckingham: Open University Press.

Patty, A. (1999) I fear massacre in our schools, *Sun-Herald*, 13 June.

Pease, B. (1997) *Men and Sexual Politics: Towards a Profeminist Practice*. Adelaide: Dulwich Centre Publications.

Polk, K. (1994) *When Men Kill: Scenarios of Masculine Violence*. Cambridge: Cambridge University Press.

Pollack, W. (1999) *Real Boys: Rescuing Our Sons from the Myths of Boyhood*. New York: Henry Holt.

Povey, H. (1998) 'That spark from heaven' or 'of the earth': Girls and boys and knowing mathematics, in A. Clark and E. Millard (eds) *Gender in the Secondary Curriculum: Balancing the Books*. London: Routledge.

Power, S., Whitty, G., Edwards, T. and Wigfall, V. (1998) Schoolboys and schoolwork: gender identification and academic achievement, *International Journal of Inclusive Education*, 2(2): 135–53.

Pringle, R. (1994) Ladies to women: Women and the professions, in N. Grieve and A. Burns (eds) *Australian Women: Contemporary Feminist Thought*. Melbourne: Oxford University Press.

Pringle, R. (1995) Destabilising patriarchy, in B. Caine and R. Pringle (eds) *Transitions: New Australian Feminisms*. St Leonards: Allen & Unwin.

Pronger, B. (1990) *The Arena of Masculinity: Sports, Homosexuality, and the Meaning of Sex*. New York: St Martin's Press.

Pyke, K. (1996) Class-based masculinities: The interdependence of gender, class, and interpersonal power, *Gender and Society*, 10(5): 527–49.

Queensland Department of Education (1994) *Enough's Enough! Sexual Harassment and Violence*. Brisbane: Queensland Department Of Education.

Randall, G. (1987) Gender differences in pupil–teacher interaction in workshops and laboratories, in G. Weiner and M. Arnot (eds) *Gender Under Scrutiny: New Inquiries in Education*. London: Hutchinson.

Reardon, B. (1985) *Sexism and the War System*. New York: Teachers College Press.

Reay, D. (1990) Working with boys, *Gender and Education*, 2(3): 269–82.

Redman, P. (1996) 'Empowering men to disempower themselves': Heterosexual masculinities, HIV and the contradictions of anti-oppressive education, in M. Mac an Ghaill (ed.) *Understanding Masculinities: Social Relations and Cultural Arenas*. Buckingham: Open University Press.

Rigby, K. (1998) Bullying at school and beyond, in P. McCarthy, M. Sheehan, S. Wilkie and W. Wilkie (eds) *Bullying: Causes, Costs and Cures*. Nathan: Beyond Bullying Association.

Roulston, K. and Mills, M. (2000) Male teachers in feminised teaching areas: Marching to the men's movement drums, *Oxford Review of Education*, 26(1): 221–37.

Sabo, D. (1994) Pigskin, patriarchy and pain, in M. Messner and D. Sabo (eds) *Sex, Violence and Power in Sports: Rethinking Masculinity*. Freedom: The Crossing Press.

Sadker, M. and Sadker, D. (1994) *Failing at Fairness: How our Schools Cheat Girls*. New York: Touchstone.

Salisbury, J. and Jackson, D. (1996) *Challenging Macho Values: Practical Ways of Working with Adolescent Boys*. London: Falmer.

Sapon-Shevin, M. (1998) Using music to teach against homophobia, in W. Letts IV and J. Sears (eds) *Queering Elementary Education: Advancing the Dialogue About Sexualities and Schooling*. Lanham: Rowman & Littlefield.

Scaife, J. (1998) Science education for all? Towards more equitable science education, in A. Clark and E. Millard (eds) *Gender in the Secondary Curriculum: Balancing the Books*. London: Routledge.

Schacht, S. (1996) Misogyny, on and off the 'pitch': The gendered world of male rugby players, *Gender and Society*, 10(5): 550–65.

Schneider, B. (1993) Put up and shut up: Workplace sexual assaults, in P. Bart and E. Moran (eds) *Violence Against Women: The Bloody Footprints*. Newbury Park, CA: Sage.

Schostak, J. (1986) *Schooling the Violent Imagination*. London: Routledge & Kegan Paul.

Scutt, J. (1990) *Even in the Best of Homes: Violence in the Family*. North Carlton: Mcculloch.

Scutt, J. (1994) *The Sexual Gerrymander*. Victoria: Spinifex.

Segal, L. (1990) *Slow Motion: Changing Masculinities Changing Men*. London: Virago.

Segal, L. and McIntosh, M. (eds) (1992) *Sex Exposed: Sexuality and the Pornography Debate*. London: Virago Press.

Seidler, V. (1994) *Unreasonable Men: Masculinity and Social Theory*. London: Routledge.

Sewell, T. (1997) *Black Masculinities and Schooling: How Black Boys Survive Modern Schooling*. Stoke on Trent: Trentham Books.

Sewell, T. (1998) Loose cannons: exploding the myth of the 'black macho' lad, in D. Epstein, J. Elwood, V. Hey and J. Maw (eds) *Failing Boys? Issues in Gender and Achievement.* Buckingham: Open University Press.

Sharp, S. and Smith, P. (eds) (1994) *Tackling Bullying in Your School.* London: Routledge.

Shoalwater, E. (1987) Critical cross-dressing: Male feminists and the woman of the year, in A. Jardine and P. Smith (eds) *Men in Feminism.* New York: Methuen.

Skelton, A. (1998) Eclipsed by Eton fields? Physical education and equal opportunities, in A. Clark and E. Millard (eds) *Gender in the Secondary Curriculum: Balancing the Books.* London: Routledge.

Skelton, C. (1996) Learning to be 'tough': The fostering of maleness in one primary school, *Gender and Education,* 3(2): 185–97.

Small, J. (1990) *Montreal December '89, Snapshot.* Fairfield: Crafty Maid Music.

Smit, L. (1992) *Private Lives and Public Domains: Home Economics and Girls' Post-School Options.* Canberra: Department of Employment, Education and Training.

Smith, P., Morita, Y., Junger-Tas, J. *et al.* (eds) (1999) *The Nature of School Bullying: A Cross National Perspective.* London: Routledge.

Smyth, W. (1987) *A Rationale for Teachers' Critical Pedagogy: A Handbook.* Victoria: Deakin University.

Spender, D. (1982) *Invisible Women: The Schooling Scandal.* London: Writers and Readers.

Spowart, N. (1999) Should we put manhood on the national curriculum for boys? *Scotsman,* 2 November.

Stanko, E. (1988) Keeping women in and out of line: Sexual harassment and occupational segregation, in S. Walby (ed.) *Gender Segregation at Work.* Milton Keynes: Open University Press.

Stanworth, M. (1987) Girls on the margins: A study of gender divisions in the classroom, in G. Weiner and M. Arnot (eds) *Gender under Scrutiny: New Inquiries in Education.* London: Hutchinson.

Stato, J. (1993) Montreal gynocide, in P. Bart and E. Moran (eds) *Violence Against Women: The Bloody Footprints.* Newbury Park, CA: Sage.

Stein, N. (1993) It happens here, too: Sexual harassment and child sexual abuse in elementary and secondary schools, in S. Biklen and D. Pollard (eds) *Gender and Education: Ninety-second Yearbook of the National Society for the Study of Education, Part 1.* Chicago, IL: The National Society for the Study of Education.

Stein, N. (1995) Sexual harassment in school, *Harvard Education Review,* 65(2): 145–62.

Steinem, G. (1999) Supremacy crimes, *Ms,* 9(5): 44–7.

Stock, E. (1991) Feminist explanations: Male power, hostility, and sexual coercion, in E. Grauerholz and M. Koralewski (eds) *Sexual Coercion: A Sourcebook on its Nature, Causes, and Prevention.* Lexington, MA: Lexington Books.

Teese, R., Davies, M., Charlton, M. and Polesel, J. (1995) *Who Wins At School? Boys and Girls in Australian Secondary Education.* Melbourne: Melbourne University.

Thorne, B. (1982) Feminist rethinking of the family: An overview, in B. Thorne and M. Yalom (eds) *Rethinking the Family: Some Feminist Questions*. New York: Longman.

Thorne, B. (1993) *Gender Play: Girls and Boys in School*. Buckingham: Open University Press.

Thornton, A. (1993) The accomplishment of masculinities: Men and sports, in T. Haddad (ed.) *Men and Masculinities: A Critical Anthology*. Toronto: Canadian Scholar's Press.

Wajcman, J. (1991) *Feminism Confronts Technology*. Pennsylvania, PA: The Pennsylvania State University Press.

Walby, S. (1997) *Gender Transformations*. London: Routledge.

Walker, H., Colvin, G. and Ramsey, E. (1995) *Antisocial Behavior in School: Strategies and Best Practices*. Pacific Grove: Brooks/Cole Publishing.

Walker, J. (1988) *Louts and Legends: Male Youth Culture in an Inner City School*. Sydney: Allen & Unwin.

Walkerdine, V. (1988) *The Mastery of Reason*. London: Routledge.

Walkerdine, V. (1989) Sex, power and pedagogy, in M. Arnot and G. Weiner (eds) *Gender and the Politics of Schooling*. London: Unwin Hyman.

Walters, M. (1997) American Gothic: Feminism, melodrama and the backlash, in A. Oakley and J. Mitchell (eds) *Who's Afraid of Feminism? Seeing Through the Backlash*. London: Penguin.

Ward, E. (1984) *Father Daughter Rape*. London: The Women's Press.

Ward, N. (1995) 'Pooftah', 'wanker', 'girl': Homophobic harassment and violence in schools. Paper presented to *Girls and Boys: Challenging Perspectives, Building Partnerships*. The third conference of the Ministerial Advisory Committee on Gender Equity, Brisbane, Queensland, April.

Waring, M. (1988) *Counting for Nothing: What Men Value and What Women are Worth*. Wellington: Allen & Unwin.

Warren, S. (1997) Who do these boys think they are? An investigation into the construction of masculinities in a primary classroom, *International Journal of Inclusive Education*, 1(2): 207–22.

Wedgwood, N. (1997) 'Spewin', Mate!' – A day at the cricket, *Social Alternatives*, 16(3): 26–30.

Weedon, C. (1987) *Feminist Practice and Poststructuralist Theory*. Oxford: Basil Blackwell.

Weiner, G. (1994) *Feminisms in Education: An Introduction*. Buckingham: Open University Press.

Weiner, G., Arnot, M. and David, M. (1997) Is the future female? Female success, male disadvantage, and changing gender patterns in education, in A. Halsey, H. Lauder, P. Brown and A. Stuart Wells (eds) *Education: Culture, Economy and Society*. Oxford: Oxford University Press.

West, C. and Fenstermaker, S. (1995) Doing difference, *Gender and Society*, 9(1): 8–37.

Westwood, S. (1990) Racism, Black masculinity and the politics of space, in J. Hearn and D. Morgan (eds) *Men, Masculinities and Social Theory*. London: Unwin Hyman.

White, J. and White, P. (1986) Teachers as political activists: Three perspectives, in A. Hartnett and M. Naish (eds) *Education and Society Today*. London: Falmer Press.

Willis, P. (1977) *Learning to Labour: How Working Class Kids Get Working Class Jobs*. Farnborough: Saxon House.

Willott, S. and Griffin, C. (1996) Men, masculinity and the challenge of long-term unemployment, in M. Mac an Ghaill (ed.) *Understanding Masculinities: Social Relations and Cultural Arenas*. Buckingham: Open University Press.

Woodhull, W. (1988) Sexuality, power, and the question of rape, in I. Diamond and L. Quinby (eds) *Feminism and Foucault: Reflections on Resistance*. Boston: Northeastern University Press.

Wright, C., Weekes, D., McGlaughlin, A. and Webb, D. (1998) Masculinised discourses within education and the construction of Black male identities amongst African Carribean youth, *British Journal of Sociology of Education*, 19(1): 75–87.

Yates, L. (2000) The 'facts of the case': Gender equity for boys as a public policy issue, in N. Lesko (ed.), *Masculinities at School*. Thousand Oaks, CA: Sage.

Yeatman, A. (1993) Voice and representation in the politics of difference, in S. Gunew and A. Yeatman (eds) *Feminism and the Politics of Difference*. St Leonards: Allen & Unwin.

Yeatman, A. (1994) *Postmodern Revisionings of the Political*. New York: Routledge.

Yeatman, A (1995a) Interlocking oppressions, in B. Caine and R. Pringle (eds) *Transitions: New Australian Feminisms*. St Leonards: Allen & Unwin.

Yeatman, A (1995b) Justice and the sovereign self, in M. Wilson and A. Yeatman (eds) *Justice and Identity: Antipodean Practices*. St Leonards: Allen & Unwin.

Young, I. (1990) *Justice and the Politics of Difference*. Princeton, NJ: Princeton University Press.

Young, I. (1995) Communication and the Other: Beyond deliberative democracy, in M. Wilson and A. Yeatman (eds) *Justice and Identity: Antipodean Practices*. St Leonards: Allen & Unwin.

Young, I. (1997) Unruly categories: A critique of Nancy Fraser's dual systems theory, *New Left Review*, 222: 147–60.

Index

SCHOOLING THE BOYS
MASCULINITIES AND PRIMARY EDUCATION

Christine Skelton

This book explores where masculinity is in primary schools. It has been argued by some commentators that a contributory factor to boys' underachievement is the predominance of women teachers in primary schools which has led to classroom management and teaching styles which 'favour' girls. As this book shows, primary schools produce a range of masculinities for pupils to draw on. A number of questions are raised: what are the tensions for boys between what the school expects from them as 'school pupils' and how they are drawn to behave as a 'boy'? How does a primary school produce certain masculine styles in its day-to-day routines? In what ways do girls respond to male practices and behaviours in the primary school classroom? The book aims to provide readers with an understanding of the background literature on boys and schooling, an insight into 'masculinity-making' in primary schools, and to offer strategies for developing gender-relevant programmes.

Contents

192pp   0 335 20695 6 (paperback)   0 335 20696 4 (hardback)

WHAT ABOUT THE BOYS?
ISSUES OF MASCULINITY IN SCHOOLS

Wayne Martino and Bob Meyenn (eds)

- How can teachers address the challenge of educating boys for life in the 21st century?
- What aspects of schooling are particularly problematic for boys?
- How do issues of class, race and sexuality impact upon boys educational experiences?

This edited collection brings together leading researchers from Australia, United Kingdom and the United States to explore issues of boys, schooling and masculinities within the context of the current concern about the education of boys. The contributors draw on detailed empirical research to highlight some important issues that are not addressed in public debates about boys in the media. Chapter topics include international perspectives on debates about boys; teaching boys; programs for boys in schools; boys and risk taking; boys and discipline; boys and sexuality; Afro-American boys; indigenous boys in Australian schools; boys and reading; boys and maths; boys, dance and sport; boys and science; girls' talk about boys. The book will be important and compelling reading for all teachers concerned with the education of boys.

Contents

c.240pp   0 335 20623 9 (paperback)   0 335 20624 7 (hardback)

MEN ENGAGING FEMINISMS
PRO-FEMINISM, BACKLASHES AND SCHOOLING

Bob Lingard and Peter Douglas

For readers concerned with the current debates about boys' education and gender justice, this is the best guide available. Bob Lingard and Peter Douglas have written a book that is judicious, very well informed, carefully argued and creative. It combines a commitment to equity with a practical concern for good schooling.

R.W. Connell, University of Sydney, Australia

Lingard and Douglas have produced a brilliant contribution to the tradition of men's pro-feminist theory and politics. This is that rare treat: a theoretically sophisticated and politically balanced intervention into an important and contentious public issue. Especially useful for teachers and educational theorists is their account of how men's negotiations with various conflicting feminist theoretical agendas play out for issues about educational policies and practices.

Sandra Harding, University of California, Los Angeles

Men Engaging Feminisms is a most engaging book, challenging both men and women to consider afresh their political commitments and practices. It argues against those who would resist such considerations about changing gender politics and it openly commits to a pro-feminist stance which is robustly argued. It is a must for all interested in issues of social justice and is particularly important for those concerned with issues of gender equity in schools.

Miriam David, Institute of Education, London University

Men Engaging Feminisms is about men's responses to feminist reforms in schooling. These have become closely intertwined with the 'what about the boys?' backlash. This and other forms of backlash are deconstructed. Written by two men from a pro-feminist perspective, *Men Engaging Feminisms* seeks to open up a dialogue about schooling and changing gender relations and changing gender order while also desiring to contribute to a more equal gender order in the future.

Contents
Men engaging feminisms in education – Contemporary masculinity politics – The structural backlash and emergent emotional economy in education – Deconstructing the 'what about the boys?' backlash – Programs for boys in schools – Towards a pro-feminist politics of alliance – Bibliography – Index.

208pp   0 335 19817 1 (paperback)   0 335 19818 X (hardback)

openup

ideas and understanding
in social science

www.**openup**.co.uk

 **Browse, search and
order online**

 **Download detailed
title information and
sample chapters***

*for selected titles

www.**openup**.co.uk